VW GOLF
GTI
1976-1986

Compiled by
R.M. Clarke

ISBN 1 869826 000

Distributed by
Brooklands Book Distribution Ltd.
'Holmerise', Seven Hills Road,
Cobham, Surrey, England

BROOKLANDS BOOKS SERIES
AC Ace & Aceca 1953-1983
AC Cobra 1962-1969
Alfa Romeo Giulia Coupés 1963-1976
Alfa Romeo Spider 1966-1981
Aston Martin Gold Portfolio 1972-1985
Austin Seven 1922-1982
Austin A30 & A35 1951-1962
Austin Healey 100 1952-1959
Austin Healey 3000 1959-1967
Austin Healey 100 & 3000 Collection No. 1
Austin Healey 'Frogeye' Sprite Collection No. 1
Austin Healey Sprite 1958-1971
Avanti 1962-1983
BMW Six Cylinder Coupés 1969-1975
BMW 1600 Collection No. 1
BMW 2002 Collection No. 1
BMW 2002 1968-1976
Bristol Cars Gold Portfolio 1946-1985
Buick Riviera 1963-1978
Cadillac Eldorado 1967-1978
Cadillac in the Sixties No. 1
Camaro 1966-1970
Chevrolet Camaro Collection No. 1
Chevelle & SS 1964-1972
Chevy II Nova & SS 1962-1973
Chrysler 300 1955-1970
Citroen Traction Avant 1934-1957
Citroen 2CV 1949-1982
Cobras & Replicas 1969-1983
Cortina 1600E & GT 1967-1970
Corvair 1959-1968
Daimler Dart & V-8 250 1959-1969
Datsun 240z & 260z 1970-1977
De Tomaso Collection No. 1
Dodge Charger 1966-1974
Excalibur Collection No. 1
Ferrari Cars 1946-1956
Ferrari Cars 1962-1966
Ferrari Cars 1969-1973
Ferrari Dino 1965-1974
Ferrari Dino 308 1974-1979
Ferrari 308 & Mondial 1980-1984
Ferrari Collection No. 1
Fiat X1/9 1972-1980
Ford Falcon 1960-1970
Ford GT40 1964-1978
Ford Mustang 1964-1967
Ford Mustang 1967-1973
Ford RS Escort 1968-1980
High Performance Escorts MkI 1968-1974
High Performance Escorts MkII 1975-1980
Hudson & Railton Cars 1936-1940
Jaguar (& S.S) Cars 1931-1937
Jaguar Cars 1948-1951
Jaguar Cars 1957-1961
Jaguar Cars 1961-1964
Jaguar Cars 1964-1968
Jaguar E-Type 1961-1966
Jaguar E-Type 1966-1971
Jaguar E-Type 1971-1975
Jaguar XKE Collection No. 1
Jaguar XJ6 1968-1972
Jaguar XJ6 Series II 1973-1979
Jaguar XJ6 & XJ12 Series III 1979-1985
Jaguar XJ12 1972-1980
Jaguar XJS 1975-1980
Jensen Cars 1946-1967
Jensen Cars 1967-1979
Jensen Interceptor Gold Portfolio 1966-1986
Jensen-Healey 1972-1976
Lamborghini Cars 1964-1970
Lamborghini Cars 1970-1975
Lamborghini Countach Collection No. 1
Lamborghini Countach & Urraco 1974-1980
Lamborghini Countach & Jalpa 1980-1985
Lancia Stratos 1972-1985
Land Rover 1948-1973
Land Rover Series II & IIa 1958-1971
Land Rover Series III 1971-1985
Lotus Cortina 1963-1970
Lotus Elan 1962-1973
Lotus Elan Collection No. 1
Lotus Elan Collection No. 2
Lotus Elite 1957-1964
Lotus Elite & Eclat 1974-1981
Lotus Esprit 1974-1981
Lotus Europa 1966-1975
Lotus Europa Collection No. 1
Lotus Seven 1957-1980
Lotus Seven Collection No. 1
Maserati 1965-1970
Maserati 1970-1975
Mazda RX-7 Collection No. 1
Mercedes 230/250/280SL 1963-1971
Mercedes 350/450SL & SLC 1971-1980
Mercedes Benz Cars 1949-1954
Mercedes Benz Cars 1954-1957
Mercedes Benz Cars 1957-1961
Mercedes Benz Competition Cars 1950-1957
Metropolitan 1954-1962

MG Cars 1929-1934
MG Cars 1935-1940
MG TC 1945-1949
MG TD 1949-1953
MG TF 1953-1955
MG Cars 1957-1959
MG Cars 1959-1962
MG Midget 1961-1980
MG MGA 1955-1962
MGA Collection No. 1
MG MGB 1962-1970
MG MGB 1970-1980
MGB GT 1965-1980
Mini Cooper 1961-1971
Morgan Cars 1960-1970
Morgan Cars 1969-1979
Morris Minor Collection No. 1
Old's Cutlass & 4-4-2 1964-1972
Oldsmobile Toronado 1966-1978
Opel GT 1968-1973
Pantera 1970-1973
Pantera & Mangusta 1969-1974
Plymouth Barracuda 1964-1974
Pontiac GTO 1964-1970
Pontiac Firebird 1967-1973
Pontiac Tempest & GTO 1961-1965
Porsche Cars 1960-1964
Porsche Cars 1964-1968
Porsche Cars 1968-1972
Porsche Cars in the Sixties
Porsche Cars 1972-1975
Porsche 356 1952-1965
Porsche 911 Collection No. 1
Porsche 911 Collection No. 2
Porsche 911 1965-1969
Porsche 911 1973-1977
Porsche 911 Carrera 1973-1977
Porsche 911 SC 1978-1983
Porsche 911 Turbo 1975-1984
Porsche 914 1969-1975
Porsche 914 Collection No. 1
Porsche 924 1975-1981
Porsche 928 Collection No. 1
Porsche 944 1981-1985
Porsche Turbo Collection No. 1
Reliant Scimitar 1964-1982
Rolls Royce Silver Cloud 1955-1965
Rolls Royce Silver Shadow 1965-1980
Range Rover 1970-1981
Rover 3 & 3.5 Litre 1958-1973
Rover P4 1949-1959
Rover P4 1955-1964
Rover 2000 + 2200 1963-1977
Rover 3500 1968-1977
Saab Sonett Collection No. 1
Saab Turbo 1976-1983
Singer Sports Cars 1933-1934
Studebaker Hawks & Larks 1956-1963
Sunbeam Alpine & Tiger 1959-1967
Thunderbird 1955-1957
Thunderbird 1958-1963
Triumph 2000-2.5-2500 1963-1977
Triumph Spitfire 1962-1980
Triumph Spitfire Collection No. 1
Triumph Stag 1970-1980
Triumph Stag Collection No. 1
Triumph TR2 & TR3 1952-1960
Triumph TR4.TR5.TR250 1961-1968
Triumph TR6 1969-1976
Triumph TR6 Collection No. 1
Triumph TR7 & TR8 1975-1981
Triumph GT6 1966-1974
Triumph Vitesse & Herald 1959-1971
TVR 1960-1980
Volkswagen Cars 1936-1956
VW Beetle 1956-1977
VW Beetle Collection No. 1
VW Golf GTi 1976-1986
VW Karmann Ghia 1955-1982
VW Scirocco 1974-1981
Volvo 1800 1960-1973
Volvo 120 Series 1956-1970

BROOKLANDS MUSCLE CARS SERIES
American Motors Muscle Cars 1966-1970
Buick Muscle Cars 1965-1970
Camaro Muscle Cars 1966-1972
Capri Muscle Cars 1969-1983
Chevrolet Muscle Cars 1966-1972
Dodge Muscle Cars 1967-1970
Mercury Muscle Cars 1966-1971
Mini Muscle Cars 1961-1979
Mopar Muscle Cars 1964-1967
Mopar Muscle Cars 1968-1971
Mustang Muscle Cars 1967-1971
Shelby Mustang Muscle Cars 1965-1970
Oldsmobile Muscle Cars 1964-1970
Plymouth Muscle Cars 1966-1971
Pontiac Muscle Cars 1966-1972
Muscle Cars Compared 1966-1971
Muscle Cars Compared Book 2 1965-1971

BROOKLANDS ROAD & TRACK SERIES
Road & Track on Alfa Romeo 1949-1963
Road & Track on Alfa Romeo 1964-1970
Road & Track on Alfa Romeo 1971-1976
Road & Track on Alfa Romeo 1977-1984
Road & Track on Aston Martin 1962-1984
Road & Track on Audi 1952-1980
Road & Track on Audi 1980-1986
Road & Track on Austin Healey 1953-1970
Road & Track on BMW Cars 1966-1974
Road & Track on BMW Cars 1975-1978
Road & Track on BMW Cars 1979-1983
Road & Track on Cobra, Shelby &
  Ford GT40 1962-1983
Road & Track on Corvette 1953-1967
Road & Track on Corvette 1968-1982
Road & Track on Corvette 1982-1986
Road & Track on Datsun Z 1970-1983
Road & Track on Ferrari 1950-1968
Road & Track on Ferrari 1968-1974
Road & Track on Ferrari 1975-1981
Road & Track on Ferrari 1981-1984
Road & Track on Fiat Sports Cars 1968-1981
Road & Track on Jaguar 1950-1960
Road & Track on Jaguar 1961-1968
Road & Track on Jaguar 1968-1974
Road & Track on Jaguar 1974-1982
Road & Track on Lamborghini 1964-1985
Road & Track on Lotus 1972-1981
Road & Track on Maserati 1952-1974
Road & Track on Maserati 1975-1983
Road & Track on Mazda 1978-1986
Road & Track on Mercedes Sports & GT Cars
  1970-1980
Road & Track on MG Sports Cars 1949-1961
Road & Track on MG Sports Cars 1962-1980
Road & Track on Pontiac 1960-1983
Road & Track on Porsche 1951-1967
Road & Track on Porsche 1968-1971
Road & Track on Porsche 1972-1975
Road & Track on Porsche 1975-1978
Road & Track on Porsche 1979-1982
Road & Track on Porsche 1982-1985
Road & Track on Rolls Royce & Bentley 1950-1965
Road & Track on Rolls Royce & Bentley 1966-1984
Road & Track on Saab 1955-1985
Road & Track on Toyota 1966-1986
Road & Track on Triumph Sports Cars 1953-1967
Road & Track on Triumph Sports Cars 1967-1974
Road & Track on Triumph Sports Cars 1974-1982
Road & Track on Volkswagen 1951-1968
Road & Track on Volkswagen 1968-1978
Road & Track on Volkswagen 1978-1985
Road & Track on Volvo 1957-1974
Road & Track on Volvo 1975-1985

BROOKLANDS CAR AND DRIVER SERIES
Car and Driver on BMW 1955-1977
Car and Driver on BMW 1977-1985
Car and Driver on Cobra, Shelby & Ford GT40
  1963-1984
Car and Driver on Datsun Z 1600 & 2000
  1966-1984
Car and Driver on Corvette 1956-1967
Car and Driver on Corvette 1968-1977
Car and Driver on Corvette 1978-1982
Car and Driver on Ferrari 1955-1962
Car and Driver on Ferrari 1963-1975
Car and Driver on Ferrari 1976-1983
Car and Driver on Mopar 1956-1967
Car and Driver on Mopar 1968-1975
Car and Driver on Pontiac 1961-1975
Car and Driver on Porsche 1955-1962
Car and Driver on Porsche 1963-1970
Car and Driver on Porsche 1970-1976
Car and Driver on Porsche 1977-1981
Car and Driver on Porsche 1982-1986
Car and Driver on Porsche 1956-1985

BROOKLANDS MOTOR & THOROUGHBRED
  & CLASSIC CAR SERIES
Motor & T & CC on Ferrari 1966-1976
Motor & T & CC on Ferrari 1976-1984
Motor & T & CC on Lotus 1979-1983
Motor & T & CC on Morris Minor 1948-1983

BROOKLANDS PRACTICAL CLASSICS SERIES
Practical Classics on MGB Restoration
Practical Classics on Midget/Sprite Restoration
Practical Classics on Mini Cooper Restoration
Practical Classics on Morris Minor Restoration

BROOKLANDS MILITARY VEHICLES SERIES
Allied Military Vehicles Collection No. 1
Allied Military Vehicles Collection No. 2
Dodge Military Vehicles Collection No. 1
Military Jeeps 1941-1945
Off Road Jeeps 1944-1971

CONTENTS

ACKNOWLEDGEMENTS

As soon as the Golf GTI was introduced in 1976 it became the 'hot hatch' to beat. What is truly amazing however, is that ten years later with its modified body and larger 16-valve engine it still holds premier place amongst this fast moving group. And proof of this will be found in the following pages.

Brooklands Books have evolved over 30 years fulfilling a small specialised need for information that is required by dedicated owners of interesting vehicles. The articles that are reproduced here are of course copyright and can only be reprinted with the permission of the original publishers. I am sure that followers of the GTI will wish to join with us in thanking the management of Autocar, Autosport, Car and Car Conversions, Car and Driver, Drive, Motor, Motor Sport, Motor Trend, Road & Track, Sporting Cars, Sports Car Mechanics, What Car? and Wheels for allowing us to include their entertaining and informative stories.

R.M. Clarke

by John Bolster

VW GOLF GTi

A change from the Beetle!

The VW Golf, in standard form, is a very popular small two-door saloon of the transverse-engined, front-wheel drive variety. With its lifting tailgate and folding rear seat, it has many of the virtues of an estate car and is excellent for the carriage of dogs, without getting their hairs on the upholstery. It is, in fact, a thoroughly modern family car, that is small enough to be nimble in traffic yet has a surprisingly spacious interior.

With a 50bhp 1100cc engine, the Golf is by no means slow, and its alternative 1600cc 75bhp power unit endows it with a useful performance. For the GTi, the fuel-injection engine of the Audi GTE is employed, and instantly the little saloon becomes a road-burner of an entirely different calibre. This 1588cc unit develops no less than 110bhp which, in a 15½cwt car, must result in a performance that, to say the least, is interesting.

The engine is fitted with the well-known Bosch K-Jetronic injection system. Full advantage has been taken of the transverse mounting to make a thoroughly neat and accessible installation, with all the components of the injection system arranged for easy adjustment. Other parts requiring servicing, such as the distributor and the alternator, are also placed where they can most easily receive attention.

Like the other VW four-cylinder engines, this one has a belt-driven camshaft. An entirely new and virtually flat cylinder head has been adopted, with different valves and larger inlet ports, the combustion chambers being in the recessed piston crowns, on the Heron system. The engine peaks at 6100rpm, but can rev all too easily far past that figure, so an ignition cut-out is very sensibly provided. The power unit is so willing that, although I tried to keep down to 6500rpm during the performance testing, I once reached the cutting-out speed accidentally, which appeared to be close on 7000rpm.

As it is considered desirable to use an air-dam for stability, there is a possibility that the airflow over the engine sump is obstructed and a built-in oil radiator makes sure that the temperature of the lubricant is moderate at all times, an oil-temperature gauge also being fitted. The engine drives directly through the clutch to the primary shaft of the two-shaft gearbox, the pinions giving the necessary offset so that, with the helical spur gear final drive to the differential, the driveshafts to the front hubs are on a line parallel to the crankshaft. The suspension has been lowered and stiffened somewhat and anti-roll bars are fitted front and rear, in conjunction with wider wheel rims and 175/70 HR13 tyres. The makers state that the roll resistance has been increased by 30

below: An air-dam adds stability.

per cent and that the cornering power is 12 per cent greater than that of the standard car.

With a 57 per cent increase in engine power, the brakes naturally have a somewhat harder task and ventilated front discs are consequently employed. At the rear, the standard trailing axle, which doubles as an anti-roll torsion bar, is fitted, but a separate bar is also coupled up and more potent dampers are used all round. It is a tribute to the excellence of the standard Golf that, with only these few ameliorations, the chassis design copes easily with the far greater performance of the GTi.

I have previously driven a GTi in Germany, as regular readers are aware. The test car which I have been using recently was not quite such a ball of fire as that former machine, but this, I think, was just a question of the mileage covered, the car in England being rather too new to have reached its apogee. Nevertheless, the performance figures were highly satisfactory, as the data panel reveals.

The engine is almost unbelievably smooth, with no rough periods, and it does not become at all noisy, even when spinning in the region of 7000rpm. As the gearbox is silent, one is encouraged to make full use of the performance, but in fact the flexibility is equally outstanding, there being not a sign of rumble at 20mph in top gear, from which the car will accelerate smoothly and swiftly. This little power unit is really more like a turbine than a piston engine and it gives the car a standard of refinement that is rare indeed among vehicles with less than six cylinders.

The gear ratios are very well staged and third, with a maximum approaching 90mph, is ideal for winding roads. Second gives fierce acceleration to 60mph and the very rapid overtaking that is possible is an excellent safety feature. Extremely quick gearchanges are easy, which augments the acceleration. The engine has no objection to continuous cruising at over 6000rpm, but of course an overdrive fifth gear would be very acceptable. However, as most of us find it inadvisable to enjoy a great deal of 100mph cruising nowadays, the need for an extra gear is not strongly felt; on the *autobahns* it might be a different matter.

Despite front-wheel drive, there is very little understeer and the response is largely neutral; when really trying one can, in fact, hang the tail out a bit. Normally, however, there is just enough understeer to ensure stability in side winds. Really, all that can be said is that the car always seems to have some cornering power in reserve and it is amusing to notice how much distance is gained through bends when another motorist attempts to follow the GTi. In ordinary use, the little machine makes a most satisfactory town and shopping car, with all the practical features of a standard Golf. The large tyres do not render the steering at all heavy and a woman would find the GTi surprisingly light to park.

There exist other small saloons, with a competition background, that have plenty of performance

and excellent handling. Where the GTi excels them all is in its refinement and comfort. However sporting a man's inclinations may be, he will find that to live all the time with a hard-sprung car soon palls. He will finish long business journeys with a headache if the body panels boom in unison with the engine, and he will get sick of gear-changing if the engine rumbles and leaps on its mountings at low revs in top gear.

The GTi is just as sporting as any of the others, but though the suspension has been stiffened, it still gives a level and comfortable ride. The seats are well shaped for lateral location and the light weight makes the task of the brakes relatively easy; a very powerful handbrake can lock the rear wheels with the greatest facility. The makers really have got the heating and ventilation right, too, which is rare indeed, and that big wiper blade on the rear window is a much-appreciated fitment, with powerful washer to match.

Perhaps the most valuable feature of this fuel-injection car is its remarkable petrol economy, even at high speeds. I averaged just over 30mpg, including all the flat-out performance testing. I made no attempt to drive economically as I was having too much fun, but it would be interesting to see how the car would perform on an economy run.

The GTi is only available with left-hand drive, which may put a few people off. Personally, I have no objection to a "left-hooker", indeed sometimes I think I prefer them, especially in the really thick fog which I had to negotiate. However, it is a matter of personal opinion and I know that some people feel quite strongly over this matter. With a wider car, steering on the left certainly is a disadvantage in England, but with a narrow little machine the inconvenience is minimal.

The position of the steering wheel apart, it is hard to find fault with the Volkswagen GTi, because it combines so well the virtues of an out-and-out competition car and a refined luxury car. If I *must* find something to criticise, let me mention the vivid red colour of the test car, which I thought unworthy of such an otherwise attractive machine, but seriously, what a change from that ghastly old Beetle!

SPECIFICATION AND PERFORMANCE DATA

Car Tested: Volkswagen Golf GTi 2-door saloon, price £3372; light alloy wheels £117.06, both including car tax and VAT.
Engine: four cylinders 79.5 x 80mm (1588cc). Compression ratio 9.5 to 1. 110bhp DIN at 6100rpm. Belt-driven overhead camshaft. Bosch K Jetronic fuel injection. Oil radiator.
Transmission: Single dry plate clutch. 4-speed all-indirect synchromesh gearbox with central remote control, ratios 0.97, 1.37, 1.94, and 3.35 to 1. Final drive by helical spur gears, ratio 3.7 to 1.
Chassis: Combined steel body and chassis. MacPherson independent front suspension with anti-roll bar. Rack and pinion steering with outside scrub radius. Torsion-beam rear axle on trailing links and coil springs with additional anti-roll bar. Servo-assisted disc/drum brakes with rear limiting valve. Bolt-on steel wheels (light alloy wheels extra), fitted 175/70 HR13 steel-braced radial-ply tyres.
Equipment: 12-volt lighting and starting. Speedometer. Rev-counter. Water temperature, oil temperature, and fuel gauges. Clock. Heating, demisting, and ventilation system. 2-speed plus intermittent windscreen wiper and rear window wiper, with washers front and rear. Heated rear window. Flashing direction indicators with hazard warning. Reversing lights.
Dimensions: Wheelbase 7ft 10.5in. Track 4ft 7.3in. Overall length 12ft 1.8in. Width 5ft 4in. Weight 15cwt 106lbs.
Performance: Maximum speed 112mph. Speeds in gears: third 88mph, second 60mph, first 32mph. Standing quarter-mile 16.9s. Acceleration: 0-30mph 3.0s, 0-50mph 6.6s, 0-60mph 8.5s, 0-80mph 16.0s.
Fuel Consumption: 30 to 36mpg.

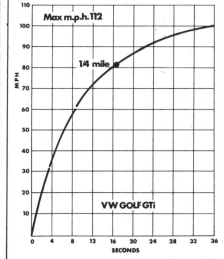

Max m.p.h. 112

1/4 mile

VW GOLF GTi

MKT 512R

STAR ROAD TEST

VOLKSWAGEN GOLF GTI

'Homologation special' remarkable for quietness and refinement as well as high performance and excellent handling and roadholding. Very good economy, so exceptional value for money. Only available in LHD form

VOLKSWAGEN HAVE made no secret of their intention to take part in various forms of motor sport, nor have they tried to conceal the fact that the Golf GTI, the subject of this test, is one instrument of that intention. The Golf GTI is being sold to the public at least partly to conform with Group I homologation regulations which require that a minimum of 5000 examples should be built.

VW are by no means the first manufacturer to do this, of course. Other companies have followed the same path for the same reasons, introducing such cars as the Ford RS2000 in consequence. The general idea is to achieve a major improvement in the performance

and roadholding of a family saloon which is inherently light, lively and nimble. If done well — and the GTI has been done very well indeed — the result is not only suitable for competition, but also a taut high-performance car entirely acceptable to the ordinary driver with sporting tastes.

The GTI is based on the standard Golf 1600, retaining the same all-independent suspension — by MacPherson struts at the front and trailing arms at the rear. But with bowl-in-piston combustion chambers, an increased compression ratio, Bosch K-Jetronic fuel injection and other modifications the output of the transversely mounted 1588 cc engine has been raised to 110 bhp. To cope with

the extra performance, ventilated disc front brakes are fitted, while to obtain the required improvement in roadholding, the ride height has been reduced, an anti-roll bar has been added at each end of the car and fatter wheels and tyres are fitted. Externally the car is distinguishable by its extended wheelarches, front spoiler and rear wiper. Inside, rally-type front seats, a rev-counter and an oil temperature gauge are also among the standard fittings.

The car created by all these modifications does well in most of the areas important to a "homologation special" but achieves much more besides: its standard of refinement is remarkable for any small production saloon, still more so for one which is highly tuned. And at £3372 it is competitively priced in its own sector of the market, unlike most German cars which are heavily penalised by the low value of the £. If Volkswagen are as successful in competition as they have been in developing this car they will prove formidable opponents.

PERFORMANCE

★★
★★
Volkswagen's basic sohc 1588 cc engine has been extensively modified to produce the power output required. Structurally the biggest change has been the adoption of bowl-in-piston combustion chambers in place of the conventional kind, but bigger inlet valves are

also fitted and the compression ratio has been raised from 8.2 : 1 to 9.5 : 1. An oil cooler is fitted to keep down the engine temperature.

The fuel is not metered by a carburetter but by a Bosch K-Jetronic continuous-flow injection system which has shown itself capable of giving outstanding results in other cars. Its most important feature is its use, in place of pressure and temperature sensors, of a direct air flow measuring device involving a floating plate which varies its position with the rate at which air is drawn into the engine and allows the fuel to be apportioned accordingly.

The net result of all these changes is to raise the power output to a claimed 110 (DIN) bhp at 6100 rpm — way above the 85 bhp of the Scirocco/Passat GLS versions of the engine, let alone the 75 bhp of an ordinary Golf 1600. Maximum torque is a healthy 101 lb ft, though developed at a very high engine speed—5000 rpm.

As might be expected, this makes the GTI a pretty brisk car, but what impressed us far more was its combination of high performance with a level of smoothness, quietness and refinement which is quite exceptional for a mass-produced 1½ litre saloon, let alone a highly tuned one. Even at its 6900 rpm limit, the engine sounds completely unfussed and its noise level remains remarkably low. Other manufacturers please copy.

Almost equally impressive was

the low-speed torque available as demonstrated by the way in which the engine would pull without hesitation from below 20 mph in top — equivalent to just over 1000 rpm. It is confirmed by the good acceleration times in top gear for each 20 mph increase in speed — 9.8s for both the 30-50 mph and the 40-60 mph increments, for example. We suspect this virtue, along with the complete lack of any flat spots or hesitations, to be due to clever manifold design combined with the excellence of the K-Jetronic fuel injection system.

Although our test car was certainly fast for a 1600, its speed and acceleration did not match Volkswagen's claims. The maximum speed, for example, was 108 mph as against a claimed 113 mph, and the 0-60 mph acceleration time was 9.6s compared with an expected time of less than 9s. VW's claims in the past have been honest and realistic, so perhaps our test car was below par.

ECONOMY

★★
★★ Unfortunately we were unable to attach our fuel flowmeter to the complex K-Jetronic injection system, but VW's claims of 50.4 mpg at a constant 50 mph and 38.2 mpg at a constant 70 mph seems entirely realistic, as do their other figures which would lead to a touring consumption of 36.7 mpg. This, incidentally, would give a range of around 360 miles from the 9.9-gallon tank.

All this fits in well with the consumption values of well over 30 mpg which we obtained when driving the car gently, and with our 28.5 mpg overall figure, which is outstandingly good in view of the performance — and another of the car's important virtues.

TRANSMISSION

★★
★★ Operated by a floor-mounted lever topped with a knob shaped like a large golf ball — but coloured black — the GTI's gearchange is a delight to use. Its light, precise action fully complements the smooth and responsive character of the engine.

The gearbox ratios are the same as the standard 1600's, but the final drive gearing has been raised — from 3.90 : 1 to 3.70 : 1 — giving 18.4 mph/1000 rpm in top. The engine pulls so well at low speeds, though, that this fairly high gearing is no disadvantage, and the car was easily able to accomplish a restart on the 1-in-3 slope. But because 90 mph can be attained in third, and because the engine is very quiet even at high rpm, it is easy to forget to change up when travelling at moderate speeds.

HANDLING

★★
★★ The GTI retains the Golf's basic suspension system — MacPherson struts at the front and trailing arms at the back — but in an extensively modified form. The torsion bar which links those rear trailing arms, for example, is augmented by an additional anti-roll bar and another anti-roll bar is fitted at the front. The spring and damper rates have been changed, the car has been lowered by nearly 1 in and it runs on 175/70 tyres fitted to 5½ in rims in place of the usual 155 tyres and 5 in rims. According to the VW engineers, the result is to cut the maximum roll angle from about 6½ deg to less than 4½ deg and to raise the maximum sustainable cornering force at a steady speed from around 0.73 g to about 0.81 g.

In our view the result is a car which corners very well indeed but does not possess the almost extraordinary precision of hand-

Left: thanks to clever packaging there is more than ample space in both the front and the rear (right) of the GTI, while the firm but very comfortable rally-type front seats are attractively upholstered in a tartan cloth.

Below: the padded sides to the well contoured front seats do mean that entry to the rear is a little restricted

Above: with the rear seat in use the boot only takes 6.6 cu ft of test suitcases but the luggage area can be considerably enlarged when it is folded as below

ling and reserves of adhesion provided by the Alfasud. But the Golf is nevertheless very nimble and responsive with mild initial understeer which means that it can be driven fast along a twisty road without much effort. At higher cornering forces, though, it begins to understeer strongly, especially on tight bends in the wet. It is also a little inconsistent at times : a bump in the road surface or a high initial rate of turn can reduce the basic understeer considerably.

The steering is low geared, but light and precise with enough feel to give some warning of impending front-end breakaway in the wet. Strangely, though, it becomes rather dead at the higher cornering speeds possible in the dry, and under hard acceleration from rest there is occasionally a trace of the added frictional stiffness combined with tuggings at the driver's hands from which the first VWs with negative offset steering originally suffered. Despite the front spoiler, too, the car is just a little unstable in a straight line at high speeds.

Above: wider, flared wheel arches, side stripes, a front spoiler, alloy wheels and wide tyres—all the accoutrements of a sporty car, but discreetly applied

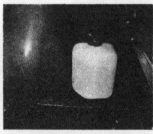

Right: the very useful rear window wash/wipe system is supplied by a plastic water bottle in the rear quarter recess, below

Right: apart from these instruments, which include a tachometer in the top half of the left-hand dial, there is a clock and an oil temperature gauge on the central console

BRAKES

★★
★★
To cope with the extra performance, the Golf's braking system has been uprated for the GTI : ventilated rather than solid discs are fitted at the front and a larger servo is provided as is a pressure relief valve for the rear circuit. As for the standard 1600 model the rear brakes are of the drum type.

This system is admirably progressive in action and also very light : a pedal force of 70 lb was enough to send the dial of our Tapley off the end of its scale, indicating a deceleration of more than 1 g. No fade was experienced during fast driving on the road, but the pedal force required rose

by 15 lb halfway through our 20-stop test. Several stops were needed before the brakes recovered from a soaking in the watersplash. The handbrake held the car securely on the 1-in-3 slope, even when the car faced downwards, but could only manage a 0.3 g retardation on the flat.

ACCOMMODATION

★★
★★
Though the Golf is little more than 12 ft long and only weighs just over 16 cwt, there's more room inside it—thanks to its front-wheel-drive and transverse engine—than in many a rear-wheel-drive car 2 ft longer and 4 cwt heavier. Thus the driver's seat has a range of adjustment which provides ample legroom for the tall, and even

when it is in its rearmost position there is enough space behind it for a person of average size — though some sharing of the available space will be called for if both driver and passenger are tall. The nearly horizontal line of the roof means that there is also good headroom in the rear seat.

The luggage space is not quite so generous, the boot taking 6.6 cu ft of our suitcases though, of course, it can be increased in size very considerably by folding the rear seat forwards. There are plenty of places to stow oddments, though. Apart from the hinged boot cover which lifts up with the tailgate but can be used as a parcel shelf, there are two small but useful cubbies in the central console, a parcel shelf under the facia on the passenger's side and an open glovebox above it.

RIDE COMFORT

★★
★
With anti-roll bars at front and rear, different spring and damper rates and a ride height reduced by nearly 1 in, the GTI's suspension has been tuned for handling rather than comfort, yet the ride is little different from that of a standard Golf 1600. Firm at all times, it is certainly a little restless and jiggly at low speeds and over small irregularities of cobblestone size. But it smoothes out at higher speeds and is well controlled on undulations, giving an entirely acceptable standard of comfort for a small saloon. There is some crash-through however, on manhole covers and the like, while cat's eyes create a lot of bump-thump.

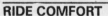

AT THE WHEEL

★★★ Perhaps the two best features of the GTI's interior are its firmly padded yet very comfortable rally-type front seats which are attractively upholstered in a tartan cloth. Their reclining backrests incorporate head restraints and provide good lumbar and lateral support, while the range of fore-and-aft adjustment is ample for tall drivers.

The major controls, such as the gearlever, handbrake and pedals are mostly well laid out, save in one respect important to a car of so sporting a character: the proximity of the central console — totally unnecessary in a front-wheel-drive vehicle with a transverse engine — to the accelerator makes it difficult to heel-and-toe.

A pair of stalks place the majority of the minor facilities under fingertip control, but the rear wash/wipe switch is tucked rather inaccessibly under the facia. This is arranged so that it is difficult to operate the wipers without a preliminary squirt of the washer — which we would prefer to control independently.

VISIBILITY

★★★ With slim, well located pillars, plenty of glass and a body with flat sides, forward visibility is good and the Golf is easily aimed through small gaps. It is also easy to judge the position of the stubby tail, but the area swept by the rear wiper (an absolutely essential item of equipment, as the tailgate window gets very dirty in wet weather) is not well placed for a left-hand-drive car used on left-hand rule roads. Similarly the mirror, with its field of view necessarily angled to the nearside, does not give the best rearward visibility and the back pillars create some obstruction at angled junctions. The light output and beam pattern of the headlamps is only fair, and the car lacks the headlamp washers we would expect to see on a high-performance sporting car of this price.

INSTRUMENTS

★★★★ In front of the driver are two well-located circular dials of reasonable size: a speedometer incorporating total and trip mileometers and a matching rev-counter incorporating fuel and water temperature gauges. These instruments are easy to read and attractively styled but calibrated in large steps. We don't like the conical glasses which cover them, but they do minimise unwanted reflections with tolerable efficiency at the expense of a little distortion.

In the central console are two additional and smaller instruments: a clock and an oil temperature gauge — an oil pressure gauge would be more useful in our opinion.

HEATING

★★★ A long-travel lever moving in a horizontal arc controls the heater temperature, while two levers above it

MOTOR ROAD TEST No 55/76 • VOLKSWAGEN GOLF GTI

PERFORMANCE

CONDITIONS

Weather	Cool and damp; wind 10-20 mph
Temperature	43°F
Barometer	30.0 in Hg
Surface	Dry tarmacadam

MAXIMUM SPEEDS

	mph	kph
Banked circuit	108.0	173.8
Best ¼ mile	112.5	181.0
Terminal speeds:		
at ¼ mile	82	132
at kilometer	98	158
at mile	106	171
Speed in gears (at 6900 rpm):		
1st	36	58
2nd	64	103
3rd	90	145

ACCELERATION FROM REST

mph	sec	kph	sec
0-30	3.3	0-40	2.4
0-40	4.9	0-60	4.4
0-50	7.0	0-80	7.0
0-60	9.6	0-100	10.3
0-70	13.0	0-120	14.5
0-80	17.0	0-140	21.0
0-90	22.7	0-160	33.6
0-100	35.3		
Stand'g ¼	17.2	Stand'g km	32.0

ACCELERATION IN TOP

mph	sec	kph	sec
20-40	10.5	40-60	6.8
30-50	9.8	60-80	5.8
40-60	9.8	80-100	6.4
50-70	10.5	100-120	7.3
60-80	12.1	120-140	9.0
70-90	14.6		

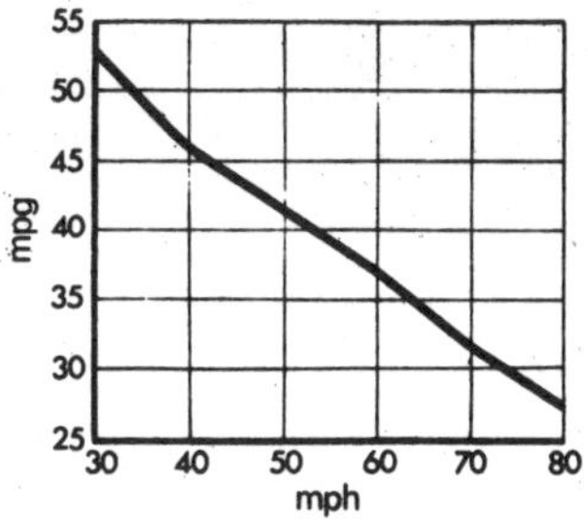

FUEL CONSUMPTION

Overall	28.5 mpg 9.9 litres/100 km
Fuel grade	100 octane 5 star rating
Tank capacity	9.9 galls 45 litres
Max range	See text
Test distance	1264 miles 2034 km

BRAKES

Pedal pressure deceleration and stopping distance from 30 mph (48 kph)

lb	kg	g	ft	m
25	11	0.55	55	17
50	23	0.97	31	10
70	32	1.00+	30	9
Handbrake		0.31	97	30

FADE

20 ½g stops at 1 min intervals from speed midway between 40 mph (64 kph) and maximum (74 mph, 119 kph)

	lb	kg
Pedal force at start	25	11
Pedal force at 10th stop	40	18
Pedal force at 20th stop	35	16

STEERING

Turning circle between kerbs	ft	m
left	31	9.5
right	30	9.1
Lock to lock	3.8 turns	
50ft diam circle	1.2 turns	

CLUTCH

	in	cm
Free pedal movement	1	2.5
Additional to disengage	2¾	7.0
Maximum pedal load	25 lb	11 kg

SPEEDOMETER (mph)

Speedo							
30	40	50	60	70	80	90	100
True mph							
28	37½	48	58	67	79	90	100

Distance recorder: 3.5 per cent fast

WEIGHT

	cwt	kg
Unladen weight*	16.2	823.0
Weight as tested	19.9	1011.0

*with fuel for approx 50 miles

Performance tests carried out by Motor's staff at the Motor Industry Research Association proving ground, Lindley.

Test data: World Copyright reserved; no unauthorised reproduction in whole or part.

GENERAL SPECIFICATION

ENGINE

Cylinders	4 in line
Capacity	1588 cc (96.9 cu in)
Bore/stroke	79.5/80.0 mm (3.13/3.15 in)
Cooling	Water
Block	Cast iron
Head	Alloy
Valves	Ohc
Valve timing	
inlet opens	9° btdc
inlet closes	41° abdc
ex opens	49° bbdc
ex closes	1° atdc
Compression	9.5 : 1
Fuel metering	Bosch K-Jetronic fuel injection
Bearings	5 main
Fuel pump	Electrical
Max power	110 bhp (DIN) at 6100 rpm
Max torque	101 lb ft (DIN) at 5000 rpm

TRANSMISSION

Type	4-speed manual
Clutch	Sdp
Internal ratios	and mph/1000 rpm:
Top	0.97 : 1/18.4
3rd	1.37 : 1/13.0
2nd	1.94 : 1/9.2
1st	3.45 : 1/5.2
Rev	3.17 : 1
Final drive	3.70 : 1

BODY/CHASSIS

Construction	Unitary
Protection	Phosphating, electrophoretic dip, zinc powder paint, PVC undersealant

SUSPENSION

Front	Independent by MacPherson struts with coil springs and anti-roll bar
Rear	Independent by trailing arms with coil springs, interconnecting torsion bar and added anti-roll bar

STEERING

Type	Rack and pinion
Assistance	No
Toe in	—
Camber	+30′ ± 30′
Castor	+20′ ± 30′
Rear toe in	0° ± 15′

BRAKES

Type	Ventilated discs/drums
Servo	Yes
Circuit	Two—diagonally split
Rear valve	Yes
Adjustment	Manual

WHEELS

Type	5½ J steel
Tyres	175/70 HR 13
Pressures	24 psi F; 24 psi R

ELECTRICAL

Battery	12V 36 Ah
Polarity	Negative earth
Generator	35A alternator
Fuses	15
Headlights	Two halogen circular

IN SERVICE

GUARANTEE

Duration ...... **12 months, unlimited mileage**

MAINTENANCE

Schedule .... **Every 10,000 miles**
Free service .... **at 600 miles**
Labour for year **1h 20m**

DO-IT-YOURSELF

Sump .... **6 pints, SAE 20W/50**
Gearbox and final drive **2.2 pints, SAE 80**
Steering gear .... **Sealed**
Coolant .... **11.4 pints**
Chassis lubrication .... **None**
Contact breaker gap ... **Approx 0.4mm**
Spark plug type ... **Bosch W225 T30**
Spark plug gap **0.6-0.7mm**
Tappets (hot)
inlet 0.2mm ± 0.05mm
exhaust 0.4mm ± 0.05mm

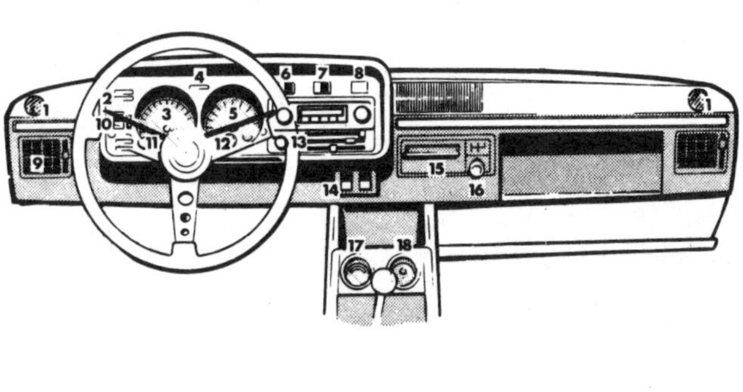

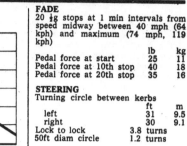

1 side-window demister
2 charge and oil pressure warning lights
3 rev-counter
4 indicator tell-tale/main beam warning
5 speedometer
6 backlight heater switch
7 hazard flasher switch
8 blank
9 fresh air vent
10 lights switch
11 indicator/horn stalk
12 wash/wipe stalk
13 heater controls
14 rear wash/wipe switch
15 ashtray
16 cigar lighter
17 oil temperature gauge
18 clock

Make: Volkswagen **Model:** Golf GTI
Makers: Volkswagenwerk AG, 3180 Wolfsburg, W. Germany
Concessionaires: Volkswagen (GB) Ltd, Volkswagen House, Brighton Road, Purley, Surrey
Price: £2882.05 plus £240.17 car tax plus £249.78 VAT equals £3372.00

★★★★ excellent ★★★★ good ★★★ average ★★ poor ★ bad

with shorter movements regulate the volumes of heated air directed to the footwell and windscreen. Symbols by this last lever rather confusingly imply that movement of it to a certain spot will bring in the booster fan, whereas this is separately controlled by a knob.

Without this booster fan the throughput of heated air is meagre, even at speed. It becomes adequate when the fan is set to its first speed, ample on the second or third, but both these are noisy. It is not easy to control the temperature finely, so the interior of the car can become stuffy when just a little heat is needed.

VENTILATION

★ ★ Like all other versions of the Golf we have tested the GTI has poor ventilation. Small cheese-cutter type vents at the ends of the facia admit fresh air, but the flow is meagre under ram pressure alone and not very strong even when fan boosted. It is insufficient to prevent the car from becoming stuffy when the heater is in use.

NOISE

★ ★ ★ Although we expect reasonable quietness of any road car sold to the public for a substantial sum of money, we would hardly be surprised to find refinement among the less striking virtues of a car introduced largely to conform with Group 1 racing homologation requirements. But we were surprised by the Golf GTI: it's not merely quiet by the standards of direct competitors like the Escort RS2000; it's quiet by the standards of any 1½-litre car. In particular, the very smooth and unfussed engine isn't obstrusive even at its 6900 rpm limit. It does take on a rather insistent drone at above 90 mph in top, but at any lower speed the car cruises in a relaxed way as there is little wind noise. There isn't much transmission noise, either, and the road noise is moderate.

EQUIPMENT

★ ★ / ★ ★ The GTI's mechanical modifications are complemented by an extensive list of additional fittings. The two rally-type front seats are the main feature of the fully carpeted interior, and the tartan cloth with which they are covered is also used for the bench seat at the rear. A rev-counter, two-speed wipers with delay, and a heater, washer and wiper for the rear window are all standard fittings, as is an additional central console incorporating two cubbies, a clock and an oil temperature gauge. Alloy wheels and tinted glass are available as extras.

FINISH

★ ★ In the past we have had cause to criticise the Golf's finish, but the GTI seemed better put together than the models previously tested. There were fewer creaks and rattles from the tailgate, and apart from a vibration in the facia audible when the engine idled, there was little to complain of.

IN SERVICE

The GTI carries the same warranty as an ordinary Golf and requires servicing at the same intervals: 10,000 miles with an oil change recommended at 5000 miles. Nor does the engine's high state of tune create any clutter under the bonnet. The oil cooler fits neatly beside the radiator and the K-Jetronic injection system does not interfere with the accessibility of other components such as the brake reservoir and distributor.

Left: a nice touch—the golf ball gearlever knob. Above: neat, simple heater controls below the radio. Below: the K-Jetronic fuel injection system dominates the under-bonnet view—the metering unit is on the right

THE RIVALS

VW GOLF GTI £3372

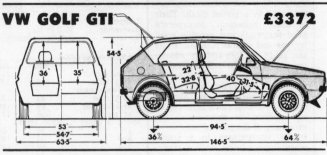

FORD ESCORT RS2000 £3279

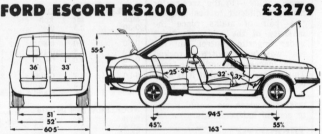

TRIUMPH DOLOMITE SPRINT £3833

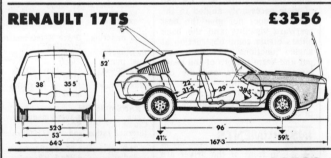

RENAULT 17TS £3556

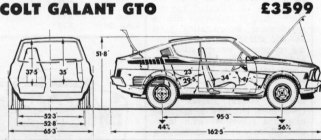

COLT GALANT GTO £3599

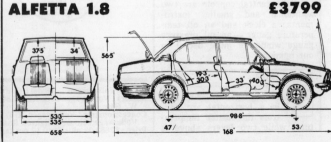

ALFETTA 1.8 £3799

Another possible competitor is the Toyota Celica Liftback GT at £3805. The GTI is unusually cheap for a German car. Report on Renault 17TS following shortly

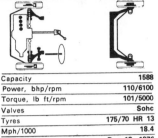

Capacity	1588
Power, bhp/rpm	110/6100
Torque, lb ft/rpm	101/5000
Valves	Sohc
Tyres	175/70 HR 13
Mph/1000	18.4
Test date	Dec 18, 1976

High performance version of Golf 1600 introduced partly to comply with Group 1 racing requirements. Bowl-in-piston combustion chambers and fuel injection help to raise output to 110 bhp; wider tyres and suspension modifications improve roadholding. Fast and very economical, but almost more remarkable for outstanding quietness and refinement. Excellent gearbox, good handling and roadholding; has many extras.

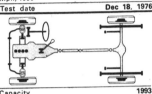

Capacity	1993
Power, bhp/rpm	110/5500
Torque, lb ft/rpm	118.5/4000
Valves	Sohc
Tyres	175/70 HR 13
Mph/1000	18.9
Test date	Sep 11, 1976

Astonishingly good value for money. This big-engined version of Ford's best-selling family saloon is an excellent example of the sporting model. Good performance and an excellent gearbox plus fun handling make it a driver's car. Economy only fair. Well finished with very comfortable front seats and excellent instrumentation. Poor rear legroom, firm almost harsh ride and a lack of refinement.

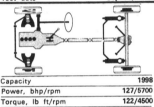

Capacity	1998
Power, bhp/rpm	127/5700
Torque, lb ft/rpm	122/4500
Valves	Sohc
Tyres	175/70 x 13
Mph/1000	23.7
Test date	July 14, 1973

One of Leyland's best cars. Conventional chassis with live axle — albeit well located — at the rear, but sophisticated 16-valve engine. One of the quickest of our selection. Responsive handling on smooth surfaces but doesn't like bumps. Well finished inside and out, versatile driving position and relaxed at speed. A prestige car, attractively priced.

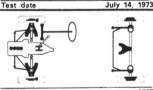

Capacity	1647
Power, bhp/rpm	98/5750
Torque, lb ft/rpm	97.6/3500
Valves	Pushrod Ohv
Tyres	155 SR 13
Mph/1000	20.2
Test date	Jan 1, 1977

Facelifted version of Renault's stylish fastback coupe with restyled interior and much improved instruments. Performance a little below average for the class but fuel consumption quite good; five-speed gearbox slightly notchy. Ride good, handling safe but unsporting. Big enough to take four adults. Unusual front seats with adjustable lateral support not particularly comfortable. Not very quiet at speed.

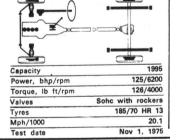

Capacity	1995
Power, bhp/rpm	125/6200
Torque, lb ft/rpm	126/4000
Valves	Sohc with rockers
Tyres	185/70 HR 13
Mph/1000	20.1
Test date	Nov 1, 1975

Sporty version of Mitsubishi's Galant, though only the platform chassis is shared. More powerful engine, stiffened suspension, wider wheels and tyres as well as bolt-on wheelarch extensions. Brisk, but not outstandingly so. Lusty low-speed torque. Superb gearchange, comfortable driving position, good heating and ventilation, and clear instrumentation. Limited accommodation and stiff ride.

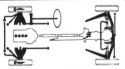

Capacity	1779
Power, bhp/rpm	122/5500
Torque, lb ft/rpm	123.3/4400
Valves	Dohc
Tyres	185/70 HR 14
Mph/1000	20.7
Test date	April 20, 1974

Technically interesting sporting Italian saloon with twin ohc engine. Has de Dion suspension and a five-speed gearbox at the rear. Apart from typical Italian driving position (pedals too close to steering wheel) a very nice car indeed, with plenty of performance allied to very good fuel consumption. Other features are very good noise suppression and outstanding roadholding and handling on all surfaces.

PERFORMANCE

	Golf GTI	Escort RS 2000	Dolomite Sprint	Renault 17TS	Galant GTO	Alfetta 1.8
Max speed, mph	108.0	108.2	112.7	103.6	107.4	111.4
Max in 4th	—	—	—	100	103	93
3rd	90	88	89	70	76	71
2nd	64	61	58	47	51	49
1st	36	33	41	27	31	21
0-60 mph, secs	9.6	8.5	8.4	11.9	11.7	9.5
30-50 mph in 4th, secs	9.8	8.4	8.0	10.0	9.8	7.2
50-70 mph in top, secs	10.5	8.0	8.7	14.3	11.2	10.8
Weight, cwt	16.2	18.1	19.8	19.3	19.8	21.2
Turning circle, ft*	30.5	29.0	29.0	31.6	31.3	32.6
50ft circle, turns	1.2	0.8	1.1	1.2	0.85	1.25
Boot capacity, cu ft	6.6	8.9	9.4	8.0	7.5	12.4

*mean of left and right

COSTS

	Golf GTI	Escort RS 2000	Dolomite Sprint	Renault 17TS	Galant GTO	Alfetta 1.8
Price, inc VAT & tax, £	3372	3279	3833	3556	3599	3799
Insurance group	—	6	6	—	—	7
Overall mpg	28.5	23.5	26.7	27.8	23.2	26.2
Touring mpg	—	27.6	33.1	33.6	31.7	29.2
Fuel grade (stars)	5	4	4	4	4	4
Tank capacity, gals	9.9	9.0	12.5	12.0	11.4	10.7
Service interval, miles	10,000	6000	6000	3000	3000	6000
Set brake pads (front) £*	14.26	9.69	4.77	12.36	6.50	6.75
Oil filter, £*	2.62	2.66	1.00	2.16	2.66	3.23
Starter motor, £*	—	47.56†	41.52	29.16†	25.00†	32.72
Windscreen, £*	31.27	26.05**	24.50**	53.35**	34.00	73.91

*inc VAT **Laminated †Exchange

EQUIPMENT

	Golf GTI	Escort RS 2000	Dolomite Sprint	Renault 17TS	Galant GTO	Alfetta 1.8
Adjustable steering			●		●	●
Carpets	●	●	●	●	●	●
Central locking						
Cigar lighter	●	●	●	●	●	●
Clock	●	●	●	●	●	●
Cloth trim	●	●	●		●	●
Dipping mirror	●	●	●	●	●	●
Dual circuit brakes	●	●		●	●	●
Electric windows						
Fresh air vents	●	●	●	●	●	●
Hazard flashers	●	●	●	●	●	●
Head restraints	●		●	●	●	
Heated rear window	●	●	●	●	●	●
Laminated screen	●			●		
Locker	●		●		●	●
Outside mirror	●	●	●	●	●	●
Petrol filler lock					●	
Radio					●	
Rear central armrest			●			
Rear wash/wipe	●					
Rev counter	●	●	●	●	●	●
Seat belts (front)		●	●		●	
Seat recline	●	●	●	●	●	●
Sliding roof						
Tinted glass					●	
Windscreen wash/wipe	●	●	●	●	●	●
Wiper delay	●	●			●	●

CONCLUSION

When a manufacturer develops a car with competition specifically in mind, we expect the result to have taut, precise handling, unusually high cornering powers and exceptional performance for its engine size. In all these respects the Golf GTI, introduced partly to conform with Group 1 racing requirements, largely met our expectations. With a maximum speed of 108 mph, for instance, it was certainly fast, even though we have good reason to believe the engine of our test car to be below par. The GTI's gearchange is very good, too, and both its handling and roadholding are excellent, while not quite matching the very high standards set by the Alfasud.

The big surprise, though, lies in the GTI's unexpected and quite remarkable quietness and refinement. A certain amount of road noise is transmitted, it is true, to the interior, but there is very little wind noise and the level of engine noise — even at high rpm — is extremely low. Add to this a competitive price which includes many useful extras and the result in our opinion is a very fine car.

The Golf GTI
A superb 110 m.p.h. VW

THE ART of civilising the high-performance engine reaches new heights of excellence as each year of increasingly regulation-bound motoring passes. Jaguar have taken such high-performance concepts as an overhead camshaft V12 and turned such engines into perfect units for limousines. Ford have 240-plus horsepower competition engines of 2-litres that will scream with rage along a forest road or tickover at a reliable albeit clattering, 1,000 r.p.m. or so, and still be ready to give clean power. Leyland score heavily with a simple s.o.h.c. 16-valve unit that combines city manners with 120 m.p.h. performance to delight the enthusiast. The Germans have the idea of a smooth punch from smaller power units well to the forefront of their priorities these days and they have joined the game with an additional sophistication: the fuel-injection sub-2-litre engine. I cannot recall a British manufacturer (or any other nationality of manufacturer on the British Market) who offers this feature on smaller engines, which is a shame for the Germans have built up a store of knowledge that has left the latest Bosch Jetronic-induced BMW, VW and Opel engines with power to spare and perfect manners.

However, there is an irony in this case. "Our" GTI Volkswagen Golf variant was a bit of a baddy. When I took it over there had been phone calls warning that this one wasn't representative, especially in performance. VW claim 0-62 m.p.h. in 9 sec., and 113 m.p.h. top speed. We were told "our" car had disgraced itself with 108 m.p.h. and 0-60 in 9.6 sec., which is still faster than any mass production 1600 that I can recall.

Priced at £3,372 in the UK, the Golf GTI comes only with left-hand drive. In the same area of the market are Ford's RS2000 (£3,729); Leyland's Dolomite Sprint (£3,833) and Opel's Kadett GT/E (£3,320). Only the Dolomite is made in Britain, though the Opel is converted to RHD here, if required.

Frankly, the VW comes out of such comparisons very well. Although it is only 1.6-litres compared with the 2.0-litre capacities of those rivals, the performance is very similar to all save the Dolomite Sprint, which is a quick car by any standard. Once you have accepted that it is left-hand drive the rest of the equipment is first class in conception and use.

I detailed the specification of both the injected Scirocco and Golf in the September 1976 issue, so I will repeat the outstanding points. The engine has new pistons on the Heron head principle and Bosch K-Jetronic fuel injection. Maximum power is 110 b.h.p. at 6,100 r.p.m. and 101 lb. ft. torque is developed at 5,000 r.p.m. Peak r.p.m. are controlled by a rev-limiter at 6,900 r.p.m. on this nearly square (79.5 by 80 mm. stroke) engine of 1,588 c.c. A normal warranty is given with the car, which retains a four-speed gearbox.

The chassis has comprehensive suspension modifications and 5½ in. alloy wheels. A larger front air dam and ventilated front disc brakes play an important part in keeping this bouncy Golf machine in play with little effort, as does an 86.8 lb. ft. torque reading,

A large front spoiler, black, wide wheel arches and wide alloy wheels distinguish the impressive Golf GTI. Its 1,588-c.c., Bosch-injected engine packs 110 b.h.p. into this little projectile (see below).

which stretches from 2,000 to 6,500 r.p.m. Inside the car has outstanding front seats from Recaro and a jazzy check cloth seat covering. A sports steering wheel is provided and there is also an oil temperature gauge, plus a central clock, which are mounted in that useless GM favourite site—low down on a centre console.

However all the description of changes made hardly prepares you for the well-mannered flyer that Golf GTI character is actually about. The seats had prepared me for a real boy racer's delight, but the car actually combines fun and efficiency in an almost frightening effectiveness within a small car.

With string back gloves whirling and teeth bared you can hurl the thing along greasy roads at simply incredible speeds on Pirelli CN36 SM radials. While the passenger flinches at the first corner, especially as he/she is on the "wrong" side, they soon share the driver's confidence in a vehicle that simply corners, stops and accelerates in a well judged harmony of components that are properly matched to each other.

The acceleration doesn't seem that surprising until you find that winding the Golf to 34 m.p.h. in 1st, 60 in 2nd and 87 m.p.h. in 3rd is bringing you the kind of performance found in 3-litre BMW saloons. However, you have no extra size to carry around, those excellently matched brakes and the agility of a 110 horsepower flea on your side! This of course leads to some disgruntlement on behalf of those who have paid large sums of money for their large cars, so it pays to demonstrate such abilities with restraint, though it is hard to stop laughing on some occasions.

Where VW's development engineers have also scored heavily compared with previous attempts to produce civilised small cars with

100-plus capabilities is on the noise front. Just under 4,000 r.p.m. brings the 70 m.p.h. speed limit up on the dial (which is marked in m.p.h.) and at this speed there is some wind noise competing idly with the crisp, but inoffensive exhaust and engine noise. Neither are at a level to be found in normal production saloons of this capacity, so the engineers have done a good job.

I said earlier that the efficiency was almost frightening. The first time I checked the fuel consumption, I just could not accept it, for the figure was 34.9 m.p.g. Well, it was not quite that good for the remainder of the test. I found on thinking a little more deeply that I had spent a lot of motorway time between 30 and 45 m.p.h. in 4th, crawling through fog, when that figure was recorded. However I averaged 28.3 m.p.g. with little oil consumed during one of the toughest tests we have run in recent years. Normally cars go through a routine week with one, or two people, but the GTI was with us over a long Christmas fortnight, and everyone seemed to thrash it mercilessly on every occasion.

There were no reports of any kind of trouble. The engine always fired up on the second turn of the key (utilising an automatic choke) and the gearchange remained lighter than most Fords despite its f.w.d. linkage, with no trace of the usual f.w.d. baulking. The brake pedal obviously had a lot more movement after 2,500 hard miles, but there was still that enviable front to rear balance with little of the locking-up tendency one might expect of a 15.9 cwt. car with generous braking capacity.

There are some snags that could be rectified easily. The first is the Hella light units which are not giving the output needed for such performance, especially in range. Secondly, there is the surprise that you cannot heel and toe, the centre console getting in the way, and thirdly there is the instrumentation. Here the problem is of scattering throughout the car, the normal water temperature and fuel gauges being awkwardly complemented by those centre console add-ons. Perhaps the answer would be a central auxiliary gauge binnacle on top of the dashboard, and the removal/simplification of the centre console to provide more foot pedal room?

Overall, a very impressive VW "hot-rod" that probably has a brighter future as a road than competition car.—J.W.

Making merry

Four fun cars that will bring a smile to even the most jaded drivers

FORD has got a great deal to answer for! For the Dagenham concern has done more for the enthusiast driver — the so-called 'Boy Racer' — than any other firm. Since the demise of the British Racing Green sports car with its soft top but rock hard ride, Ford has been responsible for providing saloon cars that will out-corner and out-perform what few two seaters there are left, as well as provide a reasonable amount of space, and at a price within the grasp of many.

Once, the go-faster element drove Mini-Coppers while a few struggled with the temperamental Lotus Cortinas, but since the advent of the Escort the tide has turned Ford's way. The enthusiasts have been queuing up to drive Escort Mexicos, RS1600s, RS1800s and latterly RS2000s. And it wasn't too long ago that Ford had this corner of the market to themselves — there was the up-market Triumph Dolomite Sprint and the special order left hand drive Opel Kadett GT/E, but that was about it.

And then, earlier this year, came a horde of go-faster specials veritably tripping over each other to attract would-be buyers . . . fuel crisis or no. Some of the manufacturers who set about turning their bread and butter cars into hot shoe shufflers had tried — half heartedly — before. Vauxhall once gave us the Firenza Droopsnoot, now they hide the

Engine

Ford

For
Lively unit; excellent gearbox; easy to maintain

Against
Noisy and rough; hard driving will mean poor economy

Talbot

For
Powerful; proven reliability; electronic ignition

Against
Lumpy, rough and temperamental in town; thirsty; unrefined

Vauxhall

For
Technically interesting; powerful and smooth

Against
Fouls plugs in town; thirsty; expensive

Volkswagen

For
Smooth; powerful; economical; good gearbox

Against
Buzzy at high speeds

Chevette 2300HS under a bushel; Talbot, née Chrysler, née Hillman developed, if that's the right word, the Avenger Tiger before using the same formula for the Talbot Sunbeam Ti; Renault hotted up their baby 5 calling it the Gordini in this country; and Volkswagen fuel injected the Golf dubbing it the GTi. The final manufacturer to enter the fray was Fiat who did a double, by squeezing 70 bhp out of their 1050 cc 127, as well as dropping a two-litre engine into a 131 shell and calling it the Mirafiori Sport.

For this test we have chosen three of the newest examples and compared them with the Daddy of them all, the RS Escort. As it turns out engine sizes and prices of the quartet vary quite considerably, but all appeal to the same sort of buyer and all provide the same sort of fun. And — as we shall see — all offer much the same performance despite it all.

The cars

Leading the group is the elder statesman, the RS2000 Custom at £5181. We did in fact test one of these cars earlier in the year (**What Car?** March '79) but as outlined in that test we were not happy with the performance figures we achieved at a streaming wet and slippery test track. Neither were Ford. This was a good excuse to put the car through the test routine once more.

The rivals chosen, all hatchbacks, are the Talbot Sunbeam Ti, the cheapest at £4528; the Vauxhall Chevette 2300HS, at £5939 the most expensive of the group; while in the middle comes the newest, the £5010 Volkswagen Golf GTi. We had hoped to also put a Renault 5 Gordini through the test routine but Renault's test fleet examples are in constant demand and so one was unavailable at the time of the test . . . another time, perhaps.

Performance

Although all four cars have four cylinder engines, the sizes of those engines vary considerably. There are a pair of 1600cc cars — the Talbot and Volkswagen — the Ford 2-litre, and topping the pile, the 2.3 litres of the Vauxhall. And yet quoted engine powers are close. Smallest is the Sunbeam with a maximum 100 bhp, the

Ford and Volkswagen both develop 110 bhp, while the Vauxhall again comes top with 135 bhp.

It's the same story on the track where performance times against the clock are uncannily similar. It's little use having masses of power if the car has to waste part of that power dragging a heavy body along, thus it should come as no surprise that the lightest car by some 2 cwt — the Golf GTi — is the quickest accelerating. From a standing start to 60 mph the German car takes just 9.2 seconds, which is no bad time for a 1600 cc car. The most powerful, and heaviest Chevette is next quickest taking 9.7 seconds, while the Ford and Talbot both take 9.9 seconds. As we said the cars all perform in much the same way as far as the stopwatches are concerned, up until mid speeds at least. The power advantage of the Chevette becomes apparent at higher speeds, though, being the quickest above 70 mph by some margin.

Over the standing 400 metres it is the Vauxhall and Volkswagen that show the others the way home, both taking 17.3 seconds, though the Vauxhall has a far higher terminal speed indicating that while the Golf has begun to run out of steam, the Chevette has just got the bit between its teeth. It should be said at this point that, once more, we were not happy with the performance of the Escort RS2000. As fate would have it, the car tested in this issue is exactly the same car as we tested in the March issue, and without the hindrance of the poor weather we improved our 0-60 mph performance times from 10.4 seconds to 9.9 seconds; Ford quote a time of 8.5 seconds. Short of blowing up an engine, we decided our times were as good as we were going to record and called it a day, deciding either Ford's claim or BPU 917T was at fault. In any case 9.9 seconds to reach 60 mph from rest is not a time to be scorned.

While the typical boy-racer might consider standing start acceleration times the most important aspect of a car's performance, we believe that more significant are top gear overtaking times. And here the Escort comes out on top, accelerating from 50-

70 mph in top in 8.9 seconds, compared with the Talbot's 9.3 seconds; the Chevette's 9.9 and the Golf's 10.4 seconds.

The Vauxhall is the only one of the group with a five speed gearbox, though in this instance direct comparisons are permissable because the Chevette's is a close ratio five speed 'box rather than the more normal four speed plus overdrive ratio five speed gearbox.

The most important aspect of performance is how the car behaves on the road, and in this case the story takes a distinct twist for two of the foursome are built primarily as club racing specials — or that is how it seems when trying to thread the Vauxhall or Talbot through busy city traffic. Both the Chevette and Sunbeam with their twin carburettors, seem to spend the bulk of their time fouling their plugs and popping and banging their way through anything that isn't a flat out blind.

To enter cars in various forms of racing or rallying, it is necessary to prove to the authorities the car is a standard road car available to all and sundry, thus some manufacturers make the barest minimum needed. We feel the 16-valve twin overhead camshaft engine of the Chevette and the twin Weber version of the Sunbeam 1.6 litre engine make both these car homologation specials — ideal for special stages and circuit racing, but out of their depth in normal traffic.

Ford are past masters of the homologation special, too. But with the RS2000 they have played safe, for the car is basically an Escort with a 2-litre Cortina engine under the bonnet and behaves in traffic in much the same way a Cortina does. Volkswagen's answer is by far the most success-ful. Rather than inserting larger engines or playing with tempera-mental twin carburettors that need expert tuning, the Golf engine has been fuel injected allowing a power boost with none of the problems faced by the rivals. Of course fuel injection is not cheap, nor did it have a good realiability record, but the Germans have been injecting engines for years and have by all accounts got it right now.

On the road it is the Golf that feels the smoothest to drive, with its delightfully free-revving attitude, the 1588 cc developing peak power at a high 6100 rpm. The Escort and Chevette both feel powerful but lack the ability to rev freely like the Golf while the pushrod Sunbeam unit feels simply archaic. For once gearchanges on all the cars can receive praise rather than rebukes, though as usual that in the Escort is the best. The small gate and an ideally placed gearlever which snicks in and out of gear means the driver is forever changing gear just for the fun of it. Changes in the other three are also good, though the Chevette, which has an unusual gear change with the top four ratios in the usual H pattern and first on its own to the left, suffers a heavy clutch.

It is usual to find speedometers a touch on the optimistic side — it probably saves quite a few licences, but the speedometer on the Escort was hopelessly optimistic while that on the Chevette under-read marginally.

Handling

With four such cars you would be forgiven for thinking that handling and roadholding capabilities should be of the highest order. You would not be disappointed, though there is one distinct leader and one distinct loser in this group. Out at the front must be the only front wheel drive car of the foursome. We have, in the past, heaped praise on the handling of all Golfs, whether 1100 cc, 1500 cc or diesel variants and the same must go for the GTi. It shares the same basic suspension set-up as other Golfs, but set slightly lower and slightly wider thanks partly to the use of fatter tyres, and the result is an agile all-rounder that corners with mild understeer but it is more than willing to help a driver hurry by lifting an inside rear wheel when asked.

Traditionally, rear wheel drive has been demanded by the enthusiast simply because it is easy to slide the rear round a corner by some unsubtle work with the right throttle foot. The result is a car that goes around corners quickly, but untidily, and a car that can catch out the unwary.

Opposite locking one's way along is fine on a test track, but it is not at home on public roads. For that reason we like the Golf so

Interior

Ford
For
Excellent Recaro seats; superb driving position
Against
Rear access poor; limited rear kneeroom

Talbot
For
Well shaped seats; hatchback
Against
Poor rearward movement of front seats; limited space in rear; sombre

Vauxhall
For
Good driving position; cheerful interior; well trimmed
Against
Poor rear space; access to rear difficult

Volkswagen
For
Firm, but comfortable seats; bright interior; good driving position
Against
Cheap finish; uninspired dash; engine noise intrudes

Instruments

Ford Escort RS 2000

1: Clock
2: Two-speed fan
3: Heater controls
4: Rev counter
5: Fuel gauge
6: Temperature
7: Oil pressure
8: Speedometer
9: Air vent
10: Lights master switch
11: Two-speed wipers
12: Indicators/dip/flash/horn
13: Rear fog lamp
14: Heated rear window
15: Cigarette lighter
16: Hazard warning lights

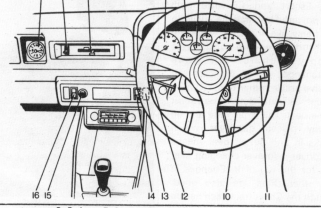

Talbot Sunbeam Ti

1: Front fog lights
2: Heater controls
3: Two-speed fan
4: Spare
5: Indicators
6: Lights/dip/flash/horn
7: Temperature
8: Oil pressure
9: Rev counter
10: Speedometer
11: Fuel gauge
12: Battery condition
13: Two-speed wipers/washers
14: Heated rear window
15: Choke
16: Rear fog lights
17: Brake test
18: Hazard warning lights
19: Rear wash wipe

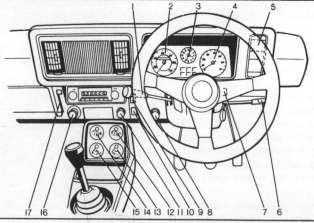

Vauxhall Chevette 2300HS

1: Two-speed wipers/washers
2: Speedometer
3: Clock
4: Rev counter
5: Lights master switch
6: Indicators/dip/flash/horn
7: Hazard flashers
8: Choke
9: Interior light
10: Heated rear window
11: Cigarette lighter
12: Voltmeter
13: Temperature gauge
14: Oil pressure gauge
15: Fuel gauge
16: Two-speed fan
17: Heater controls

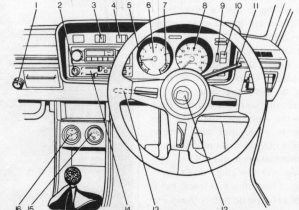

Volkswagen Golf GTi

1: Cigarette lighter
2: Three-speed heater fan
3: Hazard warning lights
4: Heated rear window
5: Temperature gauge
6: Rev counter
7: Fuel gauge
8: Speedometer
9: Panel light rheostat
10: Lights master switch
11: Two-speed wipers/intermittent rear wash-wipe
12: Horn
13: Indicators/dip/flash
14: Heater controls
15: Clock
16: Oil temperature

much, but that is not to say the Escort and Chevette do not handle well, for they do. The Escort with its rather crude rear semi-elliptic suspension nevertheless has such delightfully light and precise steering that the whole car feels well balanced, while the live-rear axled Chevette with its wide, fat tyres is difficult to unstick in the dry at least. The Vauxhall's steering — all have rack and pinion steering — is not as light as the Escort's but precise and quick, despite it having four turns lock-to-lock.

At the back comes the Sunbeam. We consider the ordinary shopping Sunbeams to be safe if a trifle dull handlers, and were looking forward to the Ti in the hope that Talbot have given th car a little more agility. They haven't. It still feels stodgy and unexciting.

As all four cars are aimed at the enthusiast, ride comfort has been sacrificed to some degree on the altar of handling. But once more it is the little Golf that comes out on top with a ride that is firm, in a typical Germanic way, but in no way uncomfortable. The car feels stiff and taut and yet is ideal transport for long journeys, while the Escort driver would soon get pretty fed up with the continual crashing and bumping as the tight suspension seemed to find all the pot-holes available. The Chevette and Sunbeam both come over as rally specials with harsh rides. Fortunately all four have excellent front seats which hold the driver and passenger in place during even the most spirited driving, especially so the Recaro seats found in the Escort.

The foursome also share the same braking arrangement with servo assisted discs at the front and drums at the rear and — thankfully — all complete their task with contemptuous ease, though the Golf has the usual VW sponginess.

Accommodation

It can be argued that these modern sports cars do not have to be particularly spacious, but even boy-racers have to do the shopping some times!

Obviously with cars that are variations on bread and butter saloons and hatchbacks, it stands to reason that they will perform mundane tasks as well — or as

Ford Escort RS2000 Custom

Familiar lines of the Escort with added RS spoiler. Boot (below) is small and crowded

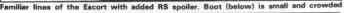

GB BPU 917T

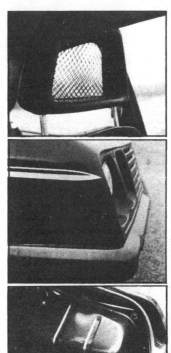

Top: controversial tennis racket head rests
Centre: rubber droop snoot disguises Ford
Above: the boot is full of petrol tank

Talbot Sunbeam Ti

Stick-on stripes and spoilers mark the Ti. Hatchback (below) is on small side

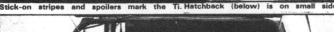

DWK 226T

Top: washer is directed through spoiler
Centre: twin Webers provide extra power
Above: stripes come unstuck with petrol

badly — as their cheaper relatives. All four have but two side doors, which means that getting to and from the rear of the cars can be a problem. And once there, room is limited anyway — especially in the three home grown cars. The Golf at least has a reasonable amount of rear leg and head room. In the front the story is not so bad, though taller drivers will find themselves at a disadvantage in the Chevette and Sunbeam as in order to allow those in the rear some room, the front seats do not adjust back far enough — and those special seats take up even more of the available space than the usual seats.

Stowage space in the rear of the cars is reasonable if not outstanding. The smallish boot of the Escort loses space to the spare wheel and petrol tank, while the boot floors of the Sunbeam and Chevette are none too deep thanks to the stowing of spare wheels underneath and the restrictions of rear wheel drive. Back seats in the three hatchbacks all fold down, however, increasing space further. The boot area of the Golf is rather narrow but much deeper than its rivals. Unlike the top of the range pedestrian Sunbeams, the Ti does not have a split rear seat arrangement which would make the car more versatile.

Interior stowage space is nothing special in any of the cars — three have small glove boxes, while the Sunbeam has none. Vauxhall and Volkswagen have given their cars a centre console with small shelves for odds and ends, while Talbot have taken a centre console *out* of the Sunbeam . . . the GLS has one, the more expensive Ti does not.

Living with the cars

The major bugbear of any tuned car is noise, and it is a problem faced by three of these four, the exception being — yet again — the civilised Golf. In contrast to the others, the Golf feels like a limousine with little wind or tyre noise, though there is a reminder that this is no ordinary Golf from the excited note of the exhaust and engine. The Ford suffers from engine noise while the most predominant noise in the Talbot is the typical asthmatic breathing of twin Webers. The Vauxhall is just plain noisy, the exhaust note is loud, the

Wide wheels and spoilers give Chevette a mean look. Hatchback (below) is useful

Top: brutal nose transforms car's looks
Centre: gauges in console are poorly placed
Above: unusual five-speed gearbox pattern

Golf GTi is understated — just one stripe. Boot (below) spoilt by intrusions

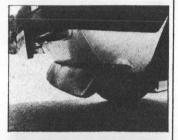

Top: nose spoiler helps stability at speed
Centre: A visual pun — a golf ball gear knob
Above: matt black 'paint' is really tape

wide tyres rumble and the engine makes sure everyone inside knows just how hard it is working.

Driving positions are generally excellent — especially so in the Escort, but none is perfect. The Vauxhall has a cluster of four dials sitting in a floor mounted console and are virtually unreadable; the Sunbeam needs more rearward adjustment to the seat, and has three spindly stalks to operate the major controls, which is one too many. The latter problem also affects the RS2000, while the Golf's floor mounted pair of dials are difficult to read at a glance — these are minor niggles however.

All four have spares stowed in the boot, upright in the case of the Ford, but beneath all the luggage in the remaining trio. All four have high loading sills, too.

Ignoring the problems of town driving as outlined in the Performance section, there could be further problems living with the Vauxhall and Talbot, and to a lesser extent with the Ford, for they all advertise the fact that they are boy-racers and attract attention to themselves. The Chevette has a neatly moulded air dam and masses of go faster stripes proclaiming its potential, while the Talbot uses black stick on stripes as if they were going out of style. The Talbot also has a air dam which in this case houses a useful pair of fog lamps. Ford designers have managed to turn a rather ordinary looking saloon into something special without recourse to stickers and stripes, but the rubber boot spoiler and "droopsnoot" nose of the RS2000 are rather obvious.

Volkswagen, on the other hand, have left the Golf too standard for some tastes. Externally the major differences are a red rim to the grille, and a matt black surround to the rear window and that's about it. Volkswagen themselves say it's case of "understatement instead of warpaint" and it's an image **What Car?** believes is probably the right one.

Heating and ventilation has come a long way in recent years since the advent of through flow ventilation and only the Sunbeam disappoints in this respect — there just doesn't seem to be enough power through the face level vents to do the job properly. Only the Vauxhall has opening rear

Car	Ford Escort RS2000	Talbot Sunbeam Ti	Vauxhall Chevette	Volkswagen Golf GTi
Price	£5181	£4433	£5939	£5135
Performance				
Max Speed (mph)	107	111	115	108
Max in 4th (mph)	—	—	93	—
Max in 3rd (mph)	90	76	72	90
Max in 2nd (mph)	63	50	51	61
Max in 1st (mph)	34	30	32	34
0-30 (sec)	3.7	3.1	3.4	3.5
0-40 (sec)	5.6	5.2	5.2	4.8
0-50 (sec)	7.4	7.0	7.1	6.9
0-60 (sec)	9.9	9.9	9.7	9.2
0-70 (sec)	13.5	13.2	12.3	12.7
0-80 (sec)	17.6	16.9	15.8	16.6
0-90 (sec)	24.1	23.3	20.1	21.6
0-400 metres (sec)	17.8	18.0	17.3	17.3
Terminal speed (mph)	81	82	87	82
30-50 in 3rd/4th/5th (sec)	8.7	8.9	7.7/12.2	9.7
40-60 in 3rd/4th/5th (sec)	8.5	8.4	7.3/9.5	9.6
50-70 in 3rd/4th/5th (sec)	8.9	9.3	6.7/9.9	10.4
Speedo error at 60 mph	12.5% fast	6% fast	1% slow	3% fast
Specifications				
Cylinders/cap (cc)	4/1993	4/1598	4/2279	4/1588
Bore x stroke (mm)	90.8 x 76.9	87.3 x 66.7	97.8 x 76.2	79.5 x 80
Valve gear	ohc	ohv	dohc	ohc
Main bearings	5	5	5	5
Power/rpm (bhp)	110/5500	100/6000	135/5500	110/6100
Torque/rpm (lbs/ft)	117.6/4000	96/4600	134/4500	96.5/5000
Steering	rack/pin	rack/pin	rack/pin	rack/pin
Turns lock to lock	3.5	3.7	4.0	3.3
Turning circle (ft)	32.8	31.5	30.2	32.8
Brakes	S/Di/Dr	S/Di/Dr	S/Di/Dr	S/Di/Dr
Suspension front	I/McP/A	I/McP/A	I/Wi/C/A	I/McP
rear	½E/Ra	4L/C	C/A	I/C/TCA
Costs				
Test mpg	19.3-23.0	18.0-19.7	15.3-18.1	23.0-30.4
Govt mpg City/56/75	25.7/37.1/27.6	21.9/34.3/00.0	17.5/34.4/28.0	23.0/41.5/32.5
Tank galls (grade)	9(4)	9.0(4)	8.4(2)	9.9(4)
Major service miles (hours)	12,000 (4.45)	10,000 (2.17)	6000 (3.6)	10,000 (2.4)
Parts costs (fitting hours)				
Front wing	£28.66 (—)	£20.00 (—)	£27.85 (7.9)	£37.41 (1.6)
Front bumper	£17.00 (—)	£23.60 (0.48)	N/A	£38.77 (0.4)
Headlamp unit	£24.47 (0.5)	£16.97 (0.5)	£23.00 (0.3)	£15.25 (0.5)
Rear light lens	£3.96 (—)	£10.10 (0.17)	£4.94 (0.2)	£11.78 (0.4)
Front brake pads	£12.88 (0.8)	£14.60 (0.53)	£14.40 (0.7)	£9.38 (0.7)
Shock absorber	£11.11 (0.8)	£14.61 (0.38)	£23.90 (0.6)	£34.07 (0.8)
Windscreen	£30.00 (1.5)	£45.00 (1.02)	£48.85 (1.9)	£33.95 (0.7)
Exhaust system	£83.90 (0.8)	£69.93 (0.58)	£74.67 (3.1)	£79.63 (1.3)
Clutch unit	£38.03 (2.4)	£34.39 (1.9)	£29.72 (0.8)	£36.76 (0.7)
Alternator	£88.11 (0.8)	£37.70 (0.35)	£35.65 (0.5)	£41.75 (0.9)
Insurance group	7/on app	4/£80-101	6/£118-133	6/£118-133
Warranty/quote	12/UL	12/UL	12/UL	12/UL + 6yr anti-corrosion
Equipment				
Alloy wheels	Yes	Yes	Yes	Yes*
Five-speed gearbox	No	No	Yes	Yes*
Electronic ignition	No	No	Yes	No
Clock	Yes	No	Yes	Yes
Front fog lights	No	Yes	No	£95.14
Rear fog lights	No	£20.22	No	One
Laminated screen	Yes	£46.13	Yes	Yes
Tinted glass	Yes	No	Yes	£109.34
Ammeter	Yes	Yes	Yes	No
Oil temperature gauge	No	No	No	Yes
Petrol cap lock	No	No	No	Yes
Radio	No	No	Yes	No
Intermittent wipe	Yes	Yes	No	Yes
Rear wash-wipe	N/A	Yes	No	Yes
*1980 models				
Dimensions				
Front headrooms (ins)	38	35	36	36.5
Front legroom (ins)	36-41	33-39.5	31-37.5	31.5-39
Steering-wheel-seat (ins)	13-19.5	11-17.5	12-18	12-19.5
Rear headroom (ins)	32	31.5	32	34
Rear kneeroom (ins)	23-29	22-29	23-29	25.5-32
Length (ins)	161.8	150.7	157.2	150.2
Wheelbase (ins)	94	95	94.2	94.5
Height (ins)	55	54.9	53.6	54.7
Boot load height (ins)	30	34	32.5	30
Boot depth (ins)	39	25-46	31-51	30-43
Boot height (ins)	21	10-28	6-24	16-39
Boot width (ins)	40-46	40-51	31-49	35-51
Overall width (ins)	61.6	63.1	62.2	64.0
Track F/R (ins)	50.8/51.8	51.8/51.3	53.4/53.2	55.3/54.0
Int width F/R (ins)	50/50	53.5/52	51/50	52/51
Weight (cwt)	18.2	17.9	18.9	15.9
Towing weight (cwt)	19.7	15.7	N/A	23.6
Payloads (lbs)	1000	970	783	926
Boot capacity (cu ft)	10.3	14.7/42.7	9/35	13/38.9

KEY. Valve gear: *ohc,* overhead camshaft; *ohv,* overhead valve; *dohc,* double overhead camshaft; *cih,* cam-in-head. **Steering:** rack/pin, rack/pin, rack and pinion; rec ball, recirculating ball; worm/nut; worm/roll, worm and roller; PA, power assistance. **Brakes:** *Di,* discs; *Dr,* Drums; *S,* servo assistance; *P,* power assistance. **Suspension:** *I,* independent; *C,* coil springs; *Tor,* torsion bar springs; *½E,* semi-elliptic springs; *Hg,* Hydragas; *Hp,* Hydropneumatic; *Wi,* wishbones; *McP,* MacPherson struts; *deD,* de Dion axle; *Ta,* trailing arm location; *STA,* semi-trailing arm location; *4L,* four link location; *3L,* three link location; *TL,* transverse link; *DA,* dead beam axle; *WL,* Watts linkage; *PR,* Panhard rod; *TCA,* torsion crank axle; *RA,* radius arms.

windows to aid air extraction, a feature that is sorely missed in the others.

Equipment

Talbot seem determined the Ti should be regarded as a club special by basing the model on the cheapest model in the range, presumably thinking the rally driver is not bothered by the lack of a cigar lighter, panel rheostat, luggage tonneau cover and split rear seat. But as a regular road car these omissions add up and give the drive the impression the car has been put together on the cheap. Vauxhall on the other hand have made sure the HS is as comfortable as possible. It has a laminated screen, tinted glass and a radio as standard, as well as alloy wheels and a five speed gearbox. The Talbot does have alloy wheels — well four of them, as the spare is a normal steel wheel.

RS2000s are available in two guises — this is the more expensive Custom version which features alloy wheels, those excellent Recaro seats, tinted glass and a remote control driver's door mirror as standard. As usual it's a German car that comes at the bottom of the list when it comes to standard equipment, though the GTi has tinted glass, a laminated windscreen and a locking petrol cap. New for 1980, will be alloy wheels and a five speed gearbox as standard — needless to say the price will be more than at present.

Costs

It's almost as if the needle has got stuck ... once again the Volkswagen Golf comes out tops. It may have fuel injection but its consumption is so far ahead of its rivals it looks almost like an economy car. The lowest mpg we achieved was 23.0 mpg, coincidentally the same as the Government test figure for the urban cycle, while the best was over 30 mpg — with a fifth gear it will be even better. In contrast, of the others, only the Escort managed to scrape above 20 mpg, and the remaining pair shocked us with their incredible thirst.

Servicing costs are going to penalise the Vauxhall owner. His Chevette needs major attention every 6000 miles, while the VW and Talbot have 10,000 mile intervals and the Ford needs looking at every 12,000 miles. Parts costs are much the same, but woe-betide any Vauxhall owner who bashes a front wing, for nearly eight hours is the quoted time to put the matter right.

Insurance costs for such high performance cars are going to be high no matter who the driver, but we found quotes favoured the Sunbeam. Ease of servicing is an important consideration and although the Escort is usually sold by Ford Rallye Sport dealers, its common running gear will provide no surprises for the bulk of Ford's 1250 dealers and agents. The two other British cars have dealer representation around 640, while Volkswagen have 360 dealers. Warranty periods are the usual 12 month and unlimited mileage deals, though Volkswagen also have a six year warranty against rust.

Verdict

It became obvious early on in this test that for everyday use there was only one winner — and that was a winner by some margin. The Golf GTi is a truly remarkable car being quick yet frugal, sporty yet practical, and understated. It is not perfect — quite. We feel the interior lacks style and we know from experience it does not take long before it gets to look shabby. We also feel there is perhaps too much painted metal around inside for the price, and perhaps a little sound insulation under the bonnet would not go amiss either.

Runner-up must be the Escort which too, is quick and practical, but loses out on refinement, interior space and roadholding. In its favour it is well priced and lacks some of the mechanical complication of the Golf. The Vauxhall and Sunbeam are in a different class altogether. We suffered near accidents at traffic lights with both cars thanks to the fouling of the plugs — the cars will pull away from lights only to stutter and near die, causing heavy braking from behind. The only answer is to rev the engine high and drop the clutch as if doing a standing start at the test track, no wonder fuel consumption was high and looks from other drivers disdainful.

For our money, it's got to be the Golf all the way.

Volkswagen Golf GTi

Still sparklingly smooth

Golf with a difference – more under the bonnet than outside, where modification are worthwile and trim changes restrained

EVER SINCE John Cooper suggested to what was then BMC that something worthwhile might be achieved in putting a more powerful engine in the Mini, there has been an irresistible attraction in the fast and nimble front-wheel-drive car. Nimble implies small, or at any rate not big; for a variety of good reasons, 2-litre and bigger front-drive cars – with the notable lone exception of the Lancia Gamma – do not lend themselves so wholly satisfactorily to good performance *and* good handling. The undoubted king of this pleasurable class is still the Volkswagen Golf GTi. We don't usually begin a Road Test with a conclusion, but it is hard to avoid saying right away that, *overall*, there is still nothing in mass production sporting saloons which quite beats the GTi. One or two competitors handle as well or a shade better – but none of them has such a superbly performing and behaving engine.

Autocar was early on to the GTi in this country, testing a left-hand-drive example (all you could get from the car's introduction at Frankfurt in 1976 up to the start of right hand sales in July 1979) in our issue of March 1977. Since then, amongst other lesser changes, VW changed the original four-speed gearbox to a five-speed (still a sports-type rather than an overdrive one) – which was a good excuse to sample this delightful machine again.

Performance
Sparklingly smooth

First of all, a brief reminder of what makes a GTi different from other Golfs: the engine is of course the main reason. It is a Bosch K-Jetronic fuel-injected version of what used to be the 1600 Golf power unit; but with bigger inlet valves, slightly more advanced cam timing, a Heron type cylinder head with dished crown pistons, higher grade main and big-end bearings and an oil cooler, it develops a DIN 110 bhp at 6,100 rpm and 103lb ft peak torque at 5,000 rpm. The original carburettor version of the 79.5 x 80mm 1,588 c.c. engine is no longer found in any Golf (it survives in the Sirocco), but when one recalls that, with its lower compression ratio (8.2 instead of the 9.5 of the GTi) and milder tune, it turns out 85 bhp at 5,600 rpm and 92lb ft at 3,800 rpm, the degree of tune of the injection engine (nearly 70 bhp per litre) is obviously high by road car standards.

The rest of the car is different in some important ways too. Wider (175/70) tyres on 5½in. aluminium alloy wheels necessitate small plastic extensions to the already pronounced wheel arch ears of the standard body, the suspension is nearly an inch lower (20mm), anti roll bars are provided at both ends, Bilstein dampers are fitted and the brakes are more heavily servo'd, with ventilated discs in front. There is a noticeable front spoiler, and you can only buy the car in one of three paint colours – metallic silver, red or black, with red coach lining round the grille.

Returning to the engine, its specification may suggest a peaky, racy thing, potentially intractable and certainly not one you'd be happy to let your timorous elderly aunt use for her local shopping expedition. In spite of that maximum torque figure, only 1,100 rpm away from the maximum power speed, the Golf GTi power unit is exactly the opposite. It would be interesting to know how much of its flexibility and sweetness is due in the first place to the extra tractability which good fuel injection confers on most cars, and how much (in part) to clever engine mounting. It will pull from surprisingly low rpm, as our fourth gear times, taken from an admittedly academic 10 mph (650 rpm), suggest – and its cold run behaviour is

typical of current Bosch injected cars. After the coldest of night stands, you simply turn the ignition key without touching the accelerator and away it goes. Equally, the cold driveaway is totally viceless, to an extent which in the hands of a thoughtless or mechanically ignorant owner could almost be harmful, for there is nothing to stop such people driving flat-out from the turn of the key.

But you don't buy any car, especially one like this, for its cold-running virtues, even if they help towards its considerable appeal. It is the way it goes that is so endearing. It is a waspish-sounding engine, with wonderful zest almost throughout its range; you cannot help being seduced by its response and total lack of any flat spots, and the way that it pulls you so vividly up the speed table. With 110 bhp to propel just under 18cwt (104 bhp per ton laden as tested), the car cannot help itself of course – it has to go, and it does – yet so comparatively smoothly.

The old four-speed car's gear ratios corresponded to 31, 54, 77 and 106 mph at power peak, so that at its 108 mph mean maximum speed it was only slightly undergeared (although VW's claim of 113 mph suggests that it was actually more markedly so). The five-speed replacement is more happily geared, the same 6,100 rpm corresponding to 30, 49, 72, 91 and 113 mph, with the engine speed on each up change dropping to a fairly progressively closing pattern – 3,750 rpm, 4,200 rpm, 4,800 and 4,900 rpm.

The test car returned a mean top speed of 111 mph, although it might have equalled VW's claim in lighter winds; the test session suffered from 10 to 25 mph wind, which is bound to have a slight effect on performance. However, the effect on the car's acceleration was less marked, so that the test example beat the claims slightly – and is comfortably faster than the four-speed original, in spite of the extra gearchange. This is probably due to the change in gearing; in overall effect, thanks to a lower final drive (3.89 instead of 3.70) and different individual gears, the

> **Volkswagen Golf GTi**
> Top-performance version of Volkswagen's best selling 1100-1600 transverse-engined front-drive two-box hatchback, with 110 bhp fuel injected version of the 1600 engine, revised suspension, special limited trim and minor body changes, now with five-speed gearbox.
>
> **PRODUCED BY:**
> *Volkswagen, AG,*
> *3180 Wofsburg,*
> *German Federal Republic.*
>
> **SOLD IN THE UK BY:**
> *Volkswagen (GB) Ltd.,*
> *Yeomans Drive,*
> *Blakelands,*
> *Milton Keynes,*
> *Buckinghamshire.*
> *(MK14 5AN)*

five-speed GTi has lower first, second and third ratios, whilst fourth is in effect a high third before the absolute true maximum speed top.

The figures tell the tale. Because of the effective transfer of weight away from the driving wheels in a front-drive car, it is very rare for such cars to break 3 sec to 30 mph – but the five-speed GTi does it in 2.9 (compared to 3.3 the original). The rest of the times are equally impressive (four-speed times in brackets): 50 comes up in 6.1 sec (7.4), 60 in 9.0 (9.8), 80 in 16.1 (19.3), 90 in 21.9 (28.7) continuing to 100 in 33.9 (which the four-speed would not reach easily within a mile in both directions). The distance times are similarly improved; the standing quarter time is now 16.9 sec (17.3), and the kilometre 31.5 (32.3).

Perhaps paradoxically, although the undeniably excellent performance of the car makes it sound like a machine best suited to the expert driver, the GTi engine is a paragon of good behaviour, in the way it is so forgiving of clumsy or lazy driving. If you haven't bothered to change down, but need suddenly to get moving, there is so much power low down that you still get away pretty smartly. Not that there is any excuse for such laziness when the gearchange is so pleasantly easy and precise, with its ideally shaped gearlever knob (a simple ball, in this case a physical pun, with its surface dimpled to resemble a golf ball). And when you are in the right gear, there is always such performance, zooming you out of a junction into a traffic gap that must be taken smartly with a marvellous whoop of exuberance. So smooth and so eager, it certainly does need the 6,750 rpm rev limiter fitted.

Economy
There when wanted

A car like the GTi is an efficient machine, in both the power and economy senses, and even when you use its performance, its economy is good. Our overall consumption of 27.7 mpg is of course worse than what most owners probably obtain, because of the high proportion of performance testing mileage – but this is still excellent for a four-seater car capable of such acceleration and top speed. 30 mpg is a much more general figure, which several of our testers bettered by at least 1 mpg. For the patient and restrained, there is better-still frugality to be wrung comparatively easily from the car.

Noise
Engine-dominated

It is certainly not the quietest of cars, by a long chalk, but most owners will not have bought it for the sake of a quiet life, and except on a long motorway run when the near-uselessness of any radio fitted becomes tiresome, the noise made by the engine and its exhaust is, to most ears, pleasing. Interestingly, it has accentuated resonant periods at 70 and 90 true (77 and 98 on the exceptionally optimistic speedometer of the test car), and is less noisy in between. There is quite a lot of wind noise too, plus an average amount of bump thump on the Cinturato CN36s fitted, although the engine noise dominates both of these.

Comfort behind is spoilt by a quite bad example of a standing wave resonance, in that the noise level is noticeably higher in the back, particularly nearer the rear quarter panels.

Road behaviour
Entertaining

The GTi steers generally very well. There is a little trace of sloppiness in its rack and pinion steering, particularly about the straight ahead, but at 3.3 turns lock to lock for a 32½ft minimum turning circle, its response is quite good, The amount of negative offset used is not too great to stop the steering effort being comparatively light, nor does it take away feel, which is pleasingly present. However, on quick take-offs, particularly if the

power is fed in early whilst rounding a tight turn, the steering tends in the common powerful front-driven-car way to stay momentarily on lock, losing the normally good self-centering. Similarly, accelerating hard over bumps produces quite a lot of fight in the steering – not unpleasantly, but it is noticeable.

In the specification, the rear suspension is described as strictly "semi-independent". That is because its trailing arms, as on all Golfs, are mechanical Siamese twins, joined transversely to each other by a box-section tube which must twist when one arm needs to move relative to the other, as in roll. On the GTi, the anti-roll stiffness this gives to the rear suspension is increased by the addition of a conventional anti-roll bar – and adding extra roll stiffness at the back relative to the front increases rear tyre slip angle when cornering, countering the naturally heavier front-tyre slip angle of a front-drive car, and has the effect of reducing understeer.

This certainly happens in the GTi, although the effect overall comes in two stages. The car has the natural straight stability of its breed, due to the right amount of initial understeer, changing to the near-neutral as you start to corner. At middling high rates, with power on, there is a little more understeer, but if thrown or swerved as the throttle is closed, it will go into a Mini-Cooper style tail slide, lifting its inside rear wheel as the roll increases noticeably. This is both a safety factor in an emergency on the public road – you would not of course drive like this normally unless in a lonely place with perfect vision, no traffic and no people – and great fun on a closed track. The high-ish build of the car, and the typically high driving position does however impart a slight topply feeling in extremis, more so than in rivals like Ford's XR3 or the Alfasud, and the inside front wheel can be made to spin comparatively easily.

Again compared with its rivals, the Golf GTi contrives to give this sort of entertaining handling and (normally) low roll without undue cost to ride. It is surprisingly good in this respect, another factor which combines with its smoothness of engine to make it more civilised than most.

The brakes are of average weight, with some noticeable initial fade which demands a surprising extra amount of shove on the pedal when briskly driving, but as our standard fade test showed, with acceptable fade resistance when made to work hard (pedal effort for the first of ten ½g stops at quarter-mile intervals from 81 mph was 40lb dropping to 32lb, and for the last stop – when the front discs had turned a dull red – was 54-48lb).

Hatch opens to expose high silled but quite generous boot

A tight bonnetful, made so particularly by the K-Jetronic air valve assembly behind battery. Generally access is considerably better than first appearances suggest

Behind the wheel
Functional

At first, the driving seat seems hard, but with experience it proves to be comfortable, with good sideways and lumbar support. For drivers of 6ft or more, and slightly shorter ones with long-ish legs, the otherwise good and typically German driving position – high, with good headroom and an excellent view

Instruments from left are 120 mph press-to-zero trip speedometer and 7,000 rpm revcounter containing fuel gauge and flanking temperature gauge (with warning system function check light), neat l.e.d. warning lamps and l.c.d. digital clock. Switches on left of instruments, are (from top) fog lamp, rear window heater, hazard and a spare space; on right are found the panel lighting dimmer and lamps switch, plus warning lamps for brakes fluid level and circuit failure. Stalks are conventional left-hand-drive, with signalling and dip on left, wipe/wash for both front and back screens on right. In centre, radio (extra) lives above conventional heater controls, and centre console with its oil temperature gauge and quite handy open pocket

HOW THE GOLF GTi PERFORMS

Figures taken at 6,500 miles by our own staff at the Motor Industry Research Association proving ground at Nuneaton. All Autocar test results are subject to world copyright and may not be reproduced in whole or in part without the Editor's written permission.

ACCELERATION

From Rest	True mph	Time (sec)	Speedo mph
	30	2.9	33
	40	4.6	43
	50	6.1	53
	60	9.0	65
	70	12.1	75
	80	16.1	87
	90	21.9	98
	100	33.9	108
	110	—	119

Standing ¼-mile: 16.9 sec, 81 mph
Standing km: 31.5 sec, 98 mph

TEST CONDITIONS:
Wind: 10-25mph
Temperature: 6 deg C (43 deg F)
Barometer: 31.6 in. Hg (1070 mbar)
Humidity: 70 per cent
Surface: dry asphalt and concrete
Test distance: 1,660 miles

MAXIMUM SPEEDS

Gear		mph	kph	rpm
Top (Mean)		111	179	6,000
(Best)		114	183	6,150
4th		101	163	6,750
3rd		79	127	6,750
2nd		54	87	6,750
1st		33	53	6,750

In Each Gear	mph	Top	4th	3rd	2nd
	10-30	—	9.2	6.1	3.5
	20-40	10.4	7.2	5.1	3.2
	30-50	9.7	6.8	4.8	3.2
	40-60	9.7	6.6	5.2	—
	50-70	11.3	7.8	7.4	—
	60-80	12.9	9.1	—	—
	70-90	15.6	10.4	—	—
	80-100	22.8	—	—	—

FUEL CONSUMPTION

Overall mpg: 27.2 (10.2 litres/100km)

Official fuel consumption figures
(ECE laboratory test conditions; not necessarily related to Autocar figures)

Urban cycle: 26.9 mpg
Stead 56 mph: 38.2 mpg
Steady 75 mph: 29.7 mpg

OIL CONSUMPTION

(SAE 20/50) negligible

WEIGHT

Kerb, 17.8 cwt/1,997 lb/906 kg
(Distribution F/R, 64.0/36.0)
Test, 21.1 cwt/2,358 lb/1,070 kg
Max payload 970 lb/440 kg

PRICES

Basic	£4,575.00
Special Car Tax	£381.25
VAT	£743.44
Total (in GB)	**£5,699.69**
Seat Belts	Standard
Licence	£70.00
Delivery charge (London)	£79.35
Number plates (approx.)	£15.00
Total on the Road (exc. insurance)	£5,864.04
EXTRAS (inc VAT)	
Metallic paint	£85.96
Sunroof	£199.33
TOTAL AS TESTED ON THE ROAD	**£5,864.04**
Insurance	Group 6/7

DIMENSIONS

Length: 150.2 in.
Width: 64.1 in.
Height: 54.9 in.

Boot capacity: 13/35.7 cu. ft.
Turning circle:
between kerbs: L 32 ft 9 in. R 32 ft. 2 in.

SPECIFICATION

ENGINE
	Transverse front, front-wheel-drive
Head/block	Al. alloy/cast iron
Cylinders	4, bored block
Main bearings	5
Cooling	Water
Fan	Electric
Bore, mm (in.)	79.5 (3.13)
Stroke, mm (in.)	80 (3.15)
Capacity, cc (in³)	1,588 (96.9)
Valve gear	Ohc
Camshaft drive	Toothed belt
Compression ratio	9.5-to-1
Ignition	Breakerless
Injection	Bosch K-Jetronic
Max power	110 bhp (DIN) at 6,100 rpm
Max torque	103 lb ft at 5,000 rpm

TRANSMISSION
Type	Five-speed
Clutch	Diaphragm spring, 7.9in. dia

Gear	Ratio	mph/1000rpm
Top	0.912	18.50
4th	1.13	14.93
3rd	1.44	11.72
2nd	2.12	7.96
1st	3.45	4.89
Final drive gear	Helical spur	
Ratio	3.89	

SUSPENSION
Front – location	Independent, MacPherson strut
springs	Coil
dampers	Telescopic
anti-roll bar	Standard
Rear – location	Semi-independent, trailing arm
springs	Coil
dampers	Telescopic
anti-roll bar	Standard

STEERING
Type	Rack and pinion
Power assistance	None
Wheel diameter	15 in.
Turns lock to lock	3.3

BRAKES
Circuits	Twin, diagonal split
Front	9.4in. dia. disc
Rear	7.1in. dia. drum
Servo	Vacuum
Handbrake	Centre lever, rear drum

WHEELS
Type	Al. alloy
Rim width	5½in.
Tyres – make	Pirelli
– type	Cinturato CN36 SM radial steel tubeless
– size	175/70HR13in.
– pressures	F 24 R 24 psi (normal driving)

EQUIPMENT
Battery	12V 36Ah
Alternator	45A
Headlamps	90/80W
Reversing lamp	Standard
Electric fuses	16
Screen wipers	2-speed + intermittent
Screen washer	Electric
Interior heater	Water valve
Air conditioning	Not available
Interior trim	Cloth seats, leatherette head-lining
Floor covering	Carpet
Jack	Screw lever
Jacking points	2 each side, under sills
Windscreen	Laminated
Underbody protection	Bitumastic/wax injected/pvc

GTi body is two-door. Front seat backs are not difficult to move out of way
Front seats hold one well sideways and although on the firm side are comfortable

forward – is spoilt by the distance between the steering wheel rim and the pedals; when the foot is lifted to brake, or, worse still, to heel and toe (otherwise easy as far as accelerator to brake pedal spacing is concerned), the knee is obstructed by the steering wheel.

Otherwise, controls are well laid out and easily understood on first meeting the car. VW have studied the digital instrument problem where clocks are concerned, and come up with the right decision – not LED (light-emitting diode) which becomes difficult to read in sunlight, but less obtrusive LCD (liquid crystal display), permanently running whether or not the ignition is on (the current drain of a liquid crystal display is negligible by car standards) and always visible thanks to dashboard illumination when side lamps are on. LEDs are used well in one of the neatest warning lamps arrangements we have seen, in the centre of the instrument pack.

In view out, the Golf is both good and bad – good in the height of the eye relative to the windows already mentioned, not so good in the thickness of the A and B-posts, and bad to an old-fashioned extent in the very heavy rear quarter panels. Front seat headrests are an obstruction to vision too, but with the aid of a screwdriver, they are removeable. Wipers are correctly pivotted to suit right hand drive, but would be better if the driver's one didn't leave quite such a large triangular area of screen upswept on the right. Given the car's shape, and the way road filth builds up on the back, the rear wiper would be better working continuously.

The heater behaves like a refined water valve one, giving some temperature variation at a constant speed as on a motorway, the comfortable setting of which is upset when conditions demand a varying speed when you join ordinary roads. It is slow to respond to any movement of the temperature control compared to the much preferable air-blending type, but has plenty of power for de-icing. Ventilation is good, with acceptable throughflow for moderate weather, although a bit limited for hot summer. Cold air vents are nicely controllable, and tolerably effective side-window demisting

is provided. Unlike too many cars, the heater does not make the glove compartment hot.

Living with the GTi

One is impressed early on by the usual good standard of finish and construction, particularly in the way that the doors shut, which many a builder of more exalted cars might do well to study – the slam is quieter than most, and there is no feeling of flimsiness or any sign of rattle. On the other hand, somewhat too much ingenuity has been applied to the steering wheel horn controls, which instead of the elaborate four-button arrangement provided would be better with a single central pad to press – much quicker to find in an emergency, and when negotiating the hairpins of a pass.

Oddment accommodation is tolerable if not generous, with lipped front shelves too narrow to take an Ordnance Survey map, but a reasonable locking glove cubby. Sun visors can be swivelled sideways as well as down, although the passenger's side one cannot be moved without disturbing the rear view mirror.

Most people seem to approve of the interior design, with its restrained functionalness, and the little bit of show in the way that the GTi-distingushing thin red line round the grille is echoed round the instrument panel and the air vents.

Golfs never have shone in rear seating, which remains poor, with insufficient kneeroom and headroom for taller passengers, and door armrests that seem tacitly to acknowledge this in their height, rather too low for larger users. The boot is correspondingly quite generous, although the high sill makes loading larger objects less easy.

The Golf range

Now that there is the Golf GLi convertible (at £6,984) the £5,700 GTi no longer occupies the most expensive place in the Golf range. Its second place means that its nearest companion in price is the 1500 automatic 5-door GLS (£5,230). Besides the other LS 1500, the worthy and endearing LD diesel, and the single 1300 LS, the range begins with the two 1100 models, starting with the 3-door N at £3,599.

HOW THE VOLKSWAGEN GOLF GTi COMPARES

VW Golf GTi £5,700

Front engine, Front drive

Capacity
1,588 c.c.

Power
110 bhp (DIN) at 6,100 rpm

Weight
1,997 lb/906 kg

Test Extra
4 April 1981

Alfa Romeo Alfasud 1.5Ti £4,400

Front engine, Front drive

Capacity
1,490 c.c.

Power
95 bhp (DIN) at 5,800 rpm

Weight
1,967 lb/893 kg

Autotest
13 September 1980

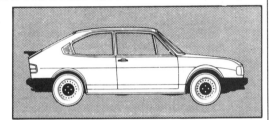

Fiat Mirafiori Sport £4,920

Front engine, Rear drive

Capacity
1,995 c.c.

Power
115 bhp (DINL(at 5,800 rpm

Weight
2,520 lb/1146 kg

Autotest
3 February 1979

Ford Escort XR3 £5,395

Front engine, Front drive

Capacity
1,596 c.c.

Power
96 bhp (DIN) at 6,000 rpm

Weight
2,040 lb/925 kg

Autotest
15 November 1980

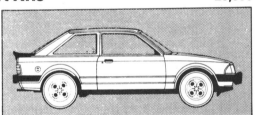

Renault 5 Gordini £5,326

Front engine, Front drive

Capacity
1,397 c.c.

Power
93 bhp (DIN) at 6,400 rpm

Weight
1,813 lb/824 kg

Autotest
28 April 1979

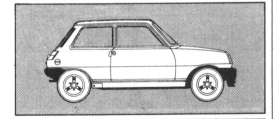

Talbot Sunbeam 1.6Ti £4,872

Front engine, Rear drive

Capacity
1,598 c.c.

Power
100 bhp (DIN) at 6,000 rpm

Weight
2,037 lb/924 kg

Autotest
12 May 1979

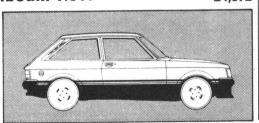

MPH & MPG

Maximum speed (mph)

Ford Escort XR3	113
VW Golf GTi	111
Fiat Mirafiori Sport	107.5
Talbot Sunbeam 1.6Ti	107
Renault 5 Gordini	107
Alfasud 1.5Ti	106

Acceleration 0-60 (sec)

VW Golf GTi	9.0
Ford Escort XR3	9.2
Alfasud 1.5Ti	10.4
Fiat Mirafiori Sport	10.7
Renault 5 Gordini	10.7
Talbot Sunbeam 1.6Ti	10.7

Overall mpg

Renault 5 Gordini	30.0
Ford Escort XR5	27.9
VW Golf GTi	27.7
Alfasud 1.5Ti	26.5
Fiat Mirafiori Sport	22.5
Talbot Sunbeam 1.6Ti	22.3

Of the cars which compete closely with the GTi, the value-for-money ones which stand out particularly are the two Italians and the Talbot; the appreciably bigger-engined (2-litre) Fiat, the delightful Alfasud 1.5Ti and the amusing if somewhat pretentiously spoilered Sunbeam all fall well below the Golf's £5,700 price – but equally, none of them is so sparkingly fast or quite so sweetly engined. Other variously similar possibilities, particularly if price is of less importance, include the GTi's close cousin, the three-box Audi 80 GLE (£7,441) which can be much slower, the BMW 320 (£6,790, 111 mph, 9.8sec, 24.6 mpg) and the still-available Triumph Dolomite Sprint (£7,119, 115 mph, 8.7sec, 23.6 mpg). Returning to the price-competitive cars, Opel's Kadett 1.3SR (£5,051, 101 mph, 14.2sec, 30.2 mpg) isn't as fast but it's handling and roadholding are slightly better than the Golf's, while Peugeot's new 305S (£5,495) might tempt until one looks at its 15 per cent greater weight and 22 per cent less power. The real contest is between the XR3 and the GTi, in which performance and economy honours, in both cases very well earned, are effectively even.

ON THE ROAD

In handling, which is of prime importance in this class, the Golf scores pretty well – very well compared to most cars – although it isn't quite as outstandingly good as the XR3 or Kadett, taking into account the limitations in all cases of front-wheel-drive, which all of these three make light of. Where the Golf is certainly better than its rivals is in ride, which is perhaps surprisingly absorbent for such a stiffly sprung design (in both normal springing and in roll). The cheeky Renault probably comes nearest, working pleasingly, accompanied in the ride stakes by the entertaining Alfasud. All of the front-drive cars here are entertaining handlers, appreciably more so than the contemporary standard for the breed. The Talbot and the Fiat are both front-engine, rear-drive cars, with handling fairly typical of their type.

The Sunbeam works well, with good predictability, although its live rear axle is a lot of unsprung weight for such a small car, and you notice this when cornering (or just riding) over bumps. The Mirafiori is fun too, and handles generally nicely for its type.

SIZE & SPACE

Legroom front/rear (in)

(seats fully back)

Fiat Mirafiori Sport	40.5/38
VW Golf GTi	40/38
Ford Escort XR3	40/38
Talbot Sunbeam 1.6Ti	40/35
Renault 5 Gordini	38/35
Alfasud 1.5Ti	34/37

One might be tempted at first to say that most buyers do not choose cars like these for their roominess – but the fact that all of them are variously practical family saloons at heart gives that supposition the lie. The Golf is a little cramped both in its driving position for tall drivers (lacking knee clearance and headroom) and in room behind. The same applies to the back seat of the XR3. The Sunbeam has a good driving position, and particularly good vision once you remove the head restraints, but rear seating is nothing to write home about. The Alfasud deserves a higher position in the table than the figures give it, since, assuming you don't mind its mildly Italian short-legs, long-arms driving stance, is a relatively generous car inside. Rear legroom on the Renault is restricted, but otherwise it isn't uncomfortable. The Escort and the Alfasud are the only cars here with truly acceptable heating systems.

VERDICT

The Alfasud, Gordini, Mirafiori and 1.6Ti form one part of this set of rivals, with closely similar performance which makes it a matter of argument which is the best of them. The economy of the Renault grows more important to more people day by day, and it is certainly a highly amusing little machine. The Talbot is a much better car than its somewhat pretentious equipment outside (not fitted to the much faster Sunbeam Lotus) might suggest, but it is thirsty. So is the Fiat – a car that will appeal greatly to people with Latin tastes who like a noisy, rorty-sounding engine; it is enjoyable without doubt, even to those who like a quieter life. Alfa's offering is still something of a front-drive classic, with much solid worth and a delightful character.

The contest however, as said earlier, is really between the Ford and the Volkswagen. Choosing between them depends finally on personal taste. If you are used to modern air blending heaters, good ventilation, and prefer its still distinctive and aerodynamic looks, then it has to be the Escort XR3, but only by a hairsbreadth. If an unusual combination of almost equally good handling and ride – the Golf rides very much better than the Escort, even if that isn't saying much – plus the most pleasing engine characteristic of the class matter more, then it is the Volkswagen, which is still a marvellous car of its size and type to drive.

VOLKSWAGEN GOLF GTI BY OETTINGER

Making the Golf swing

BY PAUL FRERE

NEITHER THE FORD Escort XR-3 nor the new Fiat Ritmo (Strada) 105TC can equal the performance of the Golf GTI, but serious competition for the Volkswagen is now emerging from two new cars soon to be marketed: the Fiat Ritmo Abarth, with the 2-liter, 125-bhp, twincam engine, and a turbocharged Renault 5 Alpine (Gordini in Great Britain) that, in contrast to the Renault 5 Turbo, retains such stock features as four seats and front-wheel drive. This challenge is worrisome for the Volkswagen of France branch as the GTI

Oettinger's solution for anemic Golfs and Rabbits is a twincam, cross-flow, 16-valve cylinder head conversion along with a higher-flow K-Jetronic fuel injection system. It's shown here on a non-factory VW. Also, note the stiffening rod attached to the strut towers.

PHOTO BY JOE RUSZ

is not only an image maker but also a significant profit maker: Fifty percent of the spark-ignition Golf models sold in France and 30 percent of all the Golfs (Rabbits) are the 110-bhp GTI.

For the French division it is essential that the GTI remains at the top of its class, but for the moment the factory has no solution compatible with its standard component policy. The turbocharged versions of the Golf have been dropped because of the difficulty in maintaining a low underhood temperature with both the exhaust and inlet systems at the rear of the engine. (Incidentally, the problem is not the same with the diesel, and the 4- and 5-cylinder versions of the VW-Audi diesel are to be marketed with a turbo.)

For the GTI the solution comes from Oettinger, a company that has specialized in tuning Volkswagen engines for more than 30 years and has been marketing a twincam 4-valve cross-flow cylinder head for the Golf for some time. Along with a Bosch K-Jetronic injection system of increased capacity, the cylinder head increases the engine's power 25 percent to 136 bhp DIN at 6500 rpm (compared with the standard version's 110 at 6100 rpm) and the maximum torque from 101 lb-ft at 5000 rpm to 116 at 5500.

The valves, which have an included angle of 24.5 degrees, are operated through inverted cup tappets. A cogged belt drives one of the camshafts; the other cam is geared to it.

Though the cylinder head bolts straight onto the standard engine, this addition necessitates a number of modifications that enhance the engine's performance and reliability. Special pistons are required to fit the new combustion chamber shape. They are forged for reliability and provide a compression ratio as high as 10.5:1. The crankshaft and connecting rods are carefully balanced, the oil pump is modified to raise the pressure and a new, extensively baffled light alloy oil sump is fitted. In order to use the revving ability of the engine, which is safe up to 8000 rpm (though it isn't prudent to exceed 7000 very often), a numerically higher final drive ratio is fitted so that the claimed maximum speed of 121 mph is reached at 7000 rpm on Uniroyal low-profile 185/60HR-14 tires, fitted as standard equipment on 6-in.-wide alloy wheels. Other modifications, apart from cosmetic ones, include an additional bolted crossmember bracing the lower front wishbone brackets and special brake pads. Otherwise, the running gear remains the same and provides an excellent compromise between acceptable comfort and excellent handling and roadholding capabilities.

Until now, anyone could buy a modified Golf GTI from Oettinger, but before Volkswagen agreed to sell it through its French branch—probably to be followed by Switzerland, Belgium and Great Britain—the model had to pass extensive tests with the result that the 16-valve Golf GTI carries the full factory warranty. It is also to be homologated in Group 4 for competition purposes as soon as 400 units are produced. For this, arrangements have been made so that Oettinger takes delivery of a number of engines and modifies them in advance. These engines are fitted to standard Golf GTIs delivered directly from the VW factory, from which the engines are removed and modified in turn. The unused parts—such as the cylinder head, pistons, etc—are returned to VW.

Four headlights, a large spoiler, special instruments and an elaborate radio are included in the car that will sell for 50 percent more than the standard GTI in France. Apart from the 121-mph maximum speed, other performance claims are 0–100 km/h (0–62 mph) in 7.6 seconds and the standing-start kilometer in 29.5 sec, claims I wouldn't question after a 180-mile drive on various types of roads. It is one of the best "fun cars" I have ever driven, and the fastest thing you can buy for secondary roads. It also shows that you can have a lot of fun without wasting fuel and that, with a properly designed engine, you can get 85 bhp per liter without using an air pump to meet the current European emission regulations.

Golf GTI Turbodiesel

Packing both fun and diesel into the Rabbit

To some, the words "fun" and "diesel" in the same sentence are enough to induce nausea. As far as they are concerned, the two concepts are as compatible as fire and water. But there are always those who will not take such things for granted. They are the free thinkers, the pioneers, the fever-headed car nuts.

Andy King claims membership in this group—unconventionals who survived the Late Great Horsepower Race. King is serious about his avocation-turned-livelihood and is the first to admit that this, his fondest piece of machinery, has a value double that of his last 427 Chevelle. He is the mover behind R&A Applied Arts, Inc. (701 Riverside Ave., Lyndhurst, NJ 07071), a progressive shop with its own ideas about cars and the state of their art.

Originally, King was an installer of aftermarket turbo kits, but as his clientele became more worldly, the idea of incor-

by Ro McGonegal
PHOTOGRAPHY BY THE AUTHOR

porating European parts to complete their cars became an obsession. Hence, the $18,000 Golf GTI (nee Rabbit LS diesel) before you. R&A has lavished a great deal of time on the Volkswagen (and Audi), simply because King believes that they are technically advanced, yet affordable to the average buyer.

What average buyer, you are asking yourself in amazement, can afford an $18,000 Rabbit? By King's admission, only a very few, but everything must have a price tag. He sees the squatty black 2-door as a testbed and as a wealth of improvements to the basic bones. Not the ultimate, but perhaps a big step toward that notion.

And being quite human, King even admits to plagiary. Our own Turbo Tour Rabbit diesel (September-December 1980 issues) provided him with the whisp

of an idea; the TT Rabbit was a creature with a high-mileage nature and a maximum comfort mentality, but it boasted little in the way of integrated suspension, spiffy cosmetics or the ability to storm to 60 miles per hour. The elfin Golf has all of these. Save for the interior appointments, every major system has been fondled or finessed, but this Rabbit has no bone-crushing suspension. It has no ragged-edge hyper-diesel or safety harness dangling from an oversize roll bar. It has personality, it has style and, most of all, it is fun to be in. At the heart of this sooty matter is a 1,457cc diesel engine with gasoline reflexes. King and his chief technician, Larry West, have hyped it with a Callaway Turbosystems hot air blower, which pumps out 73 horsepower when the boost rises 10 pounds above normal atmospheric pressure.

Internally, the engine is stock (complete with 22:1 compression ratio), but even the stock diesel operates at higher temperatures than the gasoline engine.

And when the turbo comes on, the temperature goes up even further. To keep the head from blowing off and the bearings from melting, West installed a baffled oil pan and windage tray (to keep the oil *off* the crankshaft and *in* the lubrication system); the 13-row auxiliary oil cooler supplements the Rabbit's existing equipment, and braided-steel lines are used throughout. Since the little stinker sits about 1½ inches lower than it would in the used car lot, a skidplate was tacked to the oil pan.

A Callaway remote air cleaner juts off to the side, and diesel fuel enters the system through a slightly modified gasoline engine fuel injector, which offers better dispersion than the stock diesel unit; waste is blown through a 2¼-inch exhaust system and "turbo" muffler. Although the power produced by this setup is not prodigious, it does make the diesel a smooth operator, greatly reducing the notorious "diesel lag" and instilling it with a positively gasoline-like spirit (0-60 in 12.9 seconds).

At this point, the copious undercarriage changes make good sense in the maturation process. Bilstein gas pressure inserts are very close to the "comfort" settings, providing good damping without introducing ride harshness. The GTI coil springs drop the Rabbit closer to the ground but do not compromise ride quality. An R&A lower frame stress bar keeps the mighty diesel's torque from tearing the front end in two while GMP 19mm anti-roll bars ensure the Rabbit's hairpin poise.

In the car's early stages, King had installed fat 205/60 radials at every corner, but they proved to be too much tire for too little power. The Rabbit now tiptoes around with sensible 175/70HR13 Phoenix Stahlflex steel belts mounted on BBS 6-inch wheels. European GTI ventilated discs and semi-metallic pads pull on the front wheels and drum brakes work in the rear. With them, the turbodiesel Rabbit only needs 160 feet to come down from 60 mph.

If the spider web alloys, windshield tape and "TURBO" graphics screaming from the lower panels don't twist your head, then the GTI fender flares and European front and rear bumpers might. They promote the sullen, business atti-

tude, furthered by the Foha front and Zender rear spoilers (visually sucking the car closer to the road). In someone else's rearview mirror, the R&A turbodiesel is one *baaad*-looking Lepus. It may not prod the 911 driver into mid-life crisis, but it worked really well on Chevettes and other Rabbits.

We ardently followed this procedure, dusting off the back roads of northern New Jersey and then descending upon

MPG

1980 Rabbit LS Turbo Diesel	
EPA City	42
EPA Highway	55
MT Test Loop	N.A.
Steady-state 55 mph	55
Driving range (steady-state 55 mph x fuel capacity)	577.5 miles

the midday hordes of Paramus, fairly slicing Route 17 to ribbons. At cruising speed, turbo power could easily cope with the drag of the air conditioner, but on hilly drives or murderous passing it meant leaving the fan on, dropping back to 3rd and smashing the pedal (or simply killing the switch and poking 4th for the needed pull). Maybe someday the turbo system makers could include an electrically-controlled clutch for the air conditioner compressor that would activate when full boost was called for.

When we tired of mechanical noise, King's Rabbit provided a number of delightful distractions: the beep-buzz of the Fox Super-Heterodyne radar detector; the pitch and resonance conjured by the Blaupunkt 2001 cassette, Fosgate PR-220 power amp, Jensen Triax II speakers and the Alpine fader; and the smart, uppercrust *blat* of dual Bosch air horns. Our fetish for the sweeping needle was indulged by meters for speed, rpm, oil pressure, oil temperature (good to have with a turbocharged engine), coolant temperature and the inevitable turbo boost indicator.

Perhaps the best thing about the R&A diesel is the lesson it provides. One of the world's mundane conveyances has been

graced with economical, safe, enjoyable performance, proving that there *is* such a thing as a fun-to-drive diesel. ⓂⓉ

☑ SPECIFICATIONS

GENERAL

Vehicle type	Front-engine, front-drive, 4-pass., 2-door sedan
Options on test car	Callaway Turbosystem, Momo steering wheel, VDO gauges, GTI fender flares, bumpers, A/C, sunroof, Fox radar detector, Blaupunkt stereo, power antenna
Price as tested	$18,000

ENGINE

Type	Turbocharged inline four, water cooled, cast iron block, aluminum head, 5 main bearings
Bore & stroke	3.01 x 3.15 in.
Displacement	89.7 cu. in. (1,457 cc)
Compression ratio	22:1
Fuel system	Mechanical fuel injection
Recommended fuel	No. 2 diesel
Emission control	None
Valve gear	OHC
Horsepower (SAE net)	73 at 5,000 rpm (10 lb. boost)
Power-to-weight ratio	26.6 lb./hp

DRIVETRAIN

Transmission	5-speed manual
Final drive ratio	3.90:1

DIMENSIONS

Wheelbase	94.4 in.
Track, F/R	54.7/53.5 in.
Length	151.2 in.
Width	63.4 in.
Height	53.6 in.
Ground clearance	3.9 in.
Curb weight	1,940 lb.

CAPACITIES

Fuel	10.5 gals.
Crankcase	5 qts.
Cooling system	6.3 qts.
Trunk	22.6 cu. ft.

SUSPENSION

Front	MacPherson struts, lower lateral arms, GTI coil springs, Bilstein gas pressure inserts, R&A lower frame stress bar, GMP 19mm anti-roll bar, GTI strut support caps
Rear	Torsion beam axle carriers, GTI progessively wound springs, Bilstein gas pressure shocks, 19mm anti-roll bar

STEERING

Type	Rack and pinion
Turns lock-to-lock	3.9
Turning circle, curb-to-curb	31.2 ft.

BRAKES

Front	9.4-in. GTI ventilated discs
Rear	7.1-in. drums

WHEELS AND TIRES

Wheel size	13 x 6.0 in.
Wheel type	BBS hand-cast alloy
Tire make and size	Phoenix Stahlflex 175/70HR13
Tire type	Steel-belted radial
Recommended pressure (psi), F/R	26/26

ACCELERATION

0-60 mph	12.9 secs.
Top speed	100 mph (est.)

Golf GTI

A banzai Rabbit that's loaded with enough ammunition to embarrass the Goliaths of motoring

by Jim McCraw

PHOTOGRAPHY BY JIM BROWN

Snoopy's pronouncements on happiness notwithstanding, we believe that happiness is driving a truly capable car in a sea of plain vanilla. Our feelings on this matter were recently reinforced by spending a few weeks driving a Volkswagen Golf GTI around Los Angeles. The GTI, a European sports sedan and distant relative of the American Rabbit S, is so light and nimble it allows the driver to humble a host of Goliaths like Corvettes, TR8s and Porsches—let alone the hordes of plain vanilla cars. With a GTI, you can choose off anything from 0-60, stay with it through the whoops and still stop at half as many gas stations.

The 1981 Golf GTI, available in Europe, is a factory hot rod. A classic example of parts-bin engineering applied to a proven platform, the GTI is a 3-door hatchback sedan that uses the Jetta dash and instrument panel, the Scirocco S reclining bucket seats, and the engine and close-ratio 5-speed transaxle found only in the European GTI and Scirocco. In addition, ride height is lowered about an inch with special MacPherson strut units and Bilstein shocks. The GTI uses both front and rear stabilizer bars (U.S. Rabbits have none), 5.5-inch alloy wheels and P175/70HR13 tires, ventilated front disc brakes, a slightly quicker steering ratio than European standard, a padded 4-spoke steering wheel, add-on wheel flares, a single body stripe and a minimum of badging.

The GTI engine is the keystone of the car, just about the hottest production 1.6 there is. While U.S. Rabbits currently use only a 1,715cc version of the same basic engine (to comply with U.S. emissions regulations), the GTI is the performance leader of five different engines used in European Golfs. The 1,588cc engine uses larger intake valves, 9.5:1 compression ratio, dished crowned pistons, a different camshaft, premium bearings, an oil cooler, and Bosch K-Jetronic fuel injection. With these changes, the 1,588 engine jumps from a rating of 75 to 110 horsepower at 6,100 rpm, with maximum torque of 103 pounds-feet at 5,000 rpm—an increase of 46%, with 16% more torque (103 pounds-feet versus 89). The GTI engine has a built-in rev limiter, set at 6,750 rpm, that the engine will readily activate. It also has a free-breathing exhaust system that plays beautiful music between 3,000 and shutoff. The GTI 1.6 makes almost 70 horsepower per

liter—a higher state of tune than any normally aspirated Porsche in U.S. trim—and, installed in the 1,800-pound Golf, gives it a better weight-to-power ratio (16.2 pounds/horsepower) than all the Porsches except the 928 (15.2). In addition, the GTI engine can be started instantly, floored immediately without complaint, rolled on from 1,500 rpm in 4th gear, or run for hours at maximum speed in 5th gear. There's not a weak or shaky bone in its little cast iron body.

But even light weight and an endless supply of smooth power and revs won't make a complete package without proper gearing, and the GTI transaxle provides that. Internal ratios are 3.45, 2.11, 1.44, 1.12 and .91:1 in 5th, with a new 3.89:1 final drive ratio. Thus, the driver gets a 13.4:1 overall ratio in 1st gear for maximum launches, and a 3.53:1 ratio in overdrive high gear for highway cruising, with all the ratios in between perfectly matched to the engine and each other. The ball-topped shifter is typically VW—excellent—making for lightning changes up or down.

The Golf GTI takes to a dragstrip like Brooke Shields to a camera, with similar magical results. Even without using what they call a banzai start, the GTI will hustle from 0-50 mph in a little over 6 seconds and pass 60 in 8.65, on the way to a 16.59-second quarter-mile at 82.60 mph. The GTI's 0-60 time is better than that of an Audi 5000 Turbo, a Porsche 924 Turbo or a Citation X-11 HO660, and comes quite close to a Jag XJS or Triumph TR8. Admit it—how would you feel if you were driving one of these and got smoked off by a Rabbit? Now, imagine what it's like to be the smoker instead of the smokee.

The GTI's ride and handling are equal to its engine's smoothness and output in just about any situation. Its 94.5-inch wheelbase and 64/36 front weight bias are no different than the other Golf or Rabbit models, but it does have lower ride height, quicker steering, stiffer springing, better shock absorption, more body-roll control, stouter brakes and more rubber on the road. These are the same seven things one would add to any stock car to make it into a race car, and with the power and gearing the GTI already has, it can't help but handle well. With added roll control front and rear, the GTI's normal understeer is lessened substantially, making it very easy to drive quickly on any smooth pavement. On choppy surfaces, with a lot of throttle, the front driving wheels want to take the steering out of your hands. Lifting in the middle of a tight turn will aim the car inward and unload the inside rear tire quite readily.

It really is great fun to drive a GTI because it has so much ammunition to use in so many driving situations, yet compromises so little. The overall ride quality for a short car with extra-duty suspension at the corners is very smooth, if not totally flat; the steering is quite precise everywhere but on center, where it becomes a touch vague. The brake system, an integral part of the car's handling in corners, is shared with all European VWs. The 9.4-inch front discs and 7.1-inch rear drums use a servo assist, consistently bringing the GTI down from 60-0 in 146 feet. (That's as well as a 911SC Weissach does with 11.3/11.6-inch all-discs.) The relatively high pedal pressure required is a small price to pay for dead-reliable braking performance.

What makes the GTI such an instrument of happiness is the fact that it is, after all, a Golf—a Rabbit to us. It has all the high quality, roominess, airiness and cargo capacity of any other Rabbit 3-door hatch, plus excellent sport seats, console-mounted gauges, the GTI steering wheel and just enough distinctive GTI blackout trim to let you know it's special even if nobody else on the road notices. And, amazingly enough, the Golf GTI delivers fuel economy like any other member of the VW family. Driven at posted limits around the *MT* mileage loop, the GTI returned 36.2 miles per gallon, a figure that's completely out of reach for any of the performance cars mentioned earlier. The 36-mpg figure is even more surprising when compared to the EPA rating for a 1981 VW Rabbit S with a 74-horsepower 1,715cc engine and wide-ratio economy gearing. The U.S.-made Rab-

An Open Letter to VWoA

November, 1981

Volkswagen of America
Englewood Cliffs, New Jersey

Dear VWoA:

Ten years ago in Europe the fortunes of Volkswagen were in jeopardy. The Beetle was no longer the darling of the car-buying public, and every new air-cooled VW model (1500, 1600TL, 411, etc.) was a disaster. Then, in 1975, partly due to your company's acquisition of Audi, you were able to introduce two front-wheel-drive water-cooled cars: the Golf and the Scirocco. Diehard VW enthusiasts were horrified, but consumers felt that you had at last built a "real automobile." Since then the Golf and its American counterpart, the Rabbit, have dominated the small-car scene. This is apparent in the number of Golf/Rabbit clones that have sprung up in Europe, Japan and the U.S.

The incredible success of the gasoline-powered Golf GTI (more than a quarter of a million sold) proves that there are enough people in Europe who still desire both economy and performance in one package. These are people new to the VW family, people who would never have owned a Beetle, considering it a car primarily for those who couldn't afford more. The GTI is an "in" car -- everyday transportation for a car lover who might also own a Porsche.

But Volkswagen of America seems interested in selling economy only. True, last year you sold almost 100,000 diesel Rabbits. But it is our opinion that many Americans want more from a small car than just economy and would welcome a small, high-performance gasoline-powered car. We don't subscribe to the notion that American car buyers are less demanding or sophisticated than the Europeans. So if the GTI is such a great success in Europe, why isn't it available in this country?

The U.S.-made Rabbit S is really a detuned version of the GTI with a larger displacement engine. Both use a fuel injection system. To equal the performance of a GTI, you would have to certify a new engine. Even if this cost you $250,000, and you sold only 20,000 cars, the cost of certification would add a mere $12.50 to the price of each car, an amount enthusiasts would gladly pay.

All the parts necessary to transform the Rabbit S into a genuine U.S. version of the GTI are off-the-shelf items that can be bolted on. In Europe, the GTI costs only $1,100 more than the Golf GLS. The Rabbit S lists here for $7,050; it would be easy for you to build a federalized GTI here and sell it for well under $10,000. Last year you sold nearly 9,000 Rabbit convertibles; there is no denying the demand for specialty Rabbits, even if they are expensive.

Introduction of a U.S. GTI would be an inexpensive, yet effective, way of boosting the VW image here in America.

So how about it, VWoA? Build us a Rabbit GTI and give Americans a reason to leave their Porsches at home.

Regards,

The Motor Trend Staff

The Motor Trend Staff

Volkswagen Golf GTI

✅ SPECIFICATIONS

GENERAL

Vehicle type	Front-engine, front-drive, 4-pass., 3-door hatchback sedan
Base price	$5,982
Options on test car	Sunroof
Price as tested	$7,800

ENGINE

Type	Transverse inline four, water cooled, cast iron block, aluminum head, 5 main bearings
Bore & stroke	79.5 x 80.0 mm
Displacement	1,588 cc (97 cu. in.)
Compression ratio	9.5:1
Fuel system	Fuel injection
Recommended fuel	Premium
Emission control	EEC
Valve gear	Overhead cam
Horsepower (SAE net)	110 at 6,100 rpm
Torque (lb.-ft., SAE net)	103 at 5,000 rpm
Power-to-weight ratio	16.23 lb./hp

DRIVETRAIN

Transmission	5-speed manual transaxle
Final drive ratio	3 89:1

DIMENSIONS

Wheelbase	94.5 in.
Track, F/R	55.3/53.0 in.
Length	150.2 in.
Width	64.0 in.
Height	54.7 in.
Ground clearance	6.0 in.

Max. load length w/rear seat(s) folded down	49.0 in.
Curb weight	1,786 lb.
Weight distribution, F/R	64/36%

CAPACITIES

Fuel	11.8 gals. (U.S.)
Crankcase	4.0 qts.
Cooling system	4.9 qts.
Trunk	13/39 cu. ft.

SUSPENSION

Front	MacPherson struts, coil springs, hydraulic shocks, stabilizer bar
Rear	Independent, coil springs, trailing arms, hydraulic shocks, stabilizer bar

STEERING

Type	Rack and pinion
Turns lock-to-lock	3.3
Turning circle, curb-to-curb	34.4 ft.

BRAKES

Front	9.4-in. discs
Rear	7.1-in. drums

WHEELS AND TIRES

Wheel size	13 x 5.5 in.
Wheel type	Aluminum alloy
Tire make and size	Continental P175/70HR13
Tire type	Steel-belted radial
Recommended pressure (psi), F/R	24/24

✅ TEST RESULTS

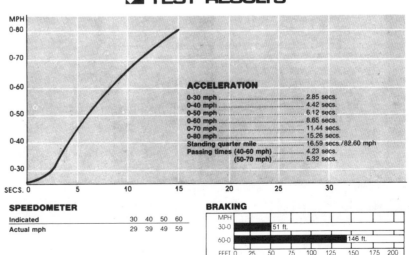

ACCELERATION

0-30 mph	2.85 secs.
0-40 mph	4.42 secs.
0-50 mph	6.12 secs.
0-60 mph	8.65 secs.
0-70 mph	11.44 secs.
0-80 mph	15.26 secs.
Standing quarter mile	16.59 secs./82.60 mph
Passing times (40-60 mph)	4.23 secs.
(50-70 mph)	5.32 secs.

SPEEDOMETER

	30	40	50	60
Indicated	30	40	50	60
Actual mph	29	39	49	59

BRAKING

MPH		
30-0	51 ft.	
60-0		146 ft.

FEET 0 25 50 75 100 125 150 175 200

---

bit S, with all the emissions and safety hardware in place, is rated at 26/40, for a combined rating of 33 mpg. On its home turf, the Golf GTI is rated at 26.9 at 75 mph, according to Common Market test procedures.

After putting the GTI through all of its paces and compiling the data, we researched our files to see what there was on the U.S. market that could do all the good things a GTI can. But there simply isn't anything available that combines the GTI's acceleration, braking, handling and fuel economy, with room for four (or two, plus 39 cubic feet of cargo). Nothing. The Rabbit S, of course, comes the closest. It has the same red accent paint, striping, console, blackout trim, wide wheels and big tires, and the wide-ratio U.S. 5-speed. But the S is down 36 horsepower and lacks the steering and suspension changes made to the GTI. The question is whether VWoA will take the time and money and make the effort necessary to bring the S up to specs for U.S. customers.

We hope they do, of course. We can see a ready market for such an able automobile, and relatively few packaging difficulties. The GTI has already been sold in numbers over several hundred thousand, so the parts are there to be bolted on. Even if VWoA were to stop short of the whole package and just add suspension, steering and the close-ratio transaxle behind the existing 74-horsepower engine, the S would be much more exciting, with a lot more scat and very little loss in overall fuel economy. Although VWoA is one of the few companies that has a real handle on CAFE ratings, it could always use more sales in areas such as the high-performance small-car segment. The current Rabbit S only *looks* like it belongs in this category.

Of course, the one thing the U.S. Rabbit

CONTINUED ON PAGE 57

Toleman's Hot VW GTi
For experienced Golfers only!

IN four brief years on the British market, Volkswagen's Golf GTi has become something of a "cult" car, attracting as much enthusiasm and affection as machines from the past like the Mini-Cooper and Lotus Cortina. So it logically follows that the "special builders" have had a hey-day with this taut little FWD Volkswagen, the result of their efforts varying from mildly stimulating to quite shattering in terms of sheer performance. Of course, with the economy as depressed as it currently is, there can be a problem persuading potential customers to part with a few thousand pounds over and above the basic GTi cost when they might feel that such money is better spent buying a more exotic car from the outset. But that doesn't prevent specialist concerns from pitching into this potentially precarious market.

Edwards of Tamworth Ltd. may not mean a great deal to many of our readers. Five years ago this Staffordshire garage business was acquired by the Toleman Group because of its MAN commercial vehicle franchise. It wasn't foremost in the Group's mind that Edwards also held a Volkswagen distributorship, but they decided to hold on to this side of the business and, when former F2 racer Rad Dougall went up to Tamworth as Edwards's Service Manager, he and Toleman Managing Director Alex Hawkridge gave considerable thought to developing performance equipment for models in the VW range. One thing led to another and now Edwards are marketing a variety of conversions to enhance Golf GTi performance. Almost as a development exercise to demonstrate what *can* be done if you're prepared to spend large sums of money, Edwards have produced a very up-market GTi road car fitted with a 2-litre 16-valve engine and decorated in the distinctive blue and white Toleman "house livery". We recently spent a week terrorising the

Essex country lanes in this tremendously quick machine and, although we've got some strong reservations about this particular overall package, we were exceedingly impressed with its sheer "punch".

Edwards have developed 1.8- and 2-litre versions of the GTi engine, available with either eight- or 16-valve heads. The car we tried was fitted with a 16-valve Oettinger head, bored and stroked to 81.5 and 94.5 mm. respectively with a 10:1 compression ratio and retaining the Bosch K-Jetronic electronic fuel injection. The intention has been to combine sheer performance and the sort of flexibility synonymous with the standard VW GTi power unit. Our feeling is that they have succeeded extremely well.

Power output is boosted by 45 b.h.p. from the normal 1,588 c.c. engine's 110 b.h.p. and the 155 b.h.p. output is accompanied by a significant increase in torque. Delivery is smooth and progressive, but the fitting of a limited slip

THE Edwards of Tamworth-built Toleman Golf GTi sports the firm's distinctive house livery, although this is specially for their Managing Director Alex Hawkridge. Below, the heart of the matter is a 2-litre fuel-injected version of the smooth four cylinder engine assembled with components supplied by Oetinger in Germany. Note the bracing bar to provide added stiffening for the bodyshell. Right, the colour-coded interior complements the external livery, but the customer can choose his own specification and choice of engine sizes.

differential, whilst theoretically conferring a traction advantage more applicable to circuit use, significantly detracts from the car's appeal for everyday motoring. It induces a peculiar feeling which suggests that the steering isn't going to respond properly when turning into a corner at speed and the "snatch" under hard acceleration from rest is alarming. It also highlights the need for a revised attitude to handling the car. It's unexpectedly sure-footed and neutral on billiard-smooth surfaces, but it's not a car to be thrown around with light-hearted abandon like the unmodified GTi. If you do approach the Toleman GTi in this manner, you'll probably wind up hating it, or having an accident — or both. If you drive it smoothly and precisely, it is a delight.

Even more impressive than the performance is the development work which has been done on the suspension. This Golf corners with no discernible roll whatsoever (again, on smooth surfaces), but there is a price to pay for the levels of adhesion and stability conferred by the use of 25 per cent. uprated springs, Koni shock-absorbers and lowered suspension working in conjunction with the 195 / 50 x 15 Fulda low profile tyres on their ATS alloy seven inch wheel rims. Frankly, for day-to-day road use, it's too stiff and on some of Essex's fast-deteriorating country lanes the limited ground clearance results in the bib spoiler touching the ground quite frequently. Rad Dougall has evolved a rubber extension to the normal bumper in the interests of improved stability in motorway crosswinds, but it's extremely vulnerable and Alex Hawkridge

admits that he took it off twice riding over snow banks in the recent wintry spell. Still, as the extension is held on by self-tapping screws, this doesn't exactly spell major disaster.

Initial tests with the Edwards performance conversions revealed that the basic Golf chassis needed some extra strengthening to deal with the loads put through it by that dramatically improved handling. Accordingly, a tubular bracing bar connects the two suspension turrets beneath the bonnet and a similar arrangement stiffens the wishbone mountings from below.

With a 0-60 mph time in the region of 7.1 sec. and a top speed of just over 135 m.p.h., this Golf is certainly no slouch. The familiar, delightful five-speed gearbox encourages one to use the full performance as frequently as possible and, in order that fast long-distance journeys may be completed with the minimum of delay, a long range fuel tank doubles the standard capacity to 15 gallons. That means a range of something around 400 miles driving reasonably quickly: during the time in our hands the GTi averaged 26.4 m.p.g. which is by no means unreasonable for a car endowed with this sort of exciting performance.

With a higher-than-standard (3.48:1) axle ratio, the Toleman GTi's acceleration is sustained at a brisk rate, even in fifth gear. In fact, for relaxed cruising it's almost a matter of necessity to get into fifth as quickly as possible. All that torque means that acceleration between 80 and 110 m.p.h. is as impressive in fourth / fifth gear as 30 to 50 m.p.h. is in second / third. The stiff suspension exaggerates the degree of road noise from the Fulda tyres, but otherwise the car is fairly quiet and drama-free. Braking is secure and

fade-free, standard calipers are deemed adequate to cope with the increased performance although larger calipers can be made available if a customer so chooses.

From a pleasing cosmetic point of view, the Toleman is fitted with a Zenda 81 body pack which includes fared-in-bumpers, boot-lid spoiler, four headlamp grille and wheel-arch extensions. All help to make the car's outward profile distinctive although I have to say that I prefer the standard matt black Golf GTi grill to the revamped product offered on this conversion.

Internally, comfort for the occupants is a prime consideration with Wolfrace 200 front seats and a Momo three-spoke steering wheel. The seats in the test car were specially trimmed in Toleman blue, designed to compliment the car's external livery. A bit striking for my taste, but not a compulsory adjunct to having this conversion carried out!

Once you're accustomed to its sensitive handling, the Toleman Golf GTi is a sheer delight for cross-country motoring. Indeed, for quick motoring on secondary roads I don't think I could nominate another machine that would be quicker. If I was ordering one I would opt to live without the limited slip differential and slightly softer suspension would be preferable, although that would probably upset the roll-free handling which is such a pleasure on smooth surfaces.

Finally, one has to consider the price. To have your own personal GTi modified with just a 2-litre, 16-valve engine will cost you £2,900, making its total cost from new around £9,400. To duplicate our test car, from scratch, would cost £12,500. An indulgence, arguably. But what a performer! — A.H.

1800 Golf GTi

Recently, a considerable demand has sprung up for small saloons with powerful engines, but which are still economical in spite of their enhanced performance. Most enthusiasts are of the opinion that the Volkswagen Golf GTi is the most attractive of these delightful little machines, of which 330,000 have been produced, and some 10,000 sold in the UK since the right-hand drive version appeared in 1979.

One would think that VW were sitting pretty, but competition in the class cannot be ignored and the difficult decision has been taken to up-rate the very successful GTi. The 1.6-litre engine has been replaced by what is virtually a new unit of 1781cc, with a fresh crankshaft of longer throw, carrying a vibration damper, which increases the stroke from 80mm to 86.4mm. Lighter pistons, in bores enlarged by 2mm to 81mm, raise the compression ratio from 9.5 to 10:1. Power output is merely up by a couple of quadrupeds to 112bhp at 5800rpm, but the big news is that the maximum torque is developed at only 3500 rpm instead of the former 5000 rpm, where a respectable 109lbf ft is forthcoming.

The maximum speed, somewhat conservatively claimed at 114mph, is not greatly altered, but the greater torque results in 0-60 mph acceleration in 8.2 secs, a by no means optimistic claim. That is in spite of raising the final drive gearing from 3.895 to 3.674:1. This, plus the need for far less gear changing due to

The 1800 version of the Golf GTi looks much the same as its little sister externally.

the augmented torque, results in a useful improvement in fuel economy. Official figures are: urban 26.6mpg, 56mph 47.9mpg, 75mph 36.7mph.

The rest of the car and the five-speed transmission remain as before. There is, however, a new onboard computer of remarkable sophistication. The required data is displayed in the centre of the instrument panel, while changes of information are secured by touching a button on the end of one of the steering column stalks. The seven functions are staged in a fixed order, each identified by a visual symbol on the display, and showing real time, journey time, journey distance, average speed, average fuel consumption, oil temperature and ambient temperature. Journey time and distance, speed and fuel consumption are stored continuously and automatically.

There are two memories, one for single journeys and the other for total

travel-distance. These can be selected by a rotary knob on the instrument panel, but to describe the full possibilities of this multifunction display would call for more space than I can command.

The price, including taxes and seat belts for five persons, is £6499.

Road Impressions

I was able to cover a useful distance in the Golf GTi 1800, both as driver and passenger, and also to recall the days of my youth by tackling the Prescott speed-hillclimb course. The bigger engine has obviously more punch and overtaking can be a very rapid process. This is a delightfully effortless car, cruising in fifth gear at any speed up to the maximum. At an easy 100mph, there is still some useful acceleration in reserve.

The original GTi had an engine as smooth as a little turbine, but the bigger unit is still remarkably free from vibra-

tion and perhaps even quieter. Certainly, there is an improvement in flexibility and the car is less dependent on the driver's use of the gear lever for its performance. Unlike some of its rivals, which tend to shake your teeth out, the Golf gives a comfortable ride.

Although the gear lever need not be used a great deal unless the driver is so minded, the change cannot be faulted and the ratios are excellently chosen. The steering is very pleasant, with plenty of castor action, and there is less understeer than with most front wheel drive cars, indeed the tail may be hung out if suitable aids are applied. As always, though, the brakes call for some criticism, lacking the instant bite that one needs when approaching the hairpin at Prescott a little too fast.

JOHN BOLSTER

TO AUSTRALIAN enthusiasts used to poor-quality roads, tight speed restrictions and a famine of exotic European cars, the autobahns of West Germany are akin to a second heaven. The roads are excellent, there are no speed limits and the motoring menu is as good as you'll get at most international shows. Probably the nicest thing of all, though, is being able to watch beautiful cars being driven *hard*.

There is something sublime about a Mercedes 500SEL racing by you with its throaty V8 roar at some 220 km/h, looking every bit as streamlined and safe as a big eagle dropping from the sky in search of prey. There is something impressive about seeing the distant flash of Porsche 928 headlights in your rearview mirror before you see the shark-shaped car storm by you in the fast lane. And there's something gratifying about hearing 12 Modenese cylinders breathing through open barrels, totally unrestricted by the bureaucracy which strangles them in any other Western country. It's like seeing a thoroughbred running across open fields after it's been cramped up in a paddock for a month.

But when you first visit a German autobahn, it's likely that a far less glamorous make of car will stick in your mind. The Volkswagen Golf GTi.

To start with, you see a lot more of the sporty little Volkswagens than you do exoticars, for they seem to dot the autobahns like mopeds stud French and Italian cities. And they always go so damn *fast*. When you see your first Golf GTi tearing along at a genuine 180 km/h you're inclined to wonder what special mods Herman the German must have added to his car. But when you see your second, and your third — all doing 180 — you start accepting the fact that the little hatchback from Wolfsburg is a superquick baby. Oddly, most of them are black. You can order your golf GTi (for about $7500 in Germany or some $10,000 in Britain) in red or silver as well, but the serious drivers invariably choose black.

The Golf GTi was released by VW in 1976. Like its little brother it proved both a runaway success and a trend-setter. Waiting lists started for the hotrod hatchback in every market it was sold. And it started the era of the small, civilised family performance car. It was a machine that combined hatchback versatility with 180 km/h. A car that combined a good price-tag with acceleration better than a Saab 900 Turbo or a Porsche 924. And a little car that combined docile city manners with excellent motorway cruising.

To the familiar Audi-developed Golf motor VW has added Bosch fuel injection, a new cylinder head with larger valves and smoother flowing inlet and exhaust manifolds. All this puts the power of the 1588 cm³ unit up to a rorting 80 kW — a massive 57 per cent increase compared to the normal Golf LS with 1.5-litre engine. An oil-cooler has also been added. The body, with deep front-chin spoiler, sits closer to the ground with altered spring and damper rates and a 12.5 mm wider track front and rear.

Bigger 175/70HR13 tyres replace the normal 155SR13 rubber. Anti-roll bars are fitted front and rear. The front discs are ventilated, while drums are retained at the back. A five-speed gearbox is standard. In other ways the car is mechanically the same as the normal Golf. The transverse ohc engine drives the front wheels. Suspension is via MacPherson struts at the front, with torsion beam axle and trailing arms at the rear. Steering is rack and pinion.

The first thing that impresses about the Golf GTi is the sheer power of the engine. With 80 kW pulling only 841 kg, the Golf races from the streetlights like an arrow from a bow. It accelerates briskly and smoothly right up to its maximum speed. The 100 km/h mark comes up in only 8.3 seconds. When you consider that's almost two seconds faster than an Alfasud Sprint Veloce and *six* seconds faster than a Ford Laser Sport, you can see that the GTi is indeed a SuperGolf. Just as impressive is the responsiveness. The fuel injection obviously helps here.

Indeed, the more you drive behind the 1.6-litre four, the more you wonder whether there is a better four-cylinder engine in the world. Apart from the excellent performance and smoothness, it is amazingly frugal. The worst fuel figure I recorded in a week of very vigorous driving was 11.4 km/l (31.4 mpg), which was on tight, mountainous roads. The best figure, cruising quickly on the motorway, was 12.2 km/l (33.5 mpg). Can any other small car return that same fuel economy/performance compromise?

Happily the Golf is just as competent when it comes to corners. The delightful rack and pinion steering gives the driver plenty of feel and allows him to throw the little car around with great confidence. The cornering is flat and neutral on fast corners. On tighter bends there's just a pleasant degree of understeer, which can be well-controlled by the throttle. Indeed, the GTi is no less than a joy on tight, windy roads, helped enormously by the light and precise five-speed gearbox — surely as nice a unit as any front-drive car has ever been fitted with.

The flat handling, however, doesn't mean a poor ride — as it does on so many other small cars. Like its equally advanced Italian rival, the Alfasud, the GTi does give a fine compromise of grip and comfort. To some softer folk the ride may still be a bit too firm — but such people

GTi
THE FASTEST BABY IN TOWN

They're black, they're small and they're fast. They burn up West Germany's autobahns at 180 km/h. They're Golf GTis. Gavin Green reports with bated breath

are unlikely to put their money into a GTi anyway. It takes a badly broken up or severely corrugated road for the ride to be uncomfortable.

Other plus points include the generous front and rear space, the ease of parking thanks to the square shape and the ease of starting after a cold night (again helped by the fuel injection).

You will realise by now that I loved the Golf GTi. But there are faults. The brakes, for instance, could be stronger. The pedal has surprisingly long travel and even when you get to the stopping point the feel is a bit too mushy. On one particularly hard section of driving the two discs and two drums were beginning to fade away. Having done many

thousands of kilometres in Alfasuds, I know the brakes on that Italian thoroughbred would have been as sharp and progressive as ever on the same road. Nonetheless, unless pushed very hard, the brakes will do an adequate job of stopping the black bombshell.

Inside I found the GTi's dashboard too plasticky and a mite too plain. Although it includes the usual tachometer (red-lined at 6300 rpm) and a coolant and oil pressure gauge, the rest of the mechanicals rely simply on warning lights. Most sports car owners would expect more. The gearshift is also mounted too far forward and does require a stretched left arm to change cogs. Appropriately the gearlever knob is styled like a golf ball.

The steering wheel is standard Golf fitment and thus disappointing on a car of this ilk. The rally-style seats, though, have excellent lateral and thigh support, are comfortable and inspire you to use the full cornering power of the well-tuned suspension and the Goodyear G800 + S tyres (mounted on alloy wheels).

Unfortunately, the Golf GTi is unlikely ever to come to Australia. Instead, enthusiasts who want good-value small performance sedans will have to rely on the likes of the Laser Sport and the Mazda 323SS. Or maybe accept the noise and discomfort of a second-hand Mini Cooper S. But in each case you'll be missing out. The Golf GTi, you see, is the world's best small sports sedan. □

Bettering the best

Driving Volkswagen's bigger-engined Golf GTi

By Michael Scarlett

IT IS a contentious thing to say — but it is probably true to label the Volkswagen Golf GTi as the best-all-round of the larger engined, high performance small saloons. The original 1.6-litre car earned this title with its unrivalled combination of smooth, very zestful performance, excellent roadholding and handling, and acceptable ride and practicality. Other cars have approached, and sometimes bettered, the Golf in one of these respects, but none achieve such high marks in all of them. The new GTi can be summed up by saying that it preserves all that was right about the old one, and adds even better performance.

The major change is the new engine. The old 1,588 c.c. ohc aluminium-alloy-head unit had a bore and stroke of 79.5×80mm, produced 110 bhp at 6,100 rpm and 101 lb.ft. at 5,000 rpm. The new one has a capacity of 1,780 c.c., derived from an 81×86.4mm bore and stroke, and is claimed to give 112 bhp at 5,800 rpm and 109 lb.ft. at 3,500 rpm — not much of a power increase (less than two per cent), but the nearly eight per cent higher peak torque is generated very usefully lower down the rev range. The new engine has longer connecting rods, which theoretically help to reduce friction. Although the five-speed gearbox remains as it should be — a sports not an overdrive box — VW have slightly increased the overall gearing, raising it from 18.5 to 19.93 mph per 1,000 rpm, so that the car should be more economical.

Otherwise, the delightful mixture is much as before. The biggest inside difference is the incorporation of a very neat and easily understood trip computer, which uses the liquid crystal display of the digital clock to show time of day (as before), elapsed journey time, distance, average speed, average mpg, engine oil temperature — an unusual and more interesting variable in this sort of car — and outside air temperature. The function desired is selected by dabbing a button on the end of the (right hand) wipe/wash stalk. The car now costs £6,500.

The old engine delighted with its smoothness and eagerness. The new one does too, resoundingly, and even more so — the gains will have to await full evaluation in a forthcoming Autotest, but subjectively the

power unit is more flexible, and certainly just as marvellously rapid. Set in the relatively light Golf three-door shell, this is one of those rare engines which never seems to be short of urge. The response is there always, snappily instant and super-willing in a way that recalls for me the satisfaction one used to get out of driving another at first sight over-engined, small-ish car, the BMW 2002. Just like the BMW, the GTi 1800 never sags — it just goes, gloriously. It is a difficult car in which to resist going fast, such is the powerful seduction it exercises over the right foot. Gear ratios are well chosen, and one's ability to seize overtaking opportunities safely

which are denied to many other cars is great.

It was wet on the day we tried the Golf, yet for a front-drive car with a two-up laden power-to-weight ratio of around 110 bhp per ton, the traction on both Michelin XVS and Firestone Wide Oval tyres was good, making exploiting the power all the easier.

VAG repeated the launch of the five-speed 1600GTi by ending the test route at the Bugatti Owners' Club Prescott hill-climb course, where journalists were allowed the privilege of playing with the car against the timing lights. Prescott demonstrated the exhilaration of the new GTi superbly, even in slippery

conditions, which held the best time of the morning down to 60.5sec; I managed sixth fastest.

As before, it steers very well, giving good steering feel and excellent accuracy. The car doesn't roll much, in spite of its twisting beam, Siamesed-trailing arm rear being easily provoked into harmlessly lifting the inside wheel. It is a very well behaved front-drive car, its tail coming out if you brake in a corner taken hard, which can help a lot. As an example of safe high performance in a small car, the GTi always was very good; in this fuller-blooded but still very civilized 1.8-litre version, it is even better.

Playing with the GTi on the hill-climb course; it can easily be provoked into harmlessly lifting the rear inside wheel

Volkswagen Rabbit GTI

VOLKSWAGEN

The car we've all been waiting for.

• The automotive business may be topsy-turvy these days, but there's still no question about where the world's best drivers' cars come from. For sheer quantity, you can't beat the Fatherland: Mercedes-Benz, Audi, BMW, Porsche, and VW turn out more great rides than the rest of the world's carmakers combined. Even the Japanese still think German cars are magic—and they're working furiously to close the gap.

So without further ado, allow us to introduce the latest autobahn panzer to grace our roads, the Volkswagen Rabbit GTI, from—wait a minute—Westmoreland County, Pennsylvania? That's right. Volkswagen of America is now producing a home-grown version of the little sedan we've been waiting for, the GTI—the perennial benchmark of high-performance European econoboxes. Better still, it works so well, you'd swear it came from Wolfsburg.

If you find this leap of faith a little

hard to accomplish, we understand. For one thing, the German-made GTI is one killer shoe box. The intense VW engineers take the three letters on the grille very seriously, and the result of all their tuning is a poor man's hot rod capable of running with BMWs on the autobahn and on twisty Bavarian back roads.

Nor was there any reason to anticipate such a car from VW of America. The cars rolling out of Pennsylvania farm country have been the farthest things from Teutonic boy racers. Since opening its U.S. plant in 1978, VW has soft-pedaled its German heritage in favor of an Americanized image. Suspensions turned flaccid, seats became bench-flat, and the flash and filigree levels rose alarmingly. If you wanted a German-style driver's car, you had to choose from one of the imported models on the dealer's floor, like the Jetta and the Scirocco.

That era, we're happy to report,

seems over. With sales off 45 percent from a year ago, VW of America is trying a whole new approach. Jim Fuller, then vice-president of Porsche+Audi, was shipped in last spring to get the lights turned back on, and a new corporate campaign—internally called "Roots"—has been established to foster a more vital image for the company.

small air dam pokes out beneath the front bumper. Moldings and bumpers are blacked out. A thin red molding encircles the grille, and simple red badges are stuck on the grille and the rear deck—just like on the German model. The only other giveaway to this car's identity lurks in the wheel wells: meaty, P185/60HR-14 Pirelli P6 tires on 14.0-

This game plan, as you might guess from the name, is for VW to "Germanize" its Americanized, U.S.-built cars. Aside from the image-making GTI—which is intended to cast a glow on the whole line—the program calls for firmer suspensions, better seats, and more understated trim across the board.

Judging by the GTI, VW seems serious enough to do it. Everything about this car is calculated to make an enthusiast salivate in anticipation. From suspension to seats, all the important parts have been uprated to full autobahn-class standards—quite an accomplishment, considering the long arm of the cost accountants.

From ten paces, the transformation is quite subtle, though still visible enough that no keen enthusiast will miss it. A

by-6.0-inch alloy wheels.

Clue number two that this is no ordinary economy car comes the second you pull open the door and slide behind the soft, molded, four-spoke Scirocco wheel. The driving environment is aggressively businesslike, but also pleasantly luxurious—more like what you'd expect in an Audi. The highlight of the interior is a pair of deeply sculptured sport seats like those found in the Scirocco, upholstered in heavy-weight corduroy—deep blue with red stripes in the case of our jet-black test car. A somewhat misshapen center console contains a clock, an oil-temperature gauge, and a voltmeter, which supplement the tach, the speedo, the fuel gauge, and the coolant-temp gauge in the instrument cluster. The final touch-

es are a golf-ball shift knob and the substitution of pseudo brushed aluminum for pseudo wood on the dash and console faces.

What you key to life on the other side of the fire wall is also something you won't find in any normal Rabbit: a 1.8-liter four-cylinder that packs more power than any other U.S.-spec Rabbit ever has—90 hp at 5500 rpm, to be exact. This 16-hp improvement over the stock powerplant is the result of a variety of revisions. The engine has been bored out from 1715cc to 1781, and compression has been bumped from 8.2:1 to 8.5. The breathing has been improved by opening up valve sizes and adding a low-restriction exhaust system with a 3mm-larger-diameter pipe.

The 1.8-liter's 22 percent power improvement is still 16 hp shy of the 1.6-liter German GTI's power peak—something the engine engineers claim is intentional. The cam from the stock 1.7-liter cooking four was retained, they say, to fatten up the midrange for better around-town response, which is sadly lacking in the high-winding German edition.

Before you roll your eyes at what sounds like an excuse, you should know that this powerplant is a delight to live with. It's spunky down low and pulls hard for the redline. The new motor muscles the 2100-pound GTI to 60 mph in a brisk 9.7 seconds, nearly 2.0 seconds faster than the standard Rabbit five-speed—and nearly a second faster than a 5.0-liter Trans Am four-speed. There's even enough power to push the boxy body through the atmosphere at 104 mph.

The new engine is more than just stronger, it's more refined as well. VW's engine team used this opportunity to reduce piston weight by twenty percent and to lengthen the connecting rods by ten percent—two key changes that com-

bine to make this engine one of the world's most velvety fours. A portion of the GTI's improved noise-and-vibration control can be traced to a most unlikely source—a new slip-joint connection between the exhaust header and the tailpipe. The upgraded system eliminates the tinny exhaust note of Rabbits past, replacing it with a mellow, expensive-sounding hum.

Another measure of driving pleasure comes through from the gearbox, a GTI unit imported from Germany. The ra-

tios are the closest you'll find this side of a race car, and they make it easy to keep the free-revving engine in the choice section of the power band.

Of course, an equal portion of the European GTI's prowess is derived from the poise its chassis shows under pressure. Here, too, VW of America has come through. Since the U.S. car is about 140 pounds heavier than its German counterpart, U.S. spring rates and shock valving had to be unique. They were chosen specifically to match the

Jim Fuller *Betting it all on performance.*

This year, it's Volkswagen's turn to worry about the fickleness of the auto-buying public. After five consecutive years of winning the EPA's fuel-economy sweepstakes with its diesels, the company suddenly finds itself in a market where nobody is worried much about mileage. That's just fine for the people who sell the Mercury Marquis, but for James R. Fuller and Volkswagen of America, it means the worst kind of trouble.

In the first six months of this year, sales of U.S.-built Rabbits were cut almost in half, nose-diving 45 percent below 1981 levels. By June the inventory of unsold Rabbits had grown to a four-month supply. The company laid off a tenth of its white-collar work force and announced that its assembly plant in Westmoreland County, Pennsylvania, would be closed for a month and a half. The opening of a second assembly plant, in suburban Detroit, had already been put off indefinitely.

Jim Fuller's assignment is simple: he's supposed to turn all this around. VW of America has created a new position—vice-president, Volkswagen Division—and put him in it. It is probably the most demanding promotion of his fast-track career.

Jim Fuller was born and raised in Boston, but you wouldn't know it to talk to him—he has mastered the Midwestern accent that is the Esperanto of the auto industry. As a teen-ager in the 1950s he lived and died by *Sportscar Graphic*, and in 1962, at the end of his freshman year in college, he joined a cooperative training program sponsored by Ford. He's been in the car business ever since.

Ford put Fuller on a fast-track management-development program, promoting him through a whirlwind of

sales, service, finance, parts, and marketing jobs. (The current head of the Ford Division, Lou Lataif, is an alumnus of the same program.) Fuller himself conducted the launches of the Torino, the Mustang II, and the Granada before leaving in 1975 to become a vice-president of Renault U.S.A. Four years later he moved to VW of America as vice-president, Porsche + Audi Division.

"I have a theory that a lot of people in management in the automobile business don't really like cars," Fuller says, explaining why he made the move. "They like management—they don't like cars. *I like cars!*" To head up Porsche + Audi, he says, "was like dying and going to heaven."

Fuller's specialty is marketing, and in his two and a half years at Porsche + Audi he paid particularly close attention to product positioning, the definition of what each line should stand for in its customers' minds. His conclusions were subsequently embodied in Porsche's "Technical Papers" advertisements and in Audi's new emphasis on its heritage of Bavarian engineering. But since he had no intention of raising expectations that his cars could not meet, Fuller also took an active role in product planning. During the development of the Porsche 944, for example, Fuller strove to answer criticisms of the Porsche 924's Audi-derived engine and too-pretty styling, pushing successfully for the adoption of a Porsche-built engine and a more aggressive look.

Porsche + Audi sales climbed seventeen percent in 1981. In May of this year, Jim Fuller was moved next door to Volkswagen to see if he can repeat the effect. Believing that many of the problems and solutions are similar, Fuller is optimistic that he can.

At Volkswagen, as at Porsche + Audi, Fuller is paying close attention to product positioning. "Volkswagen is unlike any of its principal

competitors," goes the basic positioning statement he has adopted, "in that only Volkswagen has the character of German engineering without compromise in ride and performance." From now on, Fuller says, VW will strive to build more than "just a nice little economy car."

For the Rabbit, Fuller's new emphasis on performance means a sharp reversal of the creeping Americanization that has dimmed the car's image among enthusiasts in recent years. While he refuses to blame anyone else at VW of America for the problem, Fuller affirms that the days of soft suspensions, nonsupportive seats, and baby-blue interiors are over. To a group of automotive writers he put it succinctly: "We're through Malibuing these cars around!"

In the campaign to rebuild the Rabbit's reputation for performance, "the GTI is a bit of the crown jewels," Fuller says. "We're putting a lot into that car, not just to sell the 20,000-plus cars a year, but to reinstitute, with our Sunday punch, just what this company is going to stand for."

The GTI is leading the way in which Jim Fuller intends to take the entire Volkswagen Division. He plans to tie everything from national advertising to the style of retail sales into his new theme of all-around, European-style performance. Given that disciplined effort at all levels, he thinks he can not only reverse Volkswagen's losses, but actually achieve its long-elusive goal of taking five percent of the U.S. market.

Fuller's optimism is tempered by the knowledge that his highly centralized strategy amounts to putting all his eggs in one basket. "If you err, you err grandly," he concedes. What will happen if, despite everything, VW buyers do not respond to the new course represented by the GTI? "Let me put it this way," he says. "If this doesn't work, a year and a half from now you won't have Jim Fuller to kick around anymore."

—*John Hilton*

European car's handling characteristics, however. To maintain the best possible quality control, the front struts come from VW's European supplier, and the rear shocks are Sachs units. The U.S. car does benefit from the same front and rear anti-sway bars used on the German GTI, as well as the foreign car's ventilated front disc brakes.

The first thing you notice when you put all these gourmet pieces into motion is what they *don't* do to our old friend the Rabbit. The new GTI is not a hard-edged street racer. The engine isn't shrill or peaky; the suspension doesn't jiggle or crash over the bumps. The GTI is far more sophisticated and refined than that. It will stick like glue—0.78 g is available for cornering work—but excellent roadholding is only half the story. It's also as composed and supple as the high-dollar brands over bad pavement, always on its toes through mountain switchbacks, and quick to answer your right foot at any speed. It never seems to breathe hard.

Despite short gearing—4300 rpm shows on the tach at 80 mph—the GTI is a quiet and comfortable long-distance cruiser. For long hauls or short, the front seats work wonders—this despite being handicapped by having only fore-and-aft and backrest-angle adjustments. Even the new, optional four-speaker AM/FM-stereo/cassette radio sounds plenty good.

Next to all-around performance like this, a Scirocco pales. This once-humble Rabbit, in fact, now qualifies as a full-fledged GT sedan. What ultimately makes the GTI truly significant, however, is that it's the first car sold in the U.S. to marry this level of driving satisfaction with the utility, compact dimensions, and fuel efficiency of an economy car. Our test GTI returned an impressive 26 mpg during five days of leadfooted road testing—including a morning of instrumented track tests. That happens to be exactly the same real-world mileage we netted with a stock five-speed Rabbit three-door we tested recently. What's more, if driving enjoyment in a small car is your paramount concern, you'd be hard pressed to beat the cost-benefit ratio inherent in the GTI's eight-grand admission price.

For that sum you will not be overwhelmed by clever features, a component sound system, or infinitely adjustable seats. In true German fashion, VW equips the GTI only with what's needed to get the job done, thank you. When it comes to sheer driving enjoyment, though, the new GTI currently stands in a class of one. True to its pedigree, it can make you feel great—and that's the best thing any car can do for its driver. —*Rich Ceppos*

COUNTERPOINT

• Listen, we ought to give this car a medal or something. Partly because it'll put the hurt on so many so-called sports cars in the stand-on-it-and-steer-it mode. But mostly because the GTI isn't another one of those dumb boy racers that ride like produce wagons and make power like blenders stuck on purée.

I mean, even a fast car should live up to certain minimum standards. So I don't mind that the GTI rides like a Jaguar. I can live with first-class furnishings in the passenger cabin. I can stand a smooth, powerful engine that squeezes a bunch of miles out of every gallon of gas. If this is the sacrifice I have to make for a car that does business as good as the *C/D* performance specs say the GTI does, I'm ready to bite the bullet.

Like everybody else, I expected a kind of Porsche Speedster—an uncivilized, fast little car. Imagine how lucky we are that this Eighties-style Speedster is civilized as well as fast. It's a fast little car without the nonsense. —*Michael Jordan*

As a self-proclaimed forward thinker, I'm sent into a quasi funk every time I think of what the GTI could have been. With Euro horsepower (110 DIN) and fewer black-speed decorations, this box could have left for dead every other performance car in the country.

But I am cheered back up again by thinking of what it *is*. This car just down-the-road drives better than any other sedan I've tried in the past year. The suspension has the right resilience, and the steering has the right feel. There's a wonderful sense of balance. Balance is the hardest quality to engineer in—harder by far than horsepower—and VW has done it right. You can really make some moves in this car.

Seats are nearly as difficult. For my anatomy, the GTI's buckets fit better than the best that can be done with all the knobs and squeeze bulbs in Camaros and Supras. For around $8000, I don't know of a friendlier place to sit and drive. —*Patrick Bedard*

Universal esteem for anything—automobiles, moving pictures, jelly doughnuts—is unheard-of in this office. Yet *every*body loves the Rabbit GTI, including me. But let me enter a short list of this car's deficiencies into the record for the sake of objectivity. The clutch pedal vibrates underfoot at times. It's difficult to heel-and-toe. The steering is too slow for my tastes. Lastly, the Rabbit is by now an old car, a condition I'll mention in passing without actually holding it against the GTI in any way. Let us instead say the car is mature.

The most interesting thing to me about the GTI is that it's a true original even though the idea of a sport box has been bandied about for years. The Japanese have nothing of the sort. Chevrolet can only dream of such a car. The Ford Motor Company is working hard on the Escort GT, but the fruit of its labor is not yet ripe. Now that VW has done the definitive econoracer, copying it should be easy. This is one case where cribbing is encouraged, at least by me. —*Don Sherman*

Vehicle type: front-engine, front-wheel-drive, 4-passenger, 2-door sedan

Estimated price: $8440

Option on test car: AM/FM-stereo radio/cassette

Sound system: AM/FM-stereo radio/cassette, 4 speakers

ENGINE
Type . . . . 4-in-line, iron block and aluminum head
Bore x stroke . . . . 3.19 x 3.40 in, 81.0 x 86.4mm
Displacement . . . . 109 cu in, 1781cc
Compression ratio 8.5:1
Fuel system . . . . Bosch K-Jetronic fuel injection
Emissions controls . . . . . 3-way catalytic converter, feedback
                                                          fuel-air-ratio control
Valve gear . . . . belt-driven overhead cam, solid lifters
Power (SAE net) . . . . 90 bhp @ 5500 rpm
Torque (SAE net) . . . . 105 lbs-ft @ 3250 rpm
Redline . . . . 6700 rpm

DRIVETRAIN
Transmission 5-speed
Final-drive ratio 3.89:1

Gear	Ratio	Mph/1000 rpm	Max. test speed
I	3.45	4.9	33 mph (6700 rpm)
II	2.12	7.9	53 mph (6700 rpm)
III	1.44	11.7	70 mph (6000 rpm)
IV	1.13	14.9	89 mph (6000 rpm)
V	0.91	18.5	104 mph (5600 rpm)

DIMENSIONS AND CAPACITIES
Wheelbase . . . . 94.5 in
Track, F/R . . . . 54.7/53.1 in
Length . . . . 155.3 in
Width . . . . 63.4 in
Height . . . . 55.5 in
Ground clearance . . . . 4.8 in

Curb weight . . . . 2100 lbs
Weight distribution, F/R . . . . 64.3/35.7 %
Fuel capacity . . . . 10.0 gal
Oil capacity . . . . 4.7 qt

CHASSIS/BODY
Type . . . . unit construction
Body material . . . . welded steel stampings

INTERIOR
SAE volume, front seat . . . . 43 cu ft
                        rear seat . . . . 33 cu ft
                        trunk space . . . . 14 cu ft
Front seats . . . . bucket
Recliner type . . . . infinitely adjustable
General comfort . . . . poor fair good **excellent**
Fore-and-aft support . . . . poor fair good **excellent**
Lateral support . . . . poor fair good **excellent**

SUSPENSION
F: . . . . . . ind, MacPherson strut, coil springs, anti-sway bar
R: . . . . ind, trailing arm integral with a transverse beam
                                                       and an anti-sway bar

STEERING
Type . . . . rack-and-pinion
Turns lock-to-lock 3.7
Turning circle curb-to-curb . . . . 31.2 ft

BRAKES
F: . . . . 9.4 x 0.8-in vented disc
R: . . . . 7.1 x 1.2-in cast-iron drum
Power assist . . . . vacuum

WHEELS AND TIRES
Wheel size . . . . 6.0 x 14 in
Wheel type . . . . cast aluminum
Tire make and size . . . Pirelli Cinturato P6, 185/60HR-14
Test inflation pressures, F/R . . . . 28/28 psi

CAR AND DRIVER TEST RESULTS

ACCELERATION   Seconds
Zero to 30 mph 3.0
     40 mph 4.4
     50 mph 6.6
     60 mph 9.7
     70 mph 13.3
     80 mph 19.0
     90 mph 29.5
Top-gear passing time, 30–50 mph 8.6
                     50–70 mph 11.2
Standing ¼-mile . . . . 17.1 sec @ 76 mph
Top speed . . . . 104 mph

HANDLING
Roadholding, 200-ft-dia skidpad . . . . 0.78 g
Understeer . . . . minimal **moderate** excessive

BRAKING
70–0 mph @ impending lockup . . . . 194 ft
Modulation . . . . poor fair good **excellent**

Fade . . . . **none** moderate heavy
Front-rear balance . . . . poor fair **good**

COAST-DOWN MEASUREMENTS
Road horsepower @ 50 mph . . . . 14.5 hp
Friction and tire losses @ 50 mph . . . . 5.0 hp
Aerodynamic drag @ 50 mph . . . . 9.5 hp

FUEL ECONOMY
EPA city driving . . . . **25 mpg**
EPA highway driving . . . . **37 mpg**
EPA combined driving . . . . **29 mpg**
C/D observed fuel economy . . . . **26 mpg**

INTERIOR SOUND LEVEL
Idle . . . . 61 dBA
Full-throttle acceleration . . . . 84 dBA
70-mph cruising . . . . 76 dBA
70-mph coasting . . . . 75 dBA

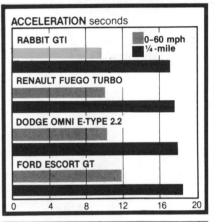

CURRENT BASE PRICE dollars x 1000

DODGE OMNI E-TYPE 2.2
VOLKSWAGEN RABBIT GTI
FORD ESCORT GT (estimated)
RENAULT FUEGO TURBO

ACCELERATION seconds

RABBIT GTI   0–60 mph   ¼-mile
RENAULT FUEGO TURBO
DODGE OMNI E-TYPE 2.2
FORD ESCORT GT

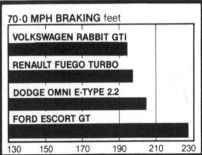

70-0 MPH BRAKING feet

VOLKSWAGEN RABBIT GTI
RENAULT FUEGO TURBO
DODGE OMNI E-TYPE 2.2
FORD ESCORT GT

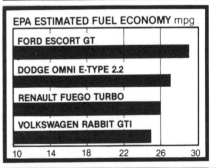

EPA ESTIMATED FUEL ECONOMY mpg

FORD ESCORT GT
DODGE OMNI E-TYPE 2.2
RENAULT FUEGO TURBO
VOLKSWAGEN RABBIT GTI

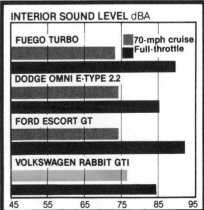

INTERIOR SOUND LEVEL dBA

FUEGO TURBO   70-mph cruise   Full-throttle
DODGE OMNI E-TYPE 2.2
FORD ESCORT GT
VOLKSWAGEN RABBIT GTI

VOLKSWAGEN GOLF GTi

Fighting off challenges from Ford and GM, VW have given their class-dominating Golf GTi a 1.8-litre engine with more torque than the old 1.6 unit, and longer gearing for better economy. Let the punches fly . . .

THE FIRST right-hand drive versions of VW's Golf GTi went on sale in the UK three years ago. The car that created the sporting hatchback market has since become its cult figure, so far vanquishing all challengers without breaking sweat. So far. With more powerful fuel-injected versions of the Ford Escort XR3 and Vauxhall Astra SR limbering up in the wings, however, the writing was on the wall for the GTi.

Now the gloves are off. Pre-empting the arrival of Ford's new hope by a few weeks, VW have raised the capacity of the GTi's jewel-like single overhead cam "four" from 1.6 to 1.8 litres, given its stronger legs a longer stride, and installed a multi-function on-board computer — all without hiking the price. The claimed benefits are even stronger performance allied to better economy and refinement: in plain figures a 114 mph top speed, 8.2 sec 0-60 mph time and 37 mpg. It seems too good to be true . . .

The 1.8-litre GTi's body, trim and chassis are identical to those of the car it replaces — with the all-new Golf on stream for next year, there would be little point in changing them now. Thus it has MacPherson struts at the front, trailing arms linked by a torsion beam at the rear, coil springs and an anti-roll bar at both ends, front disc and rear drum brakes, and rack and pinion steering. The big difference is under the bonnet, where both bore and stroke have been increased to raise the swept volume from 1,588 to 1,781cc. Physically, the new unit is actually slightly lighter than the old one thanks to its lighter pistons and crankshaft. This latter item also features improved balancing, and a torsional vibration damper, for smoother running. Greater combustion efficiency has been achieved by combining larger inlet and exhaust valves with a revised camshaft, new combustion chamber pattern, and a 10:1 compression ratio.

Shapely front seats are comfortable and have good rearward travel. Rear legroom is better than in early Golfs, but still not as good as in some rivals

The changes were designed to give an engine with an already high specific power output more torque across the rev range and less frenzied power characteristics. So although the new version of VW's Bosch K-Jetronic fuel-injected engine develops only 2 bhp more — 112 (DIN) — it does so at 5,800 instead of 6,100 rpm, while peak torque is up from 103 lb at 5,000 rpm to 109 lb ft at 3,500 rpm. With the extra muscle comes longer legs: the lower (3.65) final drive ratio gives taller overall gearing and a well judged 19.7 mph/1000 rpm in fifth, compared with 18.4 on the 1.6.

At £6,500 (the same as the old model), the 1.8 GTi clearly represents fine value, though there's no denying that the competition is tough and keenly priced, too. Ford's Escort XR3i (£6,030) only just breaks the £6,000 barrier, and there are plenty of potent hatchbacks that don't: the Colt 1400 Turbo (£5,959), Fiat's Strada 105 TC (£5,495), Alfa Romeo's Alfasud 1.5 TiX (£5,850) and the Renault 5 Gordini Turbo (£5,752). All these cars — front-wheel drive like the VW — take on the GTi at its own game with varying degrees of success. None is as accelerative as the crackerjack Golf (the Renault gets close on top speed), though the Alfasud has equally agile handling and the edge on space. The Volvo 360

GLT (£6,198 in three-door form) is also a car in the sporting hatchback mould and more fun than you might expect, albeit not as quick as its 115 bhp might suggest.

With a class-clobbering power/weight ratio and a perfect sprinting set of gear ratios in its favour, the GTi accelerates as rapidly as anything you'll find under 2 litres and goes on to reach a more than respectable top speed. On a blustery day, it lapped MIRA's banked circuit at 112.4 mph (111.6 for the 1.6 in ideal test conditions) and demonstrated the benefit of its longer gearing with a best quarter mile of 118.4 mph (113.6). The GTi sprinted from rest to 60 mph in just 8.1 sec, an outstandingly good figure and around a second better than the class average. Fourth and fifth gear flexibility is also above-par; 30-50 mph in fourth takes just 6.0 sec while the all-important 50-70 mph increment is covered in 9.1 sec in fifth.

Exceptionally free-revving and a paragon of smoothness, the new engine is also marginally more refined than the old 1.6-litre unit, proving less boomy at high revs though no less sporting in note. As before, throttle response is crisp and immediate, power delivery clean and urgent. Driven gently, the GTi feels eager.

Our overall fuel consumption of 28.8 mpg, although some way short of

VW's claimed 37 mpg, is nevertheless excellent when you consider the GTi's vivid performance and the fact that it was exploited to the full. None of the rivals with which we've compared the GTi in this test is more economical though all are slower. With an estimated touring consumption of 34 mpg, the 8.9 gallon tanks permits a maximum range of 300 miles of 4 star petrol.

As ever, the GTi's gearchange is excellent and delighted all our testers with its light, quick and baulk-free action. The four intermediate ratios are ideally spaced allowing maxima of 32, 53, 78 and 99 mph — third is an especially effective overtaking gear. The clutch is light, and progressive in its take up.

Out-gunned for sheer smooth-road grip by some of its more extravagantly-shod rivals, the excellence of the GTi's *handling* still has few peers. It's the VW's ability to corner quickly in a wide variety of situations and conditions that sets it apart. Its light, precise steering always keeps the driver well informed. Neither is he committed to understeer; the cornering balance can be fine-adjusted with throttle and brake. Mid-corner bumps deflect the suspension and not the car; basic stability is excellent. So is the ride for this type of car where even board-like unresilience isn't too frowned upon. The GTi does ride firmly and thumps heavily over short, sharp bumps around town. But comfort improves with speed as the ride smooths out; above about 50 mph the suspension displays fine control and is seldom upset. It's a pity the brakes don't inspire as much confidence as the handling. They work adequately well but there's still too much dead pedal travel, and, on our car, unwelcome graunching noises when asked to match up to the performance.

The rest is much as before. The GTi driver is well looked after with a hip-hugging Recaro-style seat which is both comfortable and well positioned in relation to the major controls. If he is six foot or taller, however, room in the back will be at a premium for long-legged passengers; more so than in an Escort or Astra, for instance, both of which are more efficiently packaged than the older design Golf. The VW's age shows up with its now unfashionably thick rear pillars, too, which create a minor blind spot at acutely angled T-junctions. Visibility in other directions is reasonable enough, but the door

The facia is ergonomically well planned

Clear instrumentation includes an instantaneous mpg gauge and change-up light (top centre), and at bottom centre the multi-function computer

The computer's six functions are summoned in set sequence by a button on the end of the wiper stalk. It has two memories, one for individual journeys and the other for cumulative travel distance

mirror is badly placed.

Inside, the areas of painted metal (red on our test car) contrast glaringly with the predominantly black trim and the materials used are hard wearing rather than plush. It all appears well screwed together and finished, however. The new on-board computer that supplements the clear and attractive instruments is the most sensible and "user friendly" we've come across, a single column stalk-end push-push button summoning the six functions in set sequence: journey duration, distance, average speed, average fuel consumption, oil temperature and outside temperature. All this is in addition to the time of day, which occupies the small liquid crystal display in the centre of the facia when none of the other data is required. Economical driving is encouraged by VW's usual economy aids — a yellow tell-tale advising on when to change up a gear and an instantaneous mpg gauge comes into action when fifth gear is engaged. We couldn't test the accuracy

of the latter, but the computer's mpg read-out was optimistic by a disappointing 11 per cent.

Heat output remains powerful and easy to regulate. The ventilation — fan boostable and independent of the heater — has a generous throughput and allows warm feet with a cool face, but the poorly sited vent on the right also cools the driver's hand on the wheel.

Overall refinement is better than before and very good for the class, with an attractive yet muted and boom-free engine note, negligible wind noise and moderate tyre roar.

At the expense of sounding interminably repetitious, this test has only one conclusion — the GTi still rules. The best car in its class has been made better: quicker, thriftier, quieter. If Ford, GM and others want to topple the GTi from its position of supremacy they do have a chance, and a fuel-injected 1.8-litre Astra SR might be the car to do it if not the XR3i. But they'll have to hurry up. Next year VW will have a new Golf.

High loading sill, but with the seat folded estate-car style the cargo deck is deep and capacious

MOTOR ROAD
VW GOLF GTi

PERFORMANCE

WEATHER CONDITIONS
Wind	10-20 mph
Temperature	50°F/10°C
Barometer	1000 mbar/29.5 in Hg
Surface	Dry tarmacadam

MAXIMUM SPEEDS
	mph	kph
Banked circuit	112.4	180.8
Best ¼ mile	118.4	190.5
Terminal Speeds:		
at ¼ mile	84	135
at kilometre	102	164
Speeds in gears (at 6,200 rpm):		
1st	32	51
2nd	53	85
3rd	78	125
4th	99	159

ACCELERATION FROM REST
mph	sec	kph	sec
0-30	3.0	0-40	2.5
0-40	4.3	0-60	3.9
0-50	5.9	0-80	5.9
0-60	8.1	0-100	8.7
0-70	10.6	0-120	12.6
0-80	15.0	0-140	18.2
0-90	19.6	0-160	28.4
0-100	28.8		
Stand'g ¼	16.2	Stand'g km	30.3

ACCELERATION IN TOP
mph	sec	kph	sec
20-40	9.7	40-60	5.9
30-50	9.1	60-80	5.7
40-60	8.9	80-100	5.5
50-70	9.1	100-120	6.6
60-80	11.2	120-140	8.3
70-90	13.2	140-160	10.6
80-100	15.8		

ACCELERATION IN 4TH
mph	sec	kph	sec
20-40	6.8	40-60	4.2
30-50	6.0	60-80	3.6
40-60	6.1	80-100	4.1
50-70	6.8	100-120	4.4
60-80	8.1	120-140	6.3
70-90	9.3	140-160	9.5
80-100	13.2		

FUEL CONSUMPTION
Overall	28.8 mpg
	9.8 litres/100 km
Govt tests	26.6 mpg (urban)
	47.9 mpg (56 mph)
	36.7 mpg (75 mph)
Fuel grade	97 octane
	4 star rating
Tank capacity	8.9 galls
	40 litres
Max range*	300 miles
	483 km
Test distance	895 miles
	1,440 km

*Based on estimated 34 mpg touring consumption.

NOISE
	dBA	Motor rating*
30 mph	65	11
50 mph	68	14
70 mph	73	19
Maximum†	81	34

*A rating where 1=30 dBA, and 100=96 dBA, and where double the number means double the loudness
†Peak noise level under full-throttle acceleration in 2nd.

SPEEDOMETER (mph)
Speedo	30 40 50 60 70 80 90 100						
True mph	27 36.5 46 55 64 73 82 91						

Distance recorder: 2.9 per cent fast

WEIGHT
	cwt	kg
Unladen weight*	16.5	838
Weight as tested	20.2	1,026

*with fuel for approx 50 miles

Performance tests carried out by Motor's staff at the Motor Industry Research Association proving ground, Lindley.

Test Data: World Copyright reserved. No reproduction in whole or part without written permission.

GENERAL SPECIFICATION

ENGINE
Cylinders	4-in-line
Capacity	1,781cc (108.6 cu in)
Bore/stroke	81/86.4mm/(3.19/3.40 in)
Cooling	Water
Block	Cast iron
Head	Alloy
Valves	Sohc
Cam drive	Belt
Compression	10:1
Fuel system	Bosch K-Jetronic fuel injection
Bearings	5 main
Max power	112 bhp (DIN) at 5,800 rpm
Max torque	109 lb ft (DIN) at 3,500 rpm

TRANSMISSION
Type	5-speed, manual
Clutch dia	7.2 in
Actuation	Cable
Internal ratios and mph/1,000 rpm	
Top	0.912:1/19.7
4th	1.130:1/15.9
3rd	1.440:1/12.5
2nd	2.120:1/8.5
1st	3.450:1/5.2
Rev	3.170:1
Final drive	3.65:1

BODY CHASSIS
Construction	Unitary, all-steel
Protection	6-year anti-corrosion guarantee

SUSPENSION
Front	Independent by MacPherson struts and lower wishbones; coil springs; anti-roll bar
Rear	Independent by trailing arms linked by torsion beam axle; coil springs; anti-roll bar

STEERING
Type	Rack and pinion
Assistance	No

BRAKES
Front	9.4 in ventilated discs
Rear	7.1 in drums
Park	On rear
Servo	Yes
Circuit	Split diagonally
Rear valve	Yes
Adjustment	Automatic

WHEELS/TYRES
Type	Alloy, 5.5J x 13
Tyres	175/70 HR 13
Pressures	24/24 psi F/R (normal)
	26/31 psi F/R (full load/ high speed)

ELECTRICAL
Battery	12V, 36 Ah
Earth	Negative
Generator	Alternator, 65A
Fuses	15
Headlights	
type	Halogen
dip	100 W total
main	120 W total

Make: Volkswagen
Model: Golf GTi
Maker: Volkswagen AG, 3180 Wolfsburg, West Germany
UK Concessionaires: VAG (UK) Ltd, Yeomans Drive, Blakelands, Milton Keynes MK14 5AN. Tel: (0908) 679121
Price: £5,217.00 plus £434.75 Car Tax and £847.76 VAT equals £6,499.51 total

TheRivals

Other rivals include the BMW 316 (£5,950), Ford's Escort XR3i (£6,030), Lancia's Delta LX (£5,965) and the Vauxhall Astra 1.6 SR (£5,867).

VW GOLF GTi — £6,500

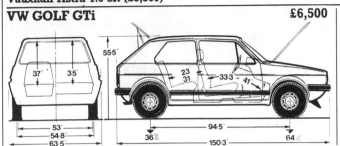

Power, bhp/rpm	112/5,800
Torque, lb ft/rpm	109/3,500
Tyres	175/70 HR 14
Weight, cwt	16.5
Max speed, mph	112.4
0-60 mph, sec	8.1
30-50 mph in 4th, sec	6.0
Overall mpg	28.8
Touring mpg	—
Fuel grade, stars	4
Boot capacity, cu ft	8.6
Test Date	November 27, 1982

Bigger-engined Golf GTi is still the hottest of the hot hatchbacks and, on balance, still the best. One of the finest "fours" in the business provides crackerjack performance with good refinement and without trauma at the petrol pumps. A delectable five-speed gearbox and real handling finesse further justify the cult status the GTi enjoys. Packaging is nothing special by today's standards and the interior is starkly appointed. But a great little car.

ALFA ROMEO ALFASUD TiX — £5,850

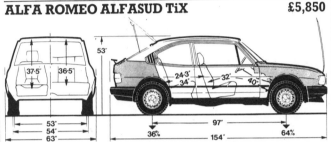

Power, bhp/rpm	95/5,800
Torque, lb ft/rpm	96/4,000
Tyres	165/70 SR 13
Weight, cwt	18.0
Max speed, mph	106.9
0-60 mph, sec	9.9
30-50 mph in 4th, sec	7.1
Overall mpg	26.1
Touring mpg	34.6
Fuel grade, stars	4
Boot capacity, cu ft	9.4
Test Date (Ti)	December 6, 1980

Now available only in 3-dr hatchback form and with recently revised (longer) gearing the Alfasud 1.5 TiX remains one of our favourites. Fine performance from combination of smooth, revvy yet torquey engine with close-ratio gearbox; with old gearing not as economical as some rivals when driven hard, but responds well to a light right foot. Superb handling, yet comfortable ride, and noise levels are low. Overall a fine driver's car that should equally be appreciated by passengers.

COLT 1400 HATCHBACK TURBO — £5,959

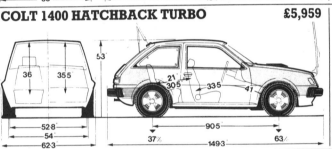

Power, bhp/rpm	105/5,500
Torque, lb ft/rpm	114/3,500
Tyres	175/70 HR 13
Weight, cwt	16.5
Max speed, mph	104.8
0-60 mph, sec	9.0
30-50 mph in 4th ("Power"), sec	9.0
Overall mpg	26.5
Touring mpg	34.2
Fuel grade, stars	4
Boot capacity, cu ft	6.0
Test Date	July 24, 1982

Colt's application of turbocharger technology has turned their 1400 Hatchback into a competent rival for the Golf GTi. It has good performance and taut, vice-free handling backed up by reasonable economy and excellent brakes. Shortcomings are restricted rear seat accommodation, poor ride comfort and an unnecessarily complex 8-speed transmission. Rather expensive, but competitively equipped.

FIAT STRADA 105 TC — £5,495

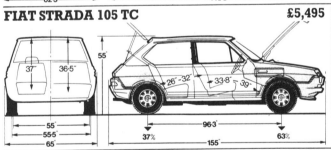

Power, bhp/rpm	105/6,100
Torque, lb ft/rpm	98/4,000
Tyres	185/60 HR 14
Weight, cwt	18.3
Max speed, mph	104.0
0-60 mph, sec	9.7
30-50 mph in 4th, sec	8.4
Overall mpg	25.5
Touring mpg	31.2
Fuel grade, stars	4
Boot capacity, cu ft	9.9
Test Date	March 6, 1982

High equipment levels and good accommodation at a keen price make the Strada very good value, but in a number of important areas — economy, gearchange, comfort, refinement and heating/ventilation — it falls somewhat short of class standards. Good smooth-road grip, but handling lacks finesse, brakes are oversensitive, and ride comfort is poor. Reasonable performance, but overall a rather disappointing car.

RENAULT GORDINI TURBO — £5,752

Power, bhp/rpm	110/6,000
Torque, lb ft/rpm	108/4,000
Tyres	155/70 HR 13
Weight, cwt	16.2
Max speed, mph	111.8
0-60 mph, sec	8.7
30-50 mph in 4th, sec	7.1
Overall mpg	28.3
Touring mpg	31.5
Fuel grade, stars	4
Boot capacity, cu ft	5.3
Test Date	June 19, 1982

A typically competent turbocharger conversion by Renault has given the R5 Gordini performance almost as good as the GTi's and respectable economy. Handling is taut and quite predictable but the steering is rather heavy and traction is lacking on the relatively narrow standard-issue rubber. The efficiently damped suspension gives acceptable ride comfort. Drawbacks are its cramped accommodation, plasticky interior trim, poor refinement, and a relatively high price.

VOLVO 360 GLT 3-door — £6,198

Power, bhp/rpm	115/6,000
Torque, lb ft/rpm	118/3,600
Tyres	185/60 HR 14
Weight, cwt	22.6
Max speed, mph	108.0
0-60 mph, sec	10.3
30-50 mph in 4th, sec	9.6
Overall mpg	24.2
Touring mpg	—
Fuel grade, stars	4
Boot capacity, cu ft	9.4
Test Date	November 6, 1982

Biggest-engined version of Volvo's smallest model really falls between cars like the GTi and Alfa's Giulietta 2.0, but makes a fine sporting hatchback nonetheless with punchy performance, well-balanced handling and a surprisingly supple ride. Build, finish and overall refinement are also good but economy and accommodation are nothing special.

Depressed? Feeling low? If you're a car enthusiast, we may have the cure for your ills. Get yourself down to your nearest Volkswagen dealer and ask to take a test drive in the new Rabbit GTI. Then call your loved ones and tell them you'll be home in a couple days, because if you're anything like us that's how long it will take you to come back down. What a car! Now, we've been fortunate enough to drive VW's Golf (Rabbit) GTi in Germany and have always come away with sensory imbalance—how can a car that looks like a Rabbit go so quickly? Then we heard an American Rabbit GTI was on the way and we feared a watered-down version with fancy trim, fancy wheels and tires, but surely no performance. Wrong, wrong, wrong. The U.S. Rabbit GTI team, headed by VW of America's Vice President for Engineering Duane Miller, has come up with a car that is the panacea for everything from the blues to the blahs.

At the press preview for the GTI, Miller explained that the initial plan was to build a more modest version of the car, adding only sport seats and "GTI-like" suspension to the Rabbit S. But it immediately became apparent that the S with the GTI suspension was a disappointment because the U.S. Rabbit weighs more than the European Golf—so the improved handling made the relative lack of horsepower seem worse than it was.

Miller says two events in Germany in 1981 made the U.S. GTI a possibility: first, the introduction of 14-in. alloy wheels for the Quantum that would also fit the Rabbit; second, a decision to develop a federalized version of the 1.8-liter high performance engine slotted for the 1983 Golf GTi. With the more powerful engine and the ability to use larger and wider wheels and tires, the engineers at VW of America felt they had the necessary ingredients to make their own GTI.

The suspension is as similar to the Golf GTi as possible, bearing in mind a weight difference of 140–200 lb. To handle the extra weight of the Rabbit, the front spring rate was made 22 percent stiffer than the Golf's (or the 1982 Rabbit's), and the rear springs were changed from progressive to linear—while their rate is the same as the Golf's, they are 29 percent stiffer than those of this year's Rabbit. Shock absorber control was also increased, and the front MacPherson struts are from the Golf GTi and give two-thirds more rebound control than stock equipment. The rear shocks are similar to those of the European GTi, but they have stiffer valving designed specifically for the American GTI.

The final touches for the Rabbit GTI were anti-roll bars front and rear (16.5 mm/20.5 mm, respectively) to minimize body roll during cornering, and the largest tires/wheels ever offered on a Rabbit or Golf: 185/60HR-14 Pirelli P6s mounted on 14 x 6-in. alloy rims. Miller claims the result is a suspension system ⟫⟫⟫→

AT A GLANCE	Volkswagen Rabbit GTI	BMW 320i	Chevrolet Citation X11
List price	est $8500	$13,290	$6754
Curb weight, lb	2070	2435	2775
Engine	inline-4	inline-4	V-6
Transmission	5-sp M	5-sp M	4-sp M
0–60 mph, sec	10.6	11.1	9.9
Standing ¼ mi, sec	17.7	18.0	17.3
Speed at end of ¼ mi, mph	76.0	77.0	80.0
Stopping distance from 60 mph, ft	153	169	154
Interior noise at 50 mph, dBA	71	69	69
Lateral acceleration, g	0.797	0.743	0.826
Slalom speed, mph	61.3	58.6	61.1
Fuel economy, mpg	29.0	26.0	19.5
Issue		2-80	10-82

VOLKSWAGEN RABBIT GTI

Street racer in a bunny suit

PHOTOS BY JOE RUSZ

that stresses balance above all else: "We believe it to be an exceptional combination of low-speed responsiveness and high-speed stability, of strong linear-range handling and 'forgiving' limit behavior. All with a ride quality that never interferes with the car's ability to double as a family sedan." An impressive declaration to be sure especially in light of the current Rabbit's strong understeer and overall lack of crispness.

The new engine is actually the old engine with some modifications. The 1982 Rabbit's engine displaces 1715 cc and boasts 74 bhp (SAE net) at 5000 rpm, with 94 lb-ft torque at 3000. The GTI powerplant has a larger bore (81.0 mm versus 79.5) to bump the displacement to 1780 cc. The cylinder head has been redesigned with larger intake and exhaust valves, and the pistons are 20 percent lighter. The compression ratio is 8.5:1 for the GTI, compared to 8.2:1 for the standard car, and the result is a bhp figure of 90 at 5500 rpm, and the torque is 105 lb-ft at 3250. VW continues to use K-Jetronic fuel injection for the new engine, along with an electronic ignition and a digital idle stabilizer to ensure excellent driveability. Adding to the engine's performance is an all-new free-flow exhaust system with large-diameter tubing and reengineered converter and muffler baffling to provide a 35-percent reduction in back pressure compared to that of the standard Rabbit.

VW has also tailored a 5-speed close-ratio gearbox to the GTI's performance capabilities, and there's a heavy-duty clutch to go with it. The final drive ratio is 3.94:1 in the GTI versus 3.89:1 in the 1982 Rabbit. The front brake discs are now vented rather than solid on this special model. Exterior changes include a flexible urethane front air dam that ties into the front fender flares, extensive use of flat-black trim all around the car, and red

grille border and red GTI nameplates. Otherwise, the GTI is a sleeper, virtually indistinguishable from any other Rabbit at a distance.

Inside, the GTI has some appropriate features that make it a serious driver's car. The sport seats are "functional duplicates" of German GTi seats, and the foam padding is imported because VW of America couldn't find a supplier with acceptable material here. There is a new 4-spoke padded steering wheel that offers excellent grip, and a tachometer and center console with additional gauges are standard. The GTI package also includes halogen headlights, left and right remote-control mirrors, the distinctive golf-ball style shift knob and rear wiper/washer.

Now that you have all of the background on what makes the Rabbit GTI different, let us tell you what really makes it different—the driving. Plain and simple, go-for-it fun, and we mean FUN! "One quick trip around the block and you won't want to give this one up," enthused one of our editors, while another described the GTI as a "Basic pocket-rocket street racer carried to subtle limits . . . The fun quotient in this sleeper is maximum!" And perhaps the most telling comment from one of us (keeping in mind that we each drive 80 to 100 different cars per year), "Here's a car I would actually buy with my own money."

And what performance would we be buying? How about 10.6 seconds, 0–60 mph? Or a quarter-mile time of 17.7 sec at 76.0 mph? For a 2200-lb car with a 1.8-liter engine, this is performance that gives grown men and women toothy smiles and enormous grins. The last Rabbit we tested ("Four Front-Wheel-Drive Sedans," February 1981) was the quickest car in that comparison test with a 0–60 mph time of 12.6 sec and a quarter-mile run of 18.7 sec at 71.0 mph (the other three cars were Ford

Escort, Honda Accord and Mazda GLC). At 10.6 sec, 0–60, the Rabbit GTI will put a lot of more expensive cars to shame—such as the Audi Coupe (11.2) or the BMW 320i (11.1), as well as running a very close second to a Saab 900 Turbo (10.0).

But straight-line acceleration is only part of the GTI's balanced performance story, because the handling capabilities may impress you even more than the power. Its road manners are so damned impressive that we just couldn't drive the car enough—any excuse to jump in it and hit the pavement and we took it. On the objective side, we measured a lateral acceleration of 0.797g, and ran through our 700-ft slalom at 61.3 mph—for comparison, we measured the Porsche 911SC (May 1980) at 0.798g on the skidpad and 59.7 mph in the slalom.

VW's Rabbit GTI is so much more than just a track car, though, it's a car built and bred for twisty mountain roads and city streets: "It corners like you won't believe with none of the tipsy feel of recent Rabbits," noted one driver following a high-speed mountain run. He added that equally impressive is the suspension's marvelous compliance that produces smooth ride characteristics to go with the crisp handling. The rack-and-pinion steering is unboosted and while slightly heavy at very low speeds, none of our drivers would care to change it at all. Feedback from the Pirelli P6 tires is excellent and the combination of steering and tires gives the driver an extremely precise feel for what is happening at the road. The close-ratio 5-speed makes you feel like you're driving a Formula Ford on the road. No matter what gear you're in, you're never at a loss for torque.

The sport seats, as VW likes to call them, are marvelously comfortable for nearly any person of any size, and they provide excellent lateral support during all the high-speed cornering every driver is going to be doing with this car. Otherwise, the interior is recognizably American Rabbit with the heavily padded vinyl dash and generally tasteful trim treatment. One criticism we have to level: without the optional air conditioning, there are no fresh air vents in the center part of the dash, and that's tacky. We also thought that the sun visors and headliner fabric look rather cheap, but all in all the color coordination and level of quality are quite good.

Well, we could go on for days singing the praises of the Rabbit GTI, but if you fancy yourself some kind of car enthusiast and hot-shoe driver, you're probably already on the way to the nearest VW dealer. If not, you better hurry. Manufacturing limits on the new 1.8 engine will restrict U.S. GTI production to 20,000 cars per year, and they should sell like lemonade in August. At an estimated price of $8500, the Rabbit GTI is the most exciting automotive news of the year. ⊚

SPECIFICATIONS

List price, all POE	est $8500
Price as tested	est $9000

Price as tested includes std equip (alloy wheels, Pirelli P6 tires, sport seats), AM/FM stereo/cassette (est $500)

GENERAL

Curb weight, lb/kg	2070	940
Test weight	2200	999
Weight dist (with driver), f/r, %	63/37	
Wheelbase, in./mm	94.5	2400
Track, front/rear	54.7/53.1	1390/1350
Length	155.3	3945
Width	63.4	1610
Height	55.5	1410
Trunk space, cu ft/liters	10.4 + 10.7	295 + 303
Fuel capacity, U.S. gal./liters	10.0	38

ENGINE

Type	sohc inline-4
Bore x stroke, in./mm	3.19 x 3.40...81.0 x 86.4
Displacement, cu in./cc	109 ...1780
Compression ratio	8.5:1
Bhp @ rpm, SAE net/kW	90/70 @ 5500
Torque @ rpm, lb-ft/Nm	105/142 @ 3250
Fuel injection	Bosch K-Jetronic
Fuel requirement	unleaded, 91-oct

DRIVETRAIN

Transmission	5-sp manual
Gear ratios: 5th (0.91)	3.58:1
4th (1.13)	4.45:1
3rd (1.44)	5.67:1
2nd (2.12)	8.35:1
1st (3.49)	13.75:1
Final drive ratio	3.94:1

CHASSIS & BODY

Layout	transverse front engine/front drive
Body/frame	unit steel
Brake system	9.4-in. (239-mm) vented discs front, 7.1 x 1.2-in. (180 x 30-mm) drums rear; vacuum asst
Wheels	cast alloy, 14 x 6J
Tires	Pirelli P6, 185/60HR-14
Steering type	rack & pinion
Turns, lock-to-lock	3.8

Suspension, front/rear: MacPherson struts, lower A-arms, coil springs, tube shocks, anti-roll bar/beam axle on trailing arms with integral anti-roll bar, coil springs, tube shocks

CALCULATED DATA

Lb/bhp (test weight)	24.4
Mph/1000 rpm (5th gear)	18.2
Engine revs/mi (60 mph)	3300
R&T steering index	1.19
Brake swept area, sq in./ton	216

ROAD TEST RESULTS

ACCELERATION

Time to distance, sec:

0–100 ft	3.5
0–500 ft	9.3
0–1320 ft (¼ mi)	17.7
Speed at end of ¼ mi, mph	76.0

Time to speed, sec:

0–30 mph	2.9
0–50 mph	7.4
0–60 mph	10.6
0–70 mph	14.6
0–80 mph	20.8

SPEEDS IN GEARS

5th gear (5900 rpm)	107
4th (6700)	98
3rd (6700)	78
2nd (6700)	54
1st (6700)	32

FUEL ECONOMY

Normal driving, mpg	29.0

BRAKES

Minimum stopping distances, ft:

From 60 mph	153
From 80 mph	264
Control in panic stop	excellent
Pedal effort for 0.5g stop, lb	17

Fade: percent increase in pedal effort to maintain 0.5g deceleration in 6 stops from 60 mph 18

Overall brake rating .... excellent

HANDLING

Lateral accel, 100-ft radius, g	0.797
Speed thru 700-ft slalom, mph	61.3

INTERIOR NOISE

Constant 30 mph, dBA	68
50 mph	71
70 mph	79

SPEEDOMETER ERROR

30 mph indicated is actually	28.0
60 mph	60.0

ACCELERATION

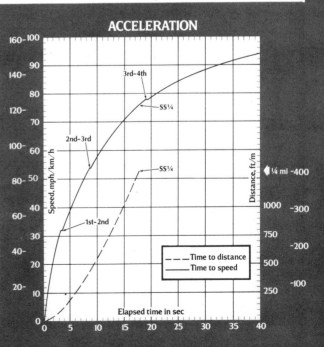

Visually, it could be any other GTI, but under the bonnet of Volkswagen's latest version is a torquier 1800cc four-cylinder engine.

Playing better Golf

Volkswagen's GTI keeps one step ahead of the opposition with its 1800cc engine. Mark Hughes has been driving one.

Since the Volkswagen Golf GTI was introduced to this country in right-hand drive form three years ago it has been universally well received, both by the press and the public. The fact that it has been acclaimed as the best sporting hatchback on the market during those three years is borne out by sales of 10,000 in Britain and more than 330,000 worldwide. While it has become something of a cult car, its status recently has been increasingly under threat from such effective new rivals as the Renault 5 Gordini Turbo and the Ford Escort XR3i, both of which undercut it on price.

Two months ago, however, Volkswagen stepped another rung up the performance ladder to maintain their market advantage by introducing an 1800cc engined GTI. The silky smooth, fuel-injected, single overhead camshaft four-cylinder unit, which has always been the best element in the GTI equation, is now an even more efficient — and economical — engine, ensuring that the existing, eight year old body shape of the Golf gets a new lease of life before the introduction of an entirely new model later this year.

Externally, the GTI 1800 is identical to the car it replaces, not even the badging announcing that there is anything different under the surface. It remains a handsome, solid-looking car, its performance potential happily understated in comparison with some of its gaudier, but slower, opponents. It is still on the expensive side in the comparison stakes, costing £500 more than the XR3i and the Gordini Turbo, but it is still unquestionably good value, especially as the price has not been increased with the higher specification. Taking the GTI's superior engineering quality, better fuel economy and 10,000 mile service intervals into account, it would probably turn out to be a better buy in the long run.

The changes to the GTI are in only three departments: the engine, a lower final drive and the addition of an on-board computer. It is under the bonnet, though, that the real difference is felt, those extra 200cc considerably improving the performance characteristics and endowing the car with noticeably more refinement.

Bore and stroke have both been increased to enlarge the swept volume from 1588cc to 1781cc, but power output is increased by only 2bhp, from 110bhp to 112bhp. Where this maximum is produced — at 5800rpm instead of 6100rpm — gives a clue to what the Volkswagen engineers were trying to acheive, but the torque characteristics give the game away. Again the maximum figure is only slightly up — from 103lbs ft to 109lbs ft — but this peak occurs at 3500rpm instead of 5000rpm. The result is a far more flexible engine, offering excellent torque over a much wider rev range.

The new unit is actually lighter than the smaller

The eight year old design still looks fresh.

engine as a result of its lighter pistons and crankshaft, while its improved balancing and the adoption of a torsional vibration damper gives smoother running. A new camshaft, larger inlet and exhaust valves and a new combustion chamber pattern increase the combustion efficiency, while warming-up time is noticeably reduced thanks to narrower water channels.

While the engine's greater efficiency on its own contributes to improving economy, its stronger pulling power allows the further economy measure of lowering the final drive ratio so that the overall gearing is now a taller 19.7mph per 1000rpm in fifth gear compared with the 18.4mph of the 1600.

Out on the road the differences to the GTI are exactly as one would expect. The engine, which was always one of the sweetest fours anywhere, is slightly more refined, but feels much more impatient. With instantaneous throttle response and bags more torque in the middle range, overtaking, particularly in the crucial 50-70mph sector, is effortless. In third and fourth gears the car leaps forward at that speed more urgently, but most of the time fifth gear is perfectly adequate for overtaking.

One of the shortcomings of the 1600 was the boominess of its engine at high speeds, which made long journeys rather tiring. Motorway cruising in the new car is more relaxed, that lower final drive and the better balancing of the engine helping to keep noise levels subdued. The precious liquid is also consumed less greedily by the 1800, the Government 75mph figure of 36.7mpg putting the 1600's 32.5mpg into perspective.

The GTI's crisp five-speed gearbox has always been a joy, and the change in final drive has not altered the excellence of the ratios. Such an eager engine and perfect gearing make the 1800 even swifter in sprinting acceleration, the 0-60mph time being reduced to 8.3secs. There isn't a quicker saloon under 2-litres available, and the efficiency which Volkswagen's engineers have been able to squeeze out of 1800cc makes one wonder whether there really is any point in the turbocharging vogue. Any turbo which can match the GTI's acceleration won't be in the same class when it comes to fuel economy.

The GTI has always been let down by brakes which, quite frankly, are a disgrace in a car of such sparkling performance. Unfortunately, the opportunity to improve the braking on the new car was not taken, the action of the pedal remaining sluggish and not sufficiently confidence inspiring. The brakes work well enough when you push really hard on the middle pedal, but you expect a sharper response from a car with such sporting character.

The suspension also remains the same — independent all round with Macpherson struts up front and trailing arms at the rear — and keeps the GTI near the head of its class. Wider tyred opponents like the XR3i perhaps have an edge on roadholding, and the Alfasud still leads the field in handling finesse, but as an all-round performer the GTI still adds up to an outstandingly nimble package. Stability in all conditions is excellent, oversteer and understeer induced as one wishes with throttle and brake.

Unlike many performance cars with resilient springing, bumpy corners do nor send the wheels skittering off line, the GTI being predictable at all times, wet or dry. Its limits are no longer in a class of their own, but few drivers would wish for higher cornering power. Although the steering wheel is a little large, there are no shortcomings in the precision and lightness of the rack and pinion set-up.

Now that the mechanical differences in the 1800 have been thoroughly covered, it must be said that the third significant change — the addition of an on-board computer — is most worthwhile. At the touch of a button on the end of the right hand stalk governing the windscreen wipers, the digital display in the centre of the instrument panel gives a read out of seven functions arranged in a fixed order: real time (that means it is a clock!), journey time, journey distance, average speed, average fuel consumption, oil temperature and outside temperature. A visual symbol identifies each function as it is selected, and a yellow knob at the top right of the panel allows the data to be stored for continuous journeys with stopping intervals of no longer than two hours. When travelling a long distance in a day, therefore, one can record the overall fuel consumption regardless of halts for fuel and refreshment. Setting the knob in the other position allows continuous recording of individual journeys up to a distance of 6200 miles, 220 gallons of petrol consumed and 100 hours of driving time.

The device proved most useful for monitoring fuel consumption, although the figure at the end of one long journey proved to be 8 per cent optimistic when compared with the accurate figure of 31.6mph deduced from the traditional brim-to-brim method of checking consumption. The new GTI also has Volkswagen's and Audi's now familiar fuel consumption gauge on which a yellow light flashes when economy dictates that the driver should change gear. A needle swings into action to register mpg when fifth gear is engaged.

Apart from this thoughtfully designed computer, the GTI's equipment is unchanged. The interior is smartly trimmed with no ostentation, the Recaro style front seats being very comfortable, firm and figure-hugging, and the all-round visibility commanding from the unusually high driving position. The Golf's design perhaps shows its age in the minor blind spot created by the broad rear pillar and the lack of room in the rear when the driver's seat is towards the end of its travel, but by small hatchback standards it is comfortable, relatively free of wind and road noise, and well finished with durable fabric for the seats and neat plastic mouldings for the facia. Although the Golf is a light car — no small saloon has a power to weight ratio as good as the GTI's — it is very solidly constructed, the doors closing with a good, firm clunk.

There is no doubt that Volkswagen's rationale behind the stop-gap GTI 1800 was to keep their pacesetting performance car one step ahead of the opposition by changing it in several ways for the better.

The GTI's handling finesse is superior to almost all of its rivals.

Nothing has been done for the sake of change, the improvements, with the exception of the dramatically better torque characteristics, being subtle rather than startling. With better performance *and* economy, the GTI's cult status can only increase in this final year of its distinguished existence.

It is with eager anticipation that we look forward to the new range of Golfs in a year's time. ∎

Above: A micro chip information centre allows the driver to compute seven functions at the touch of a button. Below: The clear instrumentation is unchanged apart from the computer display and fuel economy meter. Bottom: The badge doesn't give the 1800 game away..

The familiar fuel injected four-cylinder.

VW GOLF GTI 1800
£6,499
Specification

Cylinders/capacity	4 in-line/1781cc
Bore x stroke	81.0 x 86.4mm
Valve gear	sohc
Compression ratio	10:1
Fuel system	Bosch K-Jetronic fuel injection
Power/rpm	112bhp/5800rpm
Torque/rpm	109lbs ft/3500rpm
Gear ratios	0.912, 1.130, 1.440, 2.120, 3.450:1
Final drive	3.65:1
Steering	rack and pinion
Brakes	servo-assisted, split-circuit 9.4ins ventilated discs (front) and 7.1ins drums (rear)
Wheels	alloy 5½J x 13
Tyres	175/70 HR 13
Suspension (front)	independent Macpherson with anti-roll bar
Suspension (rear)	independent trailing arms and torsion beam axle with anti-roll bar

Dimensions

Wheelbase	94.5ins
Track (front/rear)	53.0/54.8ins
Length	150.3ins
Width	63.5ins
Weight	1896lbs

Performance

Max in fifth	114mph
Max in fourth	103mph
Max in third	83mph
Max in second	55mph
Max in first	34mph
0-30mph	3.0s
0-50mph	6.4s
0-60mph	8.3s
0-80mph	13.5s
0-100mph	24.1s

Fuel

Urban/56mph/75mph	26.6/47.9/36.7mpg
Test	30-33mpg

CLUB WARS

'What makes this a cult car and leader of the hot-hatch war when the aerodynamic cd figure of cd0.42 is no better than a BMC Austin A40 of 1959'

IT IS NOW nine years since Volkswagen launched their front-wheel-drive hatchback onto an unsuspecting public used to Beetles, and next year, ten years on, the box gets softer and more rounded styling — but still visibly a Golf.

A GTi in the new shape is a good 12 months away from an onslaught at this most competitive sector of the market, but having driven the current GTi we can conclude that if we were shopping for a hot-hatch now, we would be strongly willed to resist any temptation to wait until next year — or plumb for a competitor instead — for the current car impresses the longer you live with it.

What makes the GTi such a cult car? It is not particularly aerodynamic — ten years ago the visionaries in the motor-industry's design houses were predicting a great deal of public awareness to cd drag figures, and they were right . . . but there is nothing startling about the Golf, it has a cd drag coefficient of 0.42, exactly the same as the pioneering hatchback produced by B.M.C. in 1959, the Austin A40. It is hard to see how such a brick can be a consistent class leader, and even more, a cult car.

The projection of the Golf GTi has been a marketing department's triumph, who have pushed it into public awareness with flair and vigour.

It was not long before the giants of the motor-industry recognised the area being carved out by the 'sporting' VW and produced competitors. But as each competitor brought out a "Golf-baiter", so VW were able to calmly take something extra off the shelf and say "match that". And so it is that the GTi has steadily been improved, to stay ahead of this particular rat-race. The final move, before the revamp next year, has been to increase the engine size from 1600cc to 1800 — not to produce any more power, but increase torque and flexibility.

The new engine was a mere 75bhp 1.8 litre, originally destined for an Audi Coupe and is as compact as the old 1600 version, but rather surprisingly, it's lighter. With the aid of longer con rods, revised camshaft profile and lighter pistons, not forgetting the fuel injection, the new unit develops 112bhp at 5,800rpm.

The 1800 version of the GTi was introduced into Britain earlier in the year and immediately stepped into where the 1600 had left off, to roar away from the XR3's that had been snapping close at its heels.

There is not a lot of difference between the old and the new GTi — appearance wise they are identical. Though the newer car is just 1mph faster, the initial feeling of power and super-quick response between 2000 and 5000rpm is very noticeable.

Inside, little seems to have changed since the cars were first introduced. The front seats are very comfortable, giving support in vital areas and the driving position is excellent. The pedal layout allows easy toe and heel gear change, but some drivers may find the gear lever a shade too far forward. The rear seats are still strictly for children only and adults riding in the back would find that it becomes increasingly uncomfortable.

Our test car started first time, every time, with no complaints and it soon settles down to a steady tickover between 800 and 900rpm. The steering wheel is equipped with four horn buttons (obviously if you can't pass them . . . blast them).

You don't have to drive many miles to find that the GTi can be driven fast and effortlessly with fewer gear changes than the old model. Acceleration is superb. It's not a punch in the kidneys job as you would expect from a turbo, but a really good smooth take-off, with the back end crouching down low.

For getting past traffic in the town, the GTi is ideal. It nips from traffic light to traffic light with no effort at all. Despite its short wheel base, sporty hard suspension (which we thought better and less harsh than the Escort XR3i) and wide tyres, the GTi rides very well indeed. Being light it does have problems mastering short bumps and sudden grooves in the road surface all of which are often transmitted into the car itself . . . wide tyres do have some drawbacks.

In terms of sheer grip around the corner the GTi can perhaps just outgun the XR3, but there is precious little in it. It is the build quality that most impresses. In fact from the start of our seven day trial the car gave the ever lasting impression of stability and safety, far more than the XR3, whose doors do not shut with such a reassuring 'clunk'. The bodywork of the Golf seems to carry an air of long-lasting quality.

The brakes were excellent and bring the car to a short, sharp stop at speed, but on the car we borrowed (reputedly tested by Stirling Moss before us) the brakes tended to bind and grate at slow speeds or when approaching a junction . . . were we to run one for a longer period then we would quickly visit Richard Lloyd of GTi Engineering to try a different brake pad material, and perhaps a set of different shockabsorbers, also.

The top speed of the GTi is 112mph, a few miles an hour short of what we actually achieved on the motorway, with no fuss at all.

The car's quietness and stability at speed always impresses.

At £6,800 the cult has clearly something to do with quality as well as economy and vitality — in this day and age, refreshing values.

Tim Watson

The VW Golf GTI 1800

THE MAJORITY of people rate the Volkswagen Golf GTi, dating from 1976, as one of the best, if not *the* top small car. Some 10,000 RHD Golf GTi's have been sold in Britain since 1979, and over 330,000 have been produced. Now we have the Golf GTI 1800, which is indeed gilding refined gold. In the former bodyshell, the three-door hatchback, an engine of greater power has been installed, an increase of two b.h.p. but accomplished at 300 fewer r.p.m., and an improvement in maximum torque of 6 lb./ft., but at 1,500 lower r.p.m., over that of the 1600 Golf GTi's engine. It is this better spread of power and torque that has truly put the latest 1.8-litre Golf GTI in a class of its own.

The power and torque increases have been achieved by using a 1½ mm. bigger cylinder bore, 6.4 mm. on the piston stroke, increasing the swept volume by 193 c.c. and incorporating bigger valves, lighter pistons, a new crankshaft with a torsional vibration damper, and other internal changes, and a higher (3.65 to 1, against 3.89 to 1) final drive. The result is a captivating little car, of very significant performance. It retains the former five-speed gearbox and otherwise is much the same as the Golf 1600 (or 1500, as VAG call it) — until you drive it!

At first, emerging into the dusk and the London snarl-ups, I felt the little VW to be a thought rorty — fierce clutch, fast sporty tick-over, sports-type bucket driving-seat. This impression soon evaporated, as I discovered how very smooth the transverse 81 x 86.4 mm. (1,781 c.c.) four-cylinder overhead-camshaft fuel-injection engine is, in spite of its 10 to 1 compression-ratio, 112 (DIN) b.h.p. output at 5,800 r.p.m., and its delivery of 109 lb./ft. torque at only 3,500 r.p.m. It really is a remarkably smooth power-unit and quiet with it, at fast cruising speeds, and can be revved safely to 6,300 r.p.m. What is more, the improved torque characteristic enables it to pull away in fifth gear from below the legal town speed-limit (1,500 r.p.m.), so that one normally uses only that, normal top and third gear most of the time, engaging the two remaining lower gears in the box only for motoring in earnest, after starting off. The clutch has a rather long travel, which I noticed even though I tend to drive at far less than the full arms-stretch position, but with care it engages smoothly and any "kangaroo take-off" is obviated. The gearbox was a trifle notchy unless the clutch was fully depressed but was otherwise a delight to use, as its ratios (3.48, 2.12, 1.44, 1.13 and 0.912 to 1) are so well related.

As for performance, so smoothly and eagerly delivered, what can I say? It was not possible to check for absolute top pace, but you can put it at some 115 m.p.h. On accleration, here was a very compact 1.8-litre car that would out-pace many far bigger ones, doing 0-60 m.p.h. in about eight seconds for example, topping the performance aspirations of such as the Renault 5 Gordini Turbo, the Alfasud TiX, the Colt 1400 Turbo, the Fiat Strada 105TC, the Volvo 360GTL, the BMW 316 and what have you, apart from being faster than these and just about as economical. Marvellous!

From a personal point of view, this made a day's journey of over 330 miles from Wales to the English Midlands and back to look at some pre-war motor-racing photographs an easy accomplishment, and it was noticeable that with four adults in the VW the excellent handling was not one whit impaired — mark you, those in the back hadn't much footroom. The return run embraced traffic running through fairly congested towns, a good deal of Motorway driving, two brief stops, one to refuel, and then fast stuff along deserted Welsh A-roads. That the VW Golf GTI was able to average in the region of 48 m.p.h. overall, at a fuel consumption of 33.7 m.p.g. is a measure of the abilities of this excellent little hatchback. The cornering is predictable, with very little lean, and in this context it is significant that Volkswagen contrive a good ride from their rear suspension, when Ford and to a lesser extent Vauxhall have (until the former's Sierra) never been good at this. Only when accelerating hard did the Fulda 175/70HR13 Rasant Steel 411 radial ply tyres of the test car lose front-drive grip, while the understeer is very mild and does not embarrass the somewhat low-geared (3.3 turns, lock-to-lock) manual, rack-and-pinion steering, which is light with excellent castor-return.

The driver is held securely by the rally-type seat, and all the former good and less-good Golf aspects are unchanged, including the ugly steering-wheel with its four horn-pushes. The fascia contains the Motormeter speedometer and tachometer, the latter with fuel and heat gauges. The 1800 cruises at 3,526 r.p.m. at 70 m.p.h. in fifth gear. After switching-on the ignition little lights flash for a time and then go out, to indicate services in order, and there is a neat computer panel which will apparently tell you what your journey time, journey distance, average speed, m.p.g., oil and outside temperatures are, by pressing a button on the end of the r.h. control stalk. It also incorporates a memory-bank, for recording up to 6,200 miles, etc., I never got this right, perhaps because of inadvertently depressing the button when using the screen-wipers, and as another tester found the computer's fuel-consumption readings optimistic, I preferred to ignore it, but its easily-read, non-dazzle digital clock was appreciated. Less so was a tiny light that came on if it thought you were being unsparing of petrol — I did tend to drive to its ministrations, with a little coasting as well, but it can curb the delights of extending to the full this very lively 1800 Golf, which can improve on the acceleration of the 1600 GTi model by as much as 1.8 sec. from 50 to 70 m.p.h. and by 2.7 sec. from 60 to 80 m.p.h., in fifth-speed, for instance. In normal fast driving, however, the "econ" warning is not particularly inhibiting, but the needle that swept back and forth across the dial calibrated from 25 to 55 m.p.g. when you were in fifth gear, I also ignored. As an aside, I note that the golf-ball gear-lever knob, rather rough to handle, is retained, a nice touch of Teutonic humour. Nor did I like the screen-washers which did not clean the base-area in the driver's line of vision. On the other hand, what could be more convenient than a wash-wipe response to a flick of the r.h. stalk (turn-indicators and flick dipper from the l.h. stalk) and rear window wash-wipe by pressing on the same stalk? This underlines the fact that this latest Golf GTI is a very convenient fast car to drive. It has the expected Golf amenities of easily-read instruments, a well-sealed body asking for a window to be opened for easy-closing of its doors, nicely contrived door handles, effective door "keeps", plenty of stowages including a lockable

lid to the cubbyhole, useful rigid door pockets, a notably steady-reading fuel gauge accurate even down to the gallon or so of petrol left at the red warning mark, a lockable fuel filler-cap, and Hella headlamps good on main beam, less good when dipped. There was too much wind-roar in the region of the near-side door, however. The ride, as I have said, is very good indeed for a small car, comfortable in spite of obviously stiffish suspension, which did not quell a modicum of float once or twice over undulations, although this is of no consequence at all. Indeed, this is a beautifully balanced little car in which to put up good average speeds. For its type the heater (with three-speed fan) works well, and the services beneath the prop-up rear-hinged bonnet are all accessible, as is the VW 12-volt, 54-amp. / hr. battery.

Overall consumption of 4-star was 33.5 m.p.g., a very commendable figure considering the performance available, the nine gallon tank giving a practical range of some 300 miles. The vacuum-servo disc/drum brakes have a rather long pedal travel, but are otherwise perfectly satisfactory. It is this splendid, effortless performance that makes this THE outstanding small-car, for it goes like a little racer yet has little of the punchy, detuned rally-car aspects that might have gone with it. The Bosch fuel-injection ensured a prompt hot or cold start, and there is almost nothing to fault. At a whisker under £6,500 and that without some of the equipment most users will want as extras, the big-engined Golf GTI costs more than some cars in this class, but you get excellent value if you enjoy driving, and alloy-wheels, rear seat-belts, front air dam and two external mirrors, both adjustable from within, are provided. Servicing intervals are now at 10,000 miles. VW have, with this newest Golf, showed, once again, how best to play the small-car game. — W.B.

Thundercolt and Rabbitfoot

"Thunderbolt and Lightfoot" was a film about a close relationship between two fellows. One was older, cynical, impassive, hardened in his ways, a definite loner. The other was young, brash, exuberant, a little rough around the edges, but ingratiating. The film ending was tragic, but the two inharmonious characters were strongly portrayed and they were remembered long after the screen was dark.

The GTI Rabbit and Colt Turbo are just such characters. After spending a couple of weeks with them, changing back and forth from car to car, damning their shortcomings and marveling at their strengths—we do not have a favorite. We love them both—the Rabbit for its seasoned impassive strengths and understated potential, the Colt for its buoyant personality and the way it begs to be driven with wild abandon.

When it's time to go out to dinner or to take a nice quiet Sunday morning drive to Santa Barbara, the Rabbit is the hands-down choice. It is very refined and the only cue to its performance potential is a raspy exhaust note. The GTI goes about its job with a calm, detached efficiency, a result of the gradual development and refinement

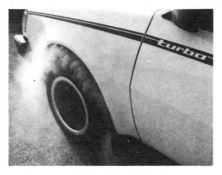

by Ron Grable

PHOTOGRAPHY BY RANDY LEFFINGWELL

Volkswagen has expended on this performance version of the ubiquitous Rabbit.

The powertrain is a sheer joy. If the mood strikes, superbunny can be driven in the "little ol' lady from Pasadena" mode. When the red mist clouds your vision, it will turn into a street racer par excellence. Maximum torque of 100 lb-ft occurs at a low 3000 rpm and max power (90 hp) at 5500 rpm, resulting in an incredibly flexible engine. It is possible to pull away from a stop in 3rd gear without any drama—just nice smooth acceleration. At the other end

of the scale, the engine breathes so well and feels so happy that unless you pay attention, it's very easy to exceed the redline (6000 rpm). The clutch engagement is linear and smooth, allowing coordinated shifts without jerking or clunking, and the short-throw gear lever has a low-effort precision that is quite enjoyable. The neutral gate is narrow, and it is possible to get 3rd gear instead of 1st occasionally (when you least expect it).

The highlights of the Rabbit's interior appointments are the standard equipment bucket seats and the 4-spoke steering wheel. The seats are among the best ever and enhance the sporty feel of the GTI. You can't drive seriously when your major concern is trying to stay behind the steering wheel. The GTI seat keeps you positioned where you can devote your energies to driving and interpreting the feedback reaching you through the steering wheel and seat.

From a chassis dynamics standpoint, the GTI displays very linear characteristics. This simply means tire slip angles and cornering force increase uniformly, and are recognized—by the driver—as a feeling of precision. The car goes where it's pointed— exactly. VW has accomplished this with

front and rear anti-roll bars (none on the base Rabbit), higher-rate springs, and stiffer shock valving. The engineers raided the Jetta's parts bin for wheels (6 x 14 in.) fitted with 185/60HR14 Pirelli P6 tires. The hardware strikes a nice compromise; it's compliant enough for everyday use but stiff enough to locate the car accurately in pitch, roll, and yaw—when the adrenaline flows.

Which brings us to the enigmatic Colt GTS Turbo. Enigmatic because it is no longer an econobox (with the turbo addition), and yet . . . what is it, exactly?

It is certainly an ego deflator—for the drivers of other sports cars. Find yourself any eager Porsche 944 and enjoy the 8.01-sec 0-60-mph acceleration of this little beastie. The same technique will work on Mazda RX-7s, Camaros, Mustangs, and many other expensive "high-performance" cars. It is a great cure for the blahs. So when you desperately need it, get in the Colt Turbo and go out and have some *fun*.

Fun is exactly what the Colt has to offer. It's not necessary to go around humbling everyone at stoplights to have fun with it. Its personality just makes you smile a lot, fling the car around, accelerate hard out of corners, and look for more corners and more Porsches, and so on.

The concept and execution of the base Colt are rooted in econothink, aimed at the market segment that places fuel economy, cost, and utility above all else. The Turbo version incorporates enhancements of creature comfort and style—necessary to attract the upscale buyer—but in many areas its Spartan origins remain all too obvious. Exterior add-ons include front air dam and rear spoiler, plus striping and Turbo decals. The Turbo variant retains the GTS high-performance suspension (unchanged), which includes gas-charged shocks, front and rear anti-roll bars, and high-rate front and rear springs that are non-linear (rising rate). In addition, the Turbo has 5 x 13-in. wheels with 165/70HR13 Michelin XVS

tires and ventilated front discs.

The interior appointments clearly indicate the frugal origins of the Colt. The seats are basic, offering little lateral support, and the dashboard does not conceal any of the heater/air conditioner ducting. No boost gauge is provided, but at full pressure you probably don't have time to look anyway.

The "Twin Stick-Super Shift" transmission is only just wonderful. The 2-speed (economy/power) selector can be shifted at any time in any gear, giving effectively an 8-speed transmission. Besides the obvious versatility of such a selection of ratios, it rivals Disney's Matterhorn ride for sheer fun. A maximum acceleration run using all eight gears requires both hands—and steering with an elbow—but is guaranteed to raise your spirits at least 10 clicks and elicit snide comments from any passengers.

So the judgement to this point: If you feel like a Samurai warrior, take the Colt. If your aggression level is not quite that

a street racer par excellence

Performance Comparison		
	GTI	COLT
0-30 mph (sec)	2.95	2.83
0-50 mph (sec)	6.76	5.83
0-60 mph (sec)	9.63	8.01
1/4 mile (sec/mph)	17.18/78.4	16.19/83.8
60-0 mph (ft)	146	145
30-0 mph (ft)	34	36
Skid pad (sec/g)	12.15/0.85	12.65/0.78
Slalom (sec)	6.94	6.80

high and you are looking forward to a nice ride with your girlfriend, it's the GTI.

In an attempt to be totally objective about these two, we spent a long day at the test track and accumulated the necessary instrumented data to separate them. From the accompanying data panel, it is obvious that the Colt Turbo is much faster than the GTI—in straight-line acceleration. Its superior power-to-weight ratio (18.3 lb/hp for the Colt, 22.3 for the GTI) gives the Turbo a 1.5-sec advantage to 60 mph, and a full second in the quarter mile, with a 5.4-mph speed advantage. Acceleration in the Colt is limited by wheelspin off the line; we tried many different starting techniques to optimize the "leave." The best starts came in 2nd-underdrive (twin-stick in "power"), because 1st underdrive or overdrive would simply send the front tires up in smoke. Controlling wheelspin by modulating the throttle doesn't work because it allows the boost to drop—which bogs the engine—and the run is kaput. We also compared acceleration with and without the "twin-stick," and the best runs in each case were within 0.05 sec. Due to the wheelspin problem, this small difference was not conclusive—so we used all eight speeds all the time simply because it made us giggle. The

Rabbit was steady, consistent, and easy to launch because of its great torque. Revs to 3000, out with the clutch, down with the accelerator, correct for the torque steer—and you're gone. No drama.

The skidpad advantage was clearly the GTI's, and demonstrated the significance of large tires and roll control. The roll angles of the Rabbit are within reason and keep the large-footprint Pirellis well planted. The Colt's Michelin XVS footprint is smaller, and the roll control is not as good—resulting in clearly inferior lateral acceleration. The Colt is rolled over, scratching away at the ground with the inside tire, and carrying almost the entire

☑ SPECIFICATIONS

Dodge Colt GTS Turbo

GENERAL
Vehicle type ....5-pass., 2-door hatchback sedan
Base price..................................$7406

ENGINE
Type and displacement........Transverse L-4, water cooled, 1600 cc (97.1 cu in.)
Bore and stroke ....77 x 86 mm (3.03 x 3.39 in.)
Induction system ....Turbocharger, ECI
Max. power (SAE net)............102 hp @ 5500 rpm
Max. torque (SAE net) ....122 lb-ft @ 3000 rpm
Recommended fuel ....91 RON unleaded

DRIVETRAIN
Transmission.............................4x2 sp. man.
Final drive 3.51:1

CHASSIS
Front suspension ....Independent, MacPherson struts, coil springs, anti-roll bar

Rear suspension ....Independent, full trailing arms, coil springs, anti-roll bar
Brakes, f/r ....9.4-in. discs/7.0-in. drums
Steering type ....Rack and pinion
Turns, lock to lock 3.9
Wheels ....13 x 5-in., steel
Tires 165/70HR13

DIMENSIONS
Curb weight ....847 kg (1865 lb)
Wheelbase ....2300 mm (90.6 in.)
Length ....3985 mm (157 in.)
Width ....1575 mm (62.1 in.)
Height ....1270 mm (49.5 in.)
Power to weight ratio............18.3 lb/hp
Fuel capacity...........................40 L (10.6 gal)

PERFORMANCE DATA
0-60 mph ....8.01 sec
Standing quarter mile ....16.19 sec/83.8 mph
Braking 60-0 ....145 ft
Skidpad ....0.78 g
Slalom ....6.80 sec
EPA rating, city/hwy..............30/39 mpg

Dodge Colt GTS

weight of the car on the outside front tire.

In our standard slalom, vehicle transient response is critical. The slalom consists of seven gates, 100 ft apart, and entry speed varies from 55 mph up (depending on vehicle capability). The Colt and GTI were very nearly equal in speed but definitely not in DQ (drama quotient). The small advantage enjoyed by the Colt results from its superior power-to-weight ratio, but flogging the Turbo through the gates at the limit is an experience in abject terror. The power comes on with the subtlety of Lyle Alzado, completely overpowering the tires, which are already in trouble trying desperately to deal with the changing side loads.

The result: allsteer, a term descriptive of a unique condition unrelated to understeer or oversteer. Seriously, the Colt is very difficult to drive fast due to its slow transient response (high roll angles, 70-series tires, and compliant suspension), and rather severe power characteristics.

The GTI is the model of front engine/front drive stability through the slalom gates, with predictable understeer under power and a suitable amount of off-throttle oversteer. The great torque characteristics of the engine allow a degree of precision that is rewarding, and allows the whole slalom procedure passes with ZDQ (zero drama quotient). Part of the credit for the ZDQ goes to the good roll control and 60 series P-6s, which make the ultimate bunny responsive and predictable.

After all the testing and comparing, we are still unable to clearly pick one over the other. The Rabbit is a satisfying, balanced performer that does almost everthing well. The Colt Turbo has some rough edges, but the way the seat pushes into your back makes up for a lot of shortcomings. So if someone comes up and says, "Here's $10,000—you can only have one of them," what would we do? Probably find two used ones for $5000 each. **[MT]**

☑ SPECIFICATIONS

Volkswagen Rabbit GTI

GENERAL
Vehicle type ....4-pass., 2-door hatchback sedan
Base price................................$8350

ENGINE
Type and displacement........Transverse L-4, liquid cooled, 1780 cc (109 cu in.)
Bore and stroke......................81 x 86.4 mm (3.19 x 3.40 in.)
Induction system ....Bosch CIS fuel injection
Max. power(SAE net) ....90 hp @ 5500 rpm
Max. torque (SAE net) ....100 lb-ft @ 3000 rpm
Recommended fuel ....87 RON unleaded

DRIVETRAIN
Transmission............................5-sp. man.
Final drive 3.58:1

CHASSIS
Front suspension....................Independent, MacPherson struts, coil springs, anti-roll bar

Rear suspension ....Interconnected trailing arms, coil springs, anti-roll bar
Brakes, f/r ....9.4-in. discs/7.1-in. drums
Steering type ....Rack and pinion
Turns, lock to lock 3.85
Wheels ....14 x 6-in. cast aluminum
Tires ....185/60HR14, steel-belted radial

DIMENSIONS
Curb weight..............................4434 kg (2011.0 lb)
Wheelbase................................2400 mm (94.5 in.)
Length ....3996 mm (157.3 in.)
Width..1630 mm (64.2 in.)
Height ....1410 mm (55.5 in.)
Power to weight ratio............22.3 lb/hp
Fuel capacity...........................40.1 L (10.0 gal)

PERFORMANCE
0-60 mph ....9.63 sec
Standing quarter mile ....17.18 sec/78.4 mph
Braking 60-0 ....146 ft
Skidpad ....0.85 g
Slalom ....6.94 sec
EPA rating, city/hwy..............26/36

Dodge Colt GTS

Volkswagen Rabbit GTI

CONTINUED FROM PAGE 29

S has that the Golf GTI doesn't is the blessing of the federal government—which leads us to explain how our test car got to L.A., and why it's been allowed to stay. It was purchased in Luxembourg, driven to Greece, and exported from Belgium to Los Angeles by John Rettie, a British citizen living and working in California as a nonresident alien. Under the law, he is entitled to bring an unfederalized car into the States and use it for a full year without penalty. At the end of the period, it must either be brought into compliance with the law or exported.

But for a U.S. citizen the laws are more stringent. A cash bond equal to the car's value must be posted; then, within a 30-day (extendable) period, the car must be federalized. If the desire to have such a slick car is strong enough to overcome the potential hassles, this is a short, but nonetheless workable, space of time—providing all the homework is done properly.

Our GTI test car has used up only a few weeks of its allotted stay here, so there's plenty of time to monitor the steps necessary to federalize it. Perhaps we'll be able to bring you some encouraging news regarding the cost of the process. In the meantime, the car will be properly equipped to cope with Southern California living. As purchased, it's a strippo, for two reasons: First, air conditioning, a near-necessity in California, isn't even offered on European models. It will either be foregone, or an aftermarket system will be installed. Second, a radio with European bands would have been useless here, so Rettie waited until the car was safely in the U.S. before thinking about a sound system for his sweet short. So, for now, he'll have to stay cool by going quickly with the windows down, and be satisfied with the music coming from the tailpipe. **[MT]**

A705 XNH

Volkswagen GOLF GTI

Fast, furious and fun, the original GTI was the definitive sporting hatch.
To make its appeal complete, all it needed was better packaging and,
in the UK at least, more reassuring brakes. On paper the new 'born again'
GTI answers the old criticisms, but on the road, how does it measure up . . .

SO SUCCESSFUL was the original Golf GTi, that it spawned imitators from virtually every major manufacturer. They came thick and fast but all fell more or less short of the mark, failing to match the original combination of cracking performance, poised handling and economy.

But the GTi's brakes were never very reassuring. They lost a good deal of feel in the conversion to righthand-drive and, for some owners, the lack of rear legroom and luggage space posed more serious practical limitations. Yet despite these minor shortcomings, the GTi was a beautifully balanced design, with strong character and identity — a real cult car.

Enough of the history. It is now 1984, the new Golf is here and, with it comes the return of the GTi. Answering the criticisms of cramped accommodation, the new version is nearly seven inches longer and over two inches wider than the car it replaces, with an extra three inches added to the wheelbase — the stretching and broadening gives it similar exterior dimensions to an Astra GTE. It is also more slippery through the air, as the Cd figure of 0.34 bears witness. The old model was around 0.4.

All of which is good news for the mainstream Golf models. On the face of it, however, the extra size and weight could seem less appealing to the performance-minded enthusiast who places more emphasis on agility and compactness. Furthermore, the new GTi's more rounded lines lack the visual punch of the original. The car looks less handy, less fun.

Underneath the skin, however, there is much that is familiar: the potent 1,781cc single overhead camshaft "four", fuelled by Bosch K-Jetronic mechanical injection; the close ratio five-speed gearbox — even the same golf-ball gear knob. It still has MacPherson struts at the front, trailing arms linked by a torsion beam at the rear, coil springs, and the anti-roll bar at both ends. Steering is by rack and pinion, braking by discs all round. Look harder and you will find subtle changes which could make the new GTi even hotter.

For a start, the engine — still with a 10.0:1 compression ratio and undersquare (81/86.4mm) bore and stroke dimensions — delivers its 112 bhp at 5,500 rpm instead of the previous 5,800 rpm; maximum torque is increased by five per cent, to 114 lb ft, and is produced at the lower engine speed of 3,100 rpm.

A larger clutch (8.3in dia) transmits this torque to the 5-speed gearbox, but there are changes here too: both final drive and fifth gear ratios have been altered, increasing the spacing between fifth and the intermediate gears. This gives intermediate gear maxima of 35, 56, 83 and 106 mph at the 6,700 rpm rev limit.

For all practical purposes the overall gearing is unchanged, fifth pulling a fairly tall 20.0 mph/1,000 rpm (previously, 19.7 mph/1,000 rpm). Tyres are 185/60 HR 14 Pirelli P6 fitted to 6J × 14 sports alloy wheels from the same maker: earlier GTis had 13 inch wheels. Now that the Golf GTi can put as much low-profile rubber on the road as rivals, it doesn't have to apologise for having "skinny" 70-series tyres.

The braking system has been improved to combat the long-standing criticisms. Disc brakes are now used at the back, complementing those (9.4 in and ventilated) at the front, and rhd cars now have the brake servo/master cylinder operated directly by the pedal, rather than by a lengthy crosslinkage.

A better GTi? Maybe. But can it really be worth £7,867? Most direct rivals undercut it by margins it's hard to ignore. For instance, the MG Maestro 1.6 — which has five doors — costs just £6,775; the Ford Escort XR3i (£6,777); the Nissan Cherry Turbo (£6,995) and the Vauxhall Astra GTE (£6,999). If performance and price are the only criteria, then add the Honda Civic CRX (£6,950), the Opel Manta GTE (£7,282), the Renault Fuego TX 2.0 (£7,350), and the twin-cam Toyota Corolla GT Coupé (£6,995) to the list.

Unusually, the engine of our test car required a few seconds churning before it fired up — progress thereafter, however, was as untemperamental as we have come to expect. The throttle action is smooth and meaty, response clean and immediate. But the once crisp, metallic-sounding exhaust note has been dulled. Now, it sounds just a little throbby.

In the light of VW's claimed 119 mph maximum speed, the 114.7 mph measured at MIRA is mildly disappointing. When you consider that the old car managed 112.4 mph it is clear that while the new model's paper aerodynamic advantage is real, it is not that significant. While the new GTi doesn't move to the top of the maximum speed league, only the Opel Manta holds a notable advantage in our comparison table. As before, the GTi is geared for sprinting, and in spite of the larger body (which has gained nearly 2 cwt in weight) it still delivers the goods.

As smooth and willing as ever, the engine spins round to the tachometer's 6,750 rpm red line with deceptive ease. The best acceleration times, however, are achieved using no more than 6,000 rpm, and even this is 500 revs beyond peak power. Accelerating from rest, the new GTi matches strides with its predecessor up to 40 mph, but lags to 60 (8.3 against 8.1 sec) and 70 mph (11.0 against 10.6 sec). Beyond this, however, the new car's more slippery shape begins to pay dividends so that, by the time 100 mph is reached, it is two seconds quicker than the old GTi. The boxed table shows how the new GTi compares with its predecessor and two of its closest rivals.

In cold figures, the margin between these fast chargers is small: all-out there really isn't much in it. The exception is the Nissan Cherry Turbo, which pips the GTi to 60 mph by three-tenths of a second. What matters more is that the new GTi feels just as quick as the old one, and where the Golf has always scored is in its throttle response and flexibility. Despite the eagerness with which it revs to the red line, it is equally content to slog away at the other end of the scale. Indeed, it will pull cleanly and uncomplainingly from below its 600 rpm idle speed.

The GTi's fourth and fifth gear acceleration is vastly better than that of its rivals as the 30 to 50 mph fourth gear time of 5.7 sec and 50 to 70 mph fifth gear time of 8.2 sec illustrate. Corresponding figures for the Escort XR3i are 7.3 sec and 11.3 sec; the Astra GTE, returns 9.2 sec and 14.5 sec. Even with its turbocharger, the Nissan Cherry can do no better, with 10.3 sec and 12.8 sec respectively. This clean, punchy lowdown power delivery is why the GTi's performance feels so usable.

Considering the performance available and that it was consistently exploited during the test, our overall fuel consumption of 30.6 mpg is a very respectable result, and one which compares favourably with the previous GTi's 28.8 mpg. Most owners should be able to approach or better our estimated 36 mpg touring figure. The message seems to be that the aerodynamic improvements brought about by VW's designers more than outweigh weight penalty. The quick-to-brim plastic fuel tank holds a useful 12.1 gallons, allowing a practical range of 436 miles.

Slick and positive on upward changes, the GTi's gearchange is not without fault, at times stubbornly baulking on the downchange into second. This is not the first time the new Golf's shift quality has failed to impress and our own long-term MG Maestro, which uses the same gearbox, suffers from a similarly indifferent action. The close-ratio gears and low overall gearing are fine for exploiting all the car's performance on the track, or for whistling along open country lanes, but they are a compromise — trading off a degree of cruising refinement and economy for sheer get-up-and-go.

The new GTi has a wider front track, more suspension travel and more compliant suspension mountings than the car it replaces. Compared with the rest of the new range, it also has a lower ride height. The low intermediate gearing and high engine torque call for excellent traction, to avoid excessive wheelspin. The GTi's chassis obliges, but it is always made obvious to the driver that the front wheels are transmitting a lot of power.

The steering — which is heavier and more prone to torque-steer effects than before — nevertheless remains direct and precise with

mph	New GTi sec	Old GTi sec	Astra GTE sec	Escort XR3i sec
0-30	3.0	3.0	2.8	2.7
0-40	4.3	4.3	4.3	4.3
0-50	6.0	5.9	6.2	6.1
0-60	8.3	8.1	8.5	8.6
0-70	11.0	10.6	11.5	11.3
0-80	14.4	15.0	14.9	15.5
0-90	18.5	19.6	21.3	20.5
0-100	26.6	28.8	30.3	28.3
Standing ¼ mile	16.5	16.2	16.5	16.1
Standing kilometre	30.5	30.3	31.2	30.3

reasonable feel, and despite the crisper turn-in and higher levels of grip offered by the low-profile tyres, the fine cornering balance and poise of earlier GTis is retained. At modest speeds, the new car corners in a pleasingly neutral fashion, with just a trace of stabilising understeer. Even when pushed to its high limits, it tends to slide all-of-a-piece. Lift off the power and it gently edges into progressive speed-sapping oversteer: it's all very forgiving and safe. First-generation GTi's would behave in much the same way, but rather more abruptly, demanding swifter and more accurate correction.

Such handling finesse has not been achieved at the expense of ride comfort either. The suspension feels a mite firmer than before, but its damping control is even better and it copes with humps and dips that would have unsettled the old GTi. Road roar is much better suppressed too, and gone is the audible thumping over broken surfaces.

The all-disc brake set-up ensures that the GTi stops as well as it goes. A trace of sponginess remains, but this is now more of an observation than a criticism. Stopping is powerful, progressive and fade-free, while the raised pedal allows an easy heel and toe action.

In the front, you sit perched up on the firmly padded but supportive "rally style" seats. There is plenty of headroom, but legroom is only just adequate for taller drivers: all the extra room is in the back.

Rear seat passengers now have as much room as in any rival, with particularly generous headroom, seat width and foot space beneath the front seats. Not only is it roomy, but the thoughtfully contoured seat, pleasingly reclined backrest, rear footwell heater ducts and seatbelts fitted as standard are further assets to passenger comfort and safety. Having taken all this trouble, it is a pity that it remains awkward for rear passengers to climb in and out. The front seat bases remain fixed when the backrests are tilted forwards, and the lower seat belt mounts threaten to trip you up too.

Boot space is much improved, but there is still a high sill to negotiate. The boot floor is uneven thanks to the intrusion of a "proper" UK-only spare wheel in a floor-well which was designed to accommodate a space-saver wheel.

Almost everything inside the car is black, relieved on our test car only by red striping on the seats and door panels. Combined with an all-black bonded headlining (whose contours prohibit the fitting of a non-VW sunroof) the result is a rather gloomy, sombre interior which seems less spacious than it really is. It gets very hot in bright sunshine too, underlining the inherent drawback of its fixed rear windows.

The control layout will be familiar to previous GTi owners. The four-spoke steering wheel and twin column stalks controlling the indicators and wash-wipe functions are carried over from the old model, while the remaining switchgear is positioned high on the facia, just out of fingertip reach.

But there are irritations: compromising the commanding driving position, all-round vision is restricted by thick pillars (especially at the rear), by mirrors that are mounted too far back and, in wet weather, by a lefthand-drive windscreen wiper pattern. Furthermore, the rear wiper has only a single sweep, flick action.

At first glance, the instrumentation seems very sparse — especially compared with the Astra GTE's six-dial instrument pack. Consider though, that the trip computer — one of the better examples of its type — also displays engine oil temperature and outside air temperature besides the usual time/distance/fuel functions and there is less to criticise, save for an optimistic speedometer (6 mph fast at 70 mph) and the trip computer's fuel readings which erred by a disgraceful 15 per cent.

For the remainder, the new GTi shares most of Golf 2's virtues and vices. It has an efficient, easily regulated air-blending heating system — but no separate fresh air ventilation. Cloth-covered moulded door trims match the seat covering and provide relief from the "plasticky" interior.

As before, the GTi is well built, but not elaborately furnished. The paint finish, exterior body panel, carpet and trim fits are all of a high order, but what is more noticeable is the *lack* of equipment that many rivals possess. True, it has a radio and the much needed driving lamps are standard, but where are the sunroof, electric windows, central locking and headlamp washers?

There is little doubt that the new GTi's virtues extend its appeal — as a family express it is certainly an improved car. Equally, as a driver's car it still feels the same — it has lost none of its magic. But in seeking a wider audience, VW have taken no more than a sideways step. For the existing GTi owner who drives solo, better brakes and improved efficiency alone are, perhaps, not quite enough to justify the upgrade.

MOTOR ROAD TEST

VW GOLF GTi

PERFORMANCE

WEATHER CONDITIONS

Wind	5-6 mph
Temperature	45 deg F/7 deg C
Barometer	29.8 in Hg 1009 mbar
Surface	Dry tarmacadam

MAXIMUM SPEEDS

	mph	kph
Banked Circuit	115.4	185.7
Best ¼ mile	118.6	190.9
Terminal speeds:		
at ¼ mile	85	137
at kilometre	103	166
Speeds in gears (at 6,700 rpm):		
1st	35	56
2nd	56	90
3rd	83	134
4th	106	171

ACCELERATION FROM REST

mph	sec	kph	sec
0-30	3.0	0-40	2.5
0-40	4.3	0-60	4.0
0-50	6.1	0-80	6.1
0-60	8.3	0-100	8.9
0-70	11.0	0-120	12.5
0-80	14.4	0-140	17.5
0-90	18.5	0-160	26.1
0-100	26.6		
Stand'g ¼	16.5	Stand'g km	30.5

ACCELERATION IN TOP

mph	sec	kph	sec
20-40	8.8	40-60	5.4
30-50	8.3	60-80	5.1
40-60	8.0	80-100	5.0
50-70	8.2	100-120	5.7
60-80	9.1	120-140	7.0
70-90	11.1	140-160	9.2
80-100	13.8		

ACCELERATION IN 4TH

mph	sec	kph	sec
20-40	6.1	40-60	3.8
30-50	5.7	60-80	3.5
40-60	5.7	80-100	3.7
50-70	6.1	100-120	4.0
60-80	6.8	120-140	5.1
70-90	8.0	140-160	8.4
80-100	11.7		

FUEL CONSUMPTION

Overall	30.6 mpg 9.2 litres/100km
Govt test	27.4 mpg (urban) 48.7 mpg (56 mph) 37.2 mpg (75 mph)
Fuel grade	98 octane 4 star rating
Tank capacity	12.1 galls 55 litres
Max range*	436 miles 701 km
Test distance	1,074 miles 1,728 km

*Based on an estimated 36 mpg touring consumption

NOISE

	dBA	Motor rating*
30 mph	68	14
50 mph	72	18
70 mph	78	28
Maximum†	82	36

*A rating where 1 = 30 dBA and 100 = 96 dBA, and where double the number means double the loudness
†Peak noise level under full-throttle acceleration in 2nd

SPEEDOMETER (mph)

Speedo	30	40	50	60	70	80	90	100
True mph	28	37	46	55	64	73	82	91

Distance recorder: 2.0 per cent fast

WEIGHT

	cwt	kg
Unladen weight*	18.4	936
Weight as tested	21.6	1,098

*with fuel for approx 50 miles

Performance tests carried out by Motor's staff at the Motor Industry Research Association proving ground, Lindley.

Test Data: World Copyright reserved. No reproduction in whole or part without written permission.

GENERAL SPECIFICATION

ENGINE

Cylinders	4-in-line
Capacity	1,781cc (108.6 cu in)
Bore/stroke	81/86.4mm (3.19/3.40in)
Cooling	Water
Block	Cast iron
Head	Alloy
Valves	Sohc
Cam drive	Toothed belt
Compression	10.0:1
Fuel system	Bosch K-Jetronic fuel injection
Ignition	Electronic
Bearings	5 main
Max power	112 bhp (DIN) at 5,500 rpm
Max torque	114 lb ft (DIN) at 3,100 rpm

TRANSMISSION

Type	5-speed manual
Clutch dia	8.3in
Actuation	Cable
Internal ratios and mph/1,000 rpm	
Top	0.89:1/20.0
4th	1.13:1/15.8
3rd	1.44:1/12.4
2nd	2.12:1/8.4
1st	3.45:1/5.2
Rev	3.17:1
Final drive	3.67:1

BODY/CHASSIS

Construction	Unitary, all steel
Protection	Galvanised steel in selected areas; sheet metal joints sealed; cataphoretic electro-priming; cavities hot wax flooded.

SUSPENSION

Front	Independent by MacPherson struts; coil springs; anti-roll bar.
Rear	Trailing arms linked by transverse torsion beam; coil springs; anti-roll bar.

STEERING

Type	Rack and pinion
Assistance	No

BRAKES

Front	9.4in ventilated discs
Rear	8.9in discs
Park	On rear
Servo	Yes
Circuit	Split diagonally
Rear valve	Yes
Adjustment	Automatic

WHEELS/TYRES

Type	Alloy, 6J × 14
Tyres	185/60 HR 14
Pressures	29/26 psi F/R (normal) 29/35 psi F/R (full load/high speed)

ELECTRICAL

Battery	12V, 45 Ah
Earth	Negative
Generator	Alternator 55 Amp
Fuses	22
Headlights	
type	Halogen
dip	110 W total
main	230 W total

Make: Volkswagen. **Model:** Golf GTi
Maker: Volkswagen AG 3180 Wolfsburg, West Germany.
UK Concessionaires: VAG (UK) Ltd, Yeomans Drive, Blakelands, Milton Keynes, Bucks. MK14 5AN. Tel (0908) 679121.
Price: £6,315.00 plus £526.25 Car Tax plus £1,026.19 VAT equals £7,867.44.

TheRivals
Other rivals include the Audi 80 1.8 Sport (£8,074), Alfa Romeo Alfasud Ti Green Cloverleaf (£6,395), BMW 318i (£8,250), Lancia Delta 1600GT (£6,250), Renault 18 Turbo (£7,995).

VOLKSWAGEN GOLF GTi   £7,867

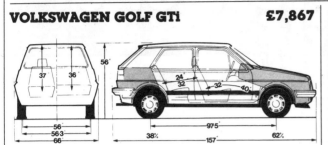

Power, bhp/rpm	112/5,500
Torque, lb/rpm	114/3,100
Tyres	185/60 HR 14
Weight, cwt	18.4
Max speed, mph	115.4
0-60 mph, sec	8.3
30-50 mph in 4th, sec	5.7
Overall mpg	30.6
Touring mpg	36.0
Fuel grade, stars	4
Boot capacity, cu ft	10.8
Test Date	May 5, 1984

Still the best of the current crop of hot hatchbacks, the new GTi no longer dominates the opposition in the performance stakes. Refined, economical and roomy, it retains its predecessor's fine ride and handling balance but suffers from heavy steering which is more influenced by front-wheel-drive torque effects. Brakes good as ever, but visibility could be better and the lack of independent ventilation is a serious shortcoming. Considerably more expensive than its direct rivals.

FORD ESCORT XR3i   £6,777

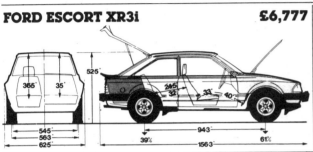

Power, bhp/rpm	105/6,000
Torque, lb ft/rpm	101/4,800
Tyres	185/60 HR 14
Weight, cwt	17.9
Max speed, mph	116.0
0-60 mph, sec	8.6
30-50 mph in 4th, sec	7.3
Overall mpg	30.7
Touring mpg	—
Fuel grade, stars	4
Boot capacity, cu ft	10.3
Test Date	January 15, 1983

Fuel injection, revised gearing and suspension modifications have made the latest version of Ford's sporting hatchback highly competitive. Performance is excellent (with the best top speed in its class) and is combined with more consistent handling and a less bone-jarring ride. Class-topping economy, efficient packaging, good heating and ventilation system and fine finish are further plusses, though mechanical refinement remains rather poor.

MG MAESTRO 1.6   £6,775

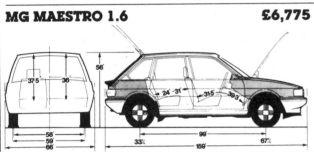

Power, bhp/rpm	103/6,000
Torque, lb ft/rpm	100/4,000
Tyres	175/65 SR 14
Weight, cwt	18.8
Max speed, mph	110.2
0-60 mph, sec	9.7
30-50 mph in 4th, sec	7.8
Overall mpg	28.5
Touring mpg	34.0
Fuel grade, stars	4
Boot capacity, cu ft	11.2
Test Date	July 16, 1983

Sporting version of the Maestro doesn't perform in the same league as the quickest of its rivals, but is no slouch and has competitive economy. Responsive handling is combined with respectable ride and refinement, good brakes. Excellent accommodation, comfortable driving position, good visibility, but gearchange and ventilation could be improved, as could some aspects of finish. Well equipped, but solid state instrumentation is unattractive and of limited functional value.

NISSAN CHERRY TURBO   £6,995

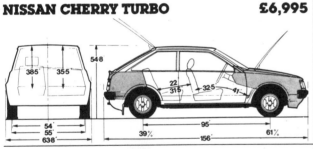

Power, bhp/rpm	114/5,600
Torque, lb ft/rpm	120.6/3,200
Tyres	175/70 HR 13
Weight, cwt	15.9
Max speed, mph	114.2
0-60 mph, sec	8.0
30-50 mph in 4th, sec	10.3
Overall mpg	28.9
Touring mpg	—
Fuel grade, stars	4
Boot capacity, cu ft	7.7
Test Date	December 10, 1983

A 1.5-litre engine with fuel injection and a turbocharger transform the normally mild-mannered Cherry into a stormer. Competitive top speed and scorching acceleration, though tall gearing means the engine has to be kept on the boil. Competitive economy but handling is no more than competent and rear legroom is poor. Slick gearchange and light controls are typically Japanese, as is comprehensive standard equipment at a competitive price. Well finished.

VAUXHALL ASTRA GTE   £6,999

Power, bhp/rpm	115/5,800
Torque, lb ft/rpm	111/4,800
Tyres	185/60 HR 14
Weight, cwt	18.8
Max speed, mph	115.8
0-60 mph, sec	8.5
30-50 mph in 4th, sec	9.2
Overall mpg	28.5
Touring mpg	—
Fuel grade, stars	4
Boot capacity, cu ft	10.3
Test Date	April 30, 1983

At last available with the power it has always deserved, the Astra, with its 1.8-litre fuel-injected engine, is smooth and potent with excellent outright performance, though tall gearing blunts its mid-range bite. Excellent handling and grip, powerful brakes, comfortable seats and a snappy gearchange complete the picture for keen drivers. Other plus points include heating and ventilation, instruments and equipment. The low speed ride is unresilient, however, and rear seat legroom poor.

VOLVO 360 GLT   £6,906

Power, bhp/rpm	115/6,000
Torque, lb ft/rpm	118/3,600
Tyres	185/60 HR 14
Weight, cwt	22.6
Max speed, mph	108.0
0-60 mph, sec	10.3
30-50 mph in 4th, sec	9.6
Overall mpg	24.2
Touring mpg	—
Fuel grade, stars	4
Boot capacity, cu ft	9.4
Test Date	November 6, 1982

Volvo's 360 GLT is perhaps a rather unlikely contender in the sporting hatchback class. The injected 2-litre overhead cam engine offers slight advantages over some rivals higher up the speed range, but performance is limited by the car's bulk. Slick gearchange and superb handling bump up the pleasure quotient, while the commanding driving position is let down slightly by only average interior packaging. All-round competence and good quality add to the car's abilities.

Over undulating rural twists, GT100 is an attractive animal

Road Runner

Professional Golf

How do you make a great car even better? GTi Engineering think they have the answer with their aftermarket add-ons for the MK 2 Golf GTi, but have they really got it right? ▶

Road Runner

Modern car design is without precedent in being intra-complementary so that changing one characteristic must tend to effect something else, and because of the car's package interdependence it's most likely that the affected 'something else' will be changed for the worse.

Now take the example of the Golf GTi. The first version wrote the hot hatchback rules. However, with the Mk2 there were initial complaints that the new car had lost some of the immediacy and throttle response so endearingly inherent in its predecessor. But further familiarisation brought nearly 100 percent approval for the dynamic features of the much different and cleverly designed new car.

The facts are that A to B, the Mk2 Golf GTi is not only marginally quicker than the old one, it's also smoother, quieter, more stable, better braked, even easier to drive and therefore even more fun over a long or short distance. So, faced with such an obviously improved machine, what can the aftermarket offer as a rational and realistic kit of feature-change components?

If anyone should know, GTi Engineering are the men. Responsible for launching the enlarged 1800 engine GTi before the German manufacturers got around to it, GTi Engineering contains a wealth of knowledge about the car. Much of that knowledge is exhibited in the company's aptly registered demonstration vehicle which we've been driving recently.

About the only components not touched are the gearbox, clutch and rear brake pads. The seats are the same too. The total price obviously reflects these extensive modifications, and fitted to a new GTi the complete package, depending on audio equipment, will cost around £11,500; that means the fitted bits cost just over £3500.

For that you'll get an RLR Plus Pac engine which comprises a sports camshaft with a gas flowed cylinder head and reprofiled inlet and exhaust seats with nimonic valves sitting in uprated double valve springs to help them close. Gases go in via a cleaned-up inlet manifold and out through a tubular 4-2-1 exhaust manifold. With an altered distributor advance curve, these modifications endow the 1800cc four cylinder engine with 135bhp, and an evocative, lumpy tickover.

Dunlop D4 195-50 VR15 tyres on attractive Ronal 6 x 15 inch alloy wheels are at the ends of a Sachs suspension kit which comprises four uprated dampers, complete with complementary springs; and the front calipers contain Mintex M 171 pad material to help kill any traces of fade during heavy applications.

That low-riding running gear combination imparts an aggressive aspect to the standard car's blandness which is otherwise enhanced by Zender body panels. These comprise a front spoiler, sill panels, wheel arch flares, rear apron panel and front auxiliary lamps, together with a Votex rear window surround.

To most eyes the aesthetics work well, and better than many other such conversions. They are, of course, mainly aesthetic in function, and the proud purchaser can make up his own mind whether such looks are worth £727 plus VAT fitted.

But this car is GTi Engineering's shop window, so it contains most items that the company has available for the Mk2 Golf. There's an extra central instrument mounting and console which contains a VDO voltmeter, plus water temperature and oil pressure gauges. Still in the centre of the dash area there's a small cassette box, and one's feet and hands are catered for GTi Engineering's very own floor mats and a pricey but pleasant steering wheel respectively.

In the same way that GTi Engineering must

have had to think carefully about which bits to offer for the Mk2 car, it's difficult to assess GT100 in the improved hot hatch stakes because it's fair to say that few people will likely go for the fully laden treatment.

Impressed, but not attracted by the styling of the standard Mk2 Golf, we were impressed with the aesthetic results of GTi Engineering modifications, even though for some of us there is a slightly excessive trace of mascara to its extremities.

Performance is not especially startling since 130bhp isn't all that much more than the 112bhp of the standard car, particularly as GTi modifications feel to have robbed the engine of some of that wonderful low down torque in the standard car. But the car is far from slow, and its 0 to 60mph acceleration time of around 7.8 seconds is perhaps its least improved straight line performance characteristic. Higher up the speed-range the modifications are better felt, and over undulating rural twists, GT100 is an attractive animal.

Straightline stability is as good as the standard car, but its response to direction changes is in a different league. At very high speed the car can be pointed at will with confidence, and with the Plus Pac engine spinning in its favourite regime, and imaginative inputs pressed into the controls, GT100 rewards the driver with consistent and accurate responses.

But the new Golf has admirable inter-dependence designed into its standard package, so something has to give. The comparative loss of bottom end flexibility that has been traded for top end power is small enough to be almost unnoticed, but the increased precision afforded by tyres and suspension has affected that so-subjective parameter, ride quality. The Dunlop D4s follow road contours more readily, but that's expected, as is increased harshness by virtue of harder suspension settings. Although it smooths out at main road speeds, we weren't enamoured either with the jiggly town ride, or the almost constant bump stop contact over comparatively minor undulations. It doesn't seem to affect the car's comportment, more the driver's orientation, as car control requirements change slightly when the stops contact.

It's a minor matter however, and the overall improvements of the modifications for a sporting driver are worth considering, and you don't *have* to buy the body bits. The essential fact is that GT100 remains a superb fun car. ∎

GTi Engineering Mk2 VW Golf GTi

ENGINE
RLR 1800 Plus Pac	£750.00
Installation (3 days)	£112.00

SUSPENSION
Sachs suspension kit	£351.00
Fitting	£45.00

WHEELS AND TYRES
Ronal 6 x 15 inch alloys	£68.90 each
Dunlop D4 195-50 VR15 tyres	£90.00 each

BRAKES
Mintex M171 front pads	£51.00

BODYWORK (Zender Series Two)
Front spoiler	£78.50
Sill panels	£84.50
Wheel arch flares	£77.00
Rear apron panel	£68.00
Front foglamps	£44.00
Votex rear window surround	£75.00
Painting and fitting kit	£300.00

INTERIOR
GTi steering wheel and boss	£70.00
VDO oil pressure gauge and sender	£36.00
VDO water temperature gauge and sender	£20.45
VDO voltmeter	£13.95
Console mounting plate	£20.50
Instrument mounting plate	£3.50
GTi engineering floor mats (set of 4)	£40.00
Cassette box	£15.00

All prices exclude VAT.

GMP Rabbit GTI

*Between living and learning,
the learning is more important.*

PHOTOGRAPHY: DON HUNTER

• Every car line must eventually face the Grim Reaper. It's true that the Citroën 2CV, the VW Beetle, and the Porsche 911 all show distinct signs of immortality, but they too, like all good things, in time will come to an end. So it is for the VW Rabbit: after a full, rich life of ten model years, the lease is finally up on its stamping dies.

As our *auf Wiedersehen* to the Rabbit, we've chosen a GTI with some of the best frills and furbelows the aftermarket has to offer. The net result is an $8350 Volkswagen dolled up with nearly $6000 worth of goodies from the abundant shelves of GMP, Inc., in Charlotte, North Carolina (704–525–0941). The GMP GTI has 22 separate changes in all, ranging in cost from a $60 rear anti-sway bar to a $600 extra-tall fifth gear. A sensible customer would mix and match to taste with an eye toward his budget, but, since this was the factory's car, it came with a full complement of alterations. We were at least given a chance to state our preference before the car was assembled, so we chose a mild state of tune under the assumption that a GTI really doesn't need much help to be a thoroughly entertaining sports sedan. If wild is more to your liking, Joe Klitzsch, the plucky proprietor of this shop, is, of course, eager to satisfy your wishes.

The engine alterations for this particular machine include a hotter camshaft, a new Bosch throttle body with a larger venturi section, and a stainless-steel exhaust system (including a tubing header but no catalyst). The transaxle's taller fifth gear, at $600, is a costly alteration, but quite effective in trimming rpm out of highway-cruise operation. (Do-it-yourselfers should be advised that only part of the transaxle need be

removed from the car for this installation. The parts for the job cost $160.) The rolling stock is a nifty set of six-by-fifteen-inch ATS wheels (available in several styles) shod with B.F. Goodrich Comp T/A 195/50VR-15 tires. Under the car is an elaborate array of anti-sway bars, Sachs shock absorbers, revised springs, and structural-reinforcement brackets. The exterior decorations are by Zender, a German skirt-and-spoiler molder, and the interior is pure Recaro. To finish off the project, GMP has selected a Kenwood stereo sound system and a very grippy Indianapolis Corsa steering wheel.

Vehicle type: front-engine, front-wheel-drive, 5-passenger, 3-door sedan
Price as tested: $14,250 (base price: $8350)
Engine type: 4-in-line, iron block and aluminum head, Bosch K-Jetronic fuel injection

Displacement	109 cu in, 1781cc
Power (manufacturer's estimate)	100 bhp @ 5500 rpm
Transmission	5-speed
Wheelbase	94.5 in
Length	155.3 in
Zero to 60 mph	9.8 sec
Zero to 90 mph	27.6 sec
Standing ¼-mile	17.3 sec @ 77 mph
Top-gear passing time, 30–50 mph	11.5 sec
50–70 mph	12.6 sec
Top speed	103 mph
Braking, 70–0 mph	203 ft
C/D observed fuel economy	27 mpg

We met the GMP GTI in Daytona Beach, Florida, in the midst of its development program. The limited back-road testing we were able to conduct pinpointed a number of weak areas, so Mr. Klitzsch returned to his Rabbit hutch to take the program several steps further. We noted that acceleration times were no better than stock; in the uprated engine's defense, it was hauling around a significantly larger payload (heavier seats, wheels, tires, spoilers, etc.). The fat tires and wheels stuck well but didn't exhibit as strong a sense of the straight-ahead direction as standard Rabbits do. Likewise, the ride was unacceptably rocky, the rear tires rubbed the fenders, and one channel of the stereo sound system was on the fritz.

Of course, many things did work quite well right out of the box. The new fifth gear (in combination with the smaller-diameter tires) drops engine rpm by. 23 percent. This does wonders for highway fuel economy and interior noise level, but there is a penalty: a significant stretching of top-gear acceleration times. We loved the Indianapolis-brand steering wheel and appreciated the form-fitting Recaro seats. A more aggressive KRX model was used for the driver, while an easier-to-enter KR was fitted on the passenger's side; all in all, the combination is a good one.

Each of you in the reading audience will have to draw your own conclusions about the aesthetic virtues of GMP's exterior trim. We will, at least, enter a vote of confidence for the Cuisinart-style wheels. Just be sure you discuss their fit with GMP before proceeding, because some wheel-well trimming is a must for clearance (particularly when wide, square-shouldered tires are used).

Theoretically, this GMP GTI should have been the be-all and end-all Rabbit, but it obviously hadn't reached its full potential at the time of our tests. Klitzsch has regrouped a bit to try new combinations of springs and ride heights, and he now has the results from several fruitful experiments under his belt. It's the live-and-learn theory of automotive development in action. Volkswagen used it religiously to give the Rabbit such a long and productive life, and now it's up to Klitzsch-class tuners to accept the baton and proceed with the program. —*Don Sherman*

SMALL CARS, BIG PERFORMANCE

Dodge Omni GLH, Honda Civic S, Mitsubishi Mirage Turbo,
Renault Encore GS, Toyota Corolla GT-S, Volkswagen Golf GTI:
Extra punch in the convenient family-size package

PHOTO BY JEFFREY R. ZWART

COMPARISON R&T ROAD TEST

SUPPOSE YOU'RE LOOKING for lots of performance for not much money, a car you can afford to buy and maintain while still having the potential for enjoyment, sport and perhaps a fling at being faster than the fancy equipment one meets on the typical mountain road.

If so, you are in luck.

Once again.

There were times in the recent past when small car and big performance were contradictions in terms. There were fast, powerful, sporting cars on the market, thank heavens, but they cost lots of money. The world's car companies were concentrating on cranking out

uninteresting economy cars.

Dull cars don't sell, so as social pressure eased, the factories heeded the obvious and began turning out more interesting versions of their smaller and more efficient packages.

This test began with a survey. The basic idea was to round up cars that offered enthusiast potential, in both speed and handling; enough practicality to be the one car in the family, and a sticker price within reason.

Be warned here, though, that performance and price are relative. We were looking for cars that move quickly and well. Brisk, which isn't the same as

breathtaking. The cars that matched our profile don't threaten the world's fastest sedans. Corvettes won't turn right rather than face a stoplight confrontation. Porsche 935s won't dwindle in our group's mirrors.

The best of this test, however, will inflict feelings of inferiority on more than one car with a better pedigree and a higher price. At the worst, this group offers fun per dollar.

In alphabetical order, the qualifiers: Dodge Omni GLH:

In principle the GLH is a classic American product, the factory hot rod. Starting point is the Omni; with trans-

66

PHOTOS BY RICHARD M. BARON & STEVE KIMBALL

verse inline-4 and front-wheel drive, it's the standard economy sedan of today.

But the GLH gets a semi-race version of the 2.2-liter powerplant. The camshaft is reprofiled, the compression ratio is increased and the ignition advance curve is tailored to come in earlier and go farther. Claimed power goes from 95 to 110 bhp.

With the engine come 15 x 6-in. wheels wearing 195/50HR-15 Goodyear Eagles. The GLH has stiffer springs and shock absorbers, larger anti-roll bars front and rear, and quicker steering. Larger vented disc brakes are borrowed from the K-car. Inside there's an added

instrument cluster, and clutch and brake pedals have been positioned to facilitate heel-and-toe downshifts.

The GLH is black with black bumpers, dual fog lamps and the usual-in-class front air dam. All complete and nicely integrated, with the bonus of being offered as a 4-door sedan.

Honda Civic S:

Honda's entry is more mix than package. The Civic Hatchback S is a combination of the useful square-back 3-door sedan and the more sporting CRX coupe. The S model 3-door comes with a 1.5-liter four coupled to a 5-speed manual transmission, fwd of course.

Michelin 175/70R-13 tires, 3-spoke steering wheel and rear anti-roll bar are also shared with the CRX. This is a rational, typically Honda approach; that is, offer the performance package with the family-style body and keep the price down by sharing components. The Civic has the smallest engine in our group and it's also the lightest car, which is also the Honda norm.

Mitsubishi Mirage Turbo:

Might as well be new is the term here. The Mirage arrived in stages. It was first sold as the Dodge/Plymouth Colt or Champ, built by Mitsubishi as they say. It was a nice little fwd hatchback. Then came a handling package and a turbo-charger option, both good in themselves but they caused the body and basic structure to be out of date.

So here's the Mirage Turbo, sold directly by Mitsubishi (but available from Dodge and Plymouth as well). The 2nd-generation coupe is also a 3-door, but longer. Mirage engine is the 1.6-liter four, turbocharged to a claimed output of 102 bhp. The new body brings with it upgraded suspension, brakes and interior. Our car had the full option list, as in air conditioning, cloth upholstery, pile carpeting, stereo radio with cassette player, even a sunroof.

The full test (R&T, October 1984) found the structure, suspension and brakes had been improved to match the engine. An impressive piece of work, we concluded.

Renault Encore GS:

This is a complete, optional package. Renault/AMC builds the Alliance and Encore of the same components, with transverse fours in a choice of displacements, stick and automatic transmissions, etc. The Encore is the smaller of the two, and it comes with a rear hatch.

The GS version has a new (in America) sohc 1.7-liter engine with fuel injection and comes only with 5-speed manual transmission. Front struts and rear shocks are gas pressurized. The GS has larger (14-in.) wheels, tuned exhaust with dual outlets, fog lamps, a front air dam and rear spoiler; a sports package added to the family car, in sum.

Toyota Corolla GT-S:

Corolla is Toyota's best-known nameplate worldwide. Because of this popularity the Corolla badge is currently used on models less alike than their name implies, witness the fwd sedans and rwd coupes.

The Corolla coupes are the older models but the GT-S is the newest of the coupes and the most sporting of the line.

The sport comes from what amounts to a new engine, in actual fact a new cylinder head atop a stronger 1.6-liter block. The head has dual overhead cams, four valves per cylinder and is timed and tuned to perform best at the upper half of the rev range.

The GT-S is this group's exception, as in north/south engine alignment and rear-wheel drive. Like the Mirage Turbo, the GT-S gets major revisions to the baseline body, and suspension and brakes upgraded to match the power. The GT-S is spruced up by adding air dam in front, spoiler in back and giant letters on the sides. The interior has adjustable driver's seat, folding rear seats, remote mirror controls, all the extras you'd expect in the class. Fun and fast is what we said in the full test (R&T, September 1984).

Volkswagen Golf GTI:

Alphabetical order isn't fair. The GTI is last in this list but it's the newest of the group, in fact the 1985 Golf GTI arrived in the midst of the tests.

The theme is old. Volkswagen used to have the Rabbit, a useful, practical family car, and the GTI used to be a Rabbit with more kick, as in upgraded suspension and tuned engine. Volkswagen can be given credit for inventing the surprisingly sporting little sedan, for this generation at least.

Then came the 1985 Golf, the Rabbit's replacement. As detailed in R&T for January 1985, the Golf is bigger and better than the Rabbit. A larger, more powerful engine and a few inches added to the wheelbase, the track and especially the rear of the passenger compartment have improved the car beyond its new numbers. (The name has been changed; there is no more Rabbit, presumably because VW wants all to know how new and improved the car is.)

The new GTI gets the traditional GTI treatment. With reprofiled camshaft, recalibrated fuel injection and a markedly higher compression ratio—from 8.5 to

GENERAL DATA

	Dodge Omni GLH	Honda Civic S	Mitsubishi Mirage Turbo	Renault Encore GS	Toyota Corolla GT-S	Volkswagen Golf GTI
Base price	$7350	$6842	$7689	$7609	$9538	$8990
Price as tested¹	$8885	$7977	$9244	$9752	$11,483	$10,450
Layout	front engine/ fwd	front engine/ fwd	front engine/ fwd	front engine/ fwd	front engine/ rwd	front engine/ fwd
Engine type	sohc inline-4	sohc inline-4	turbo sohc inline-4	sohc inline-4	dohc 4-valve inline-4	sohc inline-4
Bore x stroke, mm	87.5 x 92.0	74.0 x 86.5	76.9 x 86.0	81.0 x 83.5	81.0 x 77.0	81.0 x 86.4
Displacement, cc	2213	1488	1597	1721	1587	1781
Compression ratio	9.6:1	9.2:1	7.6:1	9.5:1	9.4:1	10.0:1
Bhp @ rpm, SAE net	110 @ 5600	76 @ 6000	102 @ 5500	78 @ 5000	112 @ 6600	100 @ 5500
Torque @ rpm, lb-ft	129 @ 3600	84 @ 3500	122 @ 3000	est 95 @ 3000	97 @ 4800	105 @ 3000
Fuel delivery	one Holley (2V)	one Keihin (3V)	Mikuni Throttle Body	Bendix Throttle Body	Bosch L-Jetronic	Bosch KE-Jetronic
Transmission	5-sp manual	5-sp manual	5-sp manual	5-sp manual	5-sp manual	5-sp manual
Gear ratios, :1	3.29/2.08/1.45 1.04/0.72	2.92/1.76/1.18 0.85/0.71	4.23/2.37/1.47 1.11/0.86	3.73/2.05/1.32 0.97/0.79	3.59/2.02/1.38 1.00/0.86	3.45/2.12/ 1.44/1.13/0.89
Final drive ratio, :1	2.78	4.27	3.47	3.56	4.30	3.94
Steering type	rack & pinion, power assist	rack & pinion	rack & pinion	rack & pinion, power assist	rack & pinion, power assist	rack & pinion, power assist
Brake system, f/r	10.1-in. vented discs/8.9 x 1.7-in. drums	9.1-in. vented discs/7.1 x 1.2-in. drums	9.4-in. vented discs/7.0 x 1.4-in. drums	9.4-in. discs/ 8.0 x 1.4-in. drums	9.2-in. vented discs/9.2-in. discs	9.4-in. vented discs/9.4-in. discs
Wheels	cast alloy, 15 x 6	steel disc, 13 x 5J	steel disc, 14 x 5½JJ	cast alloy, 14 x 5½	cast alloy, 14 x 5½J	cast alloy, 14 x 6J
Tires	Goodyear Eagle GT, 195/50HR-15	Michelin MX L, 175/70R-13	Yokohama A008, 185/60R-14	Michelin MXV, 185/60R-14	Bridgestone Potenza, 185/60R-14	Goodyear Eagle GT, P185/60HR-14
Suspension, f/r	MacPherson struts, lower A-arms, coil springs, tube shocks, anti-roll bar/beam axle on trailing arms, coil springs, tube shocks, anti-roll bar	MacPherson struts, lower A-arms, torsion bars, tube shocks, anti-roll bar/beam axle on trailing arms, Panhard rod, coil springs, tube shocks	MacPherson struts, lower A-arms, coil springs, tube shocks, anti-roll bar/trailing arms, coil springs, tube shocks, anti-roll bar	MacPherson struts, lower A-arms, coil springs, tube shocks, anti-roll bar/trailing arms, torsion bars, tube shocks, anti-roll bar	MacPherson struts, lower lateral arms, compliance struts, coil springs, tube shocks, anti-roll bar/live axle on upper & lower trailing arms, Panhard rod, coil springs, tube shocks, anti-roll bar	MacPherson struts, lower A-arms, coil springs, tube shocks, anti-roll bar/beam axle on trailing arms with integral anti-roll bar, coil springs, tube shocks, anti-roll bar

¹Price as tested includes: For the Omni GLH, std equip. (sports sus with 50-series tires, alloy wheels, GLH trim), air cond ($643), AM/FM stereo/cassette ($264), protection grp ($144), rear-window heat ($132), rear-window wiper/washer ($120), misc options ($232); for the Civic S, AM/FM stereo/cassette ($515), air cond ($510), misc options ($110); for the Mirage Turbo, air cond ($630), elect. sunroof ($425), AM/FM stereo/cassette ($400), rear wiper/washer ($100); for the Encore GS, air cond ($673), AM/FM stereo/cassette ($440), keyless central locking ($227), power assisted steering ($221), cruise control ($179), rear-window heat ($137), diagnostic panel ($132), misc options ($134); for the Corolla GT-S, std equip. (16-valve dohc engine, 60-series tires, alloy wheels), air cond ($670), elect. sunroof ($445), AM/FM stereo/ cassette ($365), power assisted steering ($205), cruise control ($160), rear wiper/washer ($100); for the Rabbit GTI, air cond ($695), AM/FM stereo/cassette ($495), power assisted steering ($230), misc options ($40)

10.0:1—the shared 1.8-liter engine goes from 85 to 100 claimed bhp. Four of the gearbox's five internal ratios are juggled, putting them closer together and the final drive ratio is numerically higher, so the engine can more readily spend more time in the higher speeds, where its strength lies.

Shocks and springs are stiffer, but not too much because the GTI gets anti-roll bars front and rear. Wheels are alloy and larger (14 x 6 instead of 13 x 5½ in.) and tires are too, 185/60HR-14 Goodyear Eagle GT. Front brakes are vented disc while the Golf's rear drums are replaced with solid discs.

The GTI comes only as a 2-door hatchback, although it naturally benefits from the Golf body's improved dimensions, especially in the rear.

Track & Road

BECAUSE THESE cars were picked on the basis of implied performance, they were tested at their limits, courtesy of Willow Springs International Raceway in Rosamond, California. They are road, even family, cars as well, so the timed results aren't the basis for final scores. But the lap times do reveal some useful data.

The Mirage narrowly took best time of the day. Willow Springs is 2400 ft above sea level and track day was hot, as in 111 degrees Fahrenheit. In particular, altitude bothers turbocharged engines less than unstuffed engines, which could have affected the results.

Even so, the Mirage was impressive. This is a great engine in a good chassis. There's plenty of cornering power. Mitsubishi engineers have brought the suspension up to the level of the engine and the car has good balance, something the earlier Colt turbo lacked.

The Mirage doesn't feel like a front-drive car; well, at least it reveals no drawbacks. There's no torque steer in the upper gears, for instance. But the Mirage requires fwd techniques. On the limit it can be rushed into the corner and braked hard, until the back gets wiggly. Stomp on the gas and the power comes on, strong and smooth, and hauls the car around the corner. Intermediate gear ratios seem suited to the power curve; more likely the ratios are right because the curve is so uncurvy.

The Toyota was slightly slower, which doesn't mean slow. This is also a completely revised car and it also has a great engine in a good chassis.

But the gearing is wrong, and it hurts.

Other things being equal, rear drive is more fun and more controllable than front drive. Rear-drive cars can be steered with wheel or throttle, that is, at either end. Weight distribution is usually more equal and the car can be braked harder.

The GT-S was impressive in its full test and the expectation was the Toyota would win the track session.

But no. The GT-S was a fraction of a second slower than the Mirage because there were times and places when the engine's power couldn't be used. The GT-S is a benign understeerer, just right. It responds to steering input and goes where it's pointed. It can be braked into turns, pitched sideways under power, all the rewarding qualities a fast car needs.

It's just that the jump from 2nd to 3rd is too wide and the jump from 4th to 5th isn't wide enough. The dohc, 4-valve engine only works when it's wound up, while shifting down into 2nd or up into 5th took more time than was gained. So the best laps came from using 3rd and 4th only; the driver was just sitting there, cruising and unable to use the power.

The GLH came next, thanks to torque and tires. Cornering power was measured through a steady-speed turn and the Omni was the best, mostly because it has the largest tires.

The hot rod GLH is fun on the track. Hurled into a turn, it takes a set, bulls

PERFORMANCE

	Dodge Omni GLH	Honda Civic S	Mitsubishi Mirage Turbo	Renault Encore GS	Toyota Corolla GT-S	Volkswagen Golf GTI
Acceleration:						
Time to distance, sec:						
0–100 ft	3.0	3.8	3.4	3.5	3.6	3.3
0–500 ft	8.9	9.9	9.7	9.7	9.9	8.9
0–1320 ft	17.2	18.2	18.1	19.3	18.6	16.9
Speed at end of						
¼ mi, mph	80.5	76.0	76.5	74.0	79.5	79.0
Time to speed, sec:						
0–30 mph	2.9	3.9	3.2	3.2	3.1	2.8
0–50 mph	6.8	7.1	7.2	7.9	7.3	6.3
0–60 mph	9.4	11.1	10.4	11.5	10.5	9.0
0–80 mph	16.9	20.6	20.2	21.5	19.0	17.5
Top speed, mph	110	100	108	100	115	107
Fuel economy, mpg	25.5	28.0	25.0	30.5	27.0	27.0
Brakes:						
Stopping distance, ft, from:						
60 mph	161	166	137	153	147	147
80 mph	270	272	240	259	256	249
Pedal effort for						
0.5g stop, lb	19	20	14	14	24	32
Fade, % increase in effort, 6 stops from						
60 mph @ 0.5g	26	nil	nil	21	nil	16
Overall brake rating	very good	very good	excellent	excellent	excellent	excellent
Handling:						
Willow Springs lap time,						
min:sec	1:55.53	1:57.65	1:55.00	1:59.05	1:55.35	1:55.80
Slalom speed, mph	59.8	61.6	61.7	56.5	60.8	62.4
Interior noise, dBA:						
Idle in neutral	54	50	50	52	49	55
Maximum in 1st gear	84	82	76	82	85	73
Constant 30 mph	65	62	63	66	65	68
50 mph	71	67	67	73	69	68
70 mph	75	74	73	75	75	74

CALCULATED DATA

	Dodge Omni GLH	Honda Civic S	Mitsubishi Mirage Turbo	Renault Encore GS	Toyota Corolla GT-S	Volkswagen Golf GTI
Lb/bhp (test weight)	22.7	27.6	23.0	31.1	23.6	23.0
Mph/1000 rpm (5th gear)	24.0	20.8	22.2	23.4	17.1	19.7
Engine revs/mi (60 mph)	2500	2880	2700	2580	3500	3050
Piston travel, ft/mi	1510	1635	1525	1415	1800	1730
R&T steering index	0.88	1.13	1.22	0.97	1.03	1.14
Brake swept area,						
sq in./ton	227	194	203	181	204	195

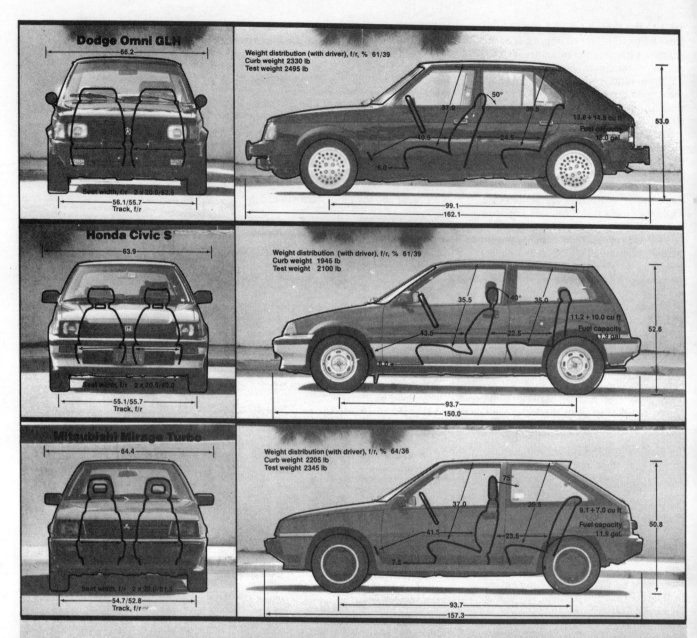

Dodge Omni GLH
66.2
Weight distribution (with driver), f/r, % 61/39
Curb weight 2330 lb
Test weight 2495 lb
50°
37.0 36.5
40.5 24.5
13.8 + 14.5 cu ft
Fuel capacity
13.0 gal.
53.0
6.0
Seat width, f/r 2 x 20.0/52.5
56.1/55.7
Track, f/r
99.1
162.1

Honda Civic S
63.9
Weight distribution (with driver), f/r, % 51/39
Curb weight 1945 lb
Test weight 2100 lb
35.5 40° 35.0
43.5 22.5
11.2 + 10.0 cu ft
Fuel capacity
1.9 gal.
52.6
5.0
Seat width, f/r 2 x 20.5/40.0
55.1/55.7
Track, f/r
93.7
150.0

Mitsubishi Mirage Turbo
64.4
Weight distribution (with driver), f/r, % 64/36
Curb weight 2205 lb
Test weight 2345 lb
75°
37.0 35.5
41.5 23.5
9.1 + 7.0 cu ft
Fuel capacity
11.9 gal.
50.8
7.5
Seat width, f/r 2 x 20.0/51.5
54.7/52.8
Track, f/r
93.7
157.3

through and punches out. Precision isn't the word here. At the limit, the inside wheel lifts, advertised by a gradual lightening of the steering. Shifting is heavy and vague, and the brakes are difficult to modulate. The GLH works, albeit it's work to drive.

The Golf GTI is much the same, but less. This is both good and bad. It's bad in the sense that the GTI has smaller tires and less cornering power, a smaller engine and less speed.

The numbers don't tell the full story. The good here is the very real improvement, new vs old GTI. Volkswagen has clearly taken all needed steps to eliminate any and all fwd torque steer. All steering is now done by the driver, aided and abetted by the clear messages coming from the front wheels. It's precise and secure.

Next, the extra wheel travel of the new suspension has been put to good use. The ride is firm (more anon) but controlled through all its travel. Where the GLH takes a set, the GTI assumes an attitude. Coming into the turn, the GTI moves its rear wheels out, then holds firm. The front end does the work, with flexible understeer keeping the car in line. On the bumps and heaves and pavement patches, where the GLH bulls and the Mirage skitters, the GTI conforms. Secure is the word we need here.

The Honda's only flaw comes with the design; a good 1.5-liter engine can't beat a good 1.7 or 2.2. The Civic S is the lightest, though, and it's nimble. There are no tricks. It's nicely balanced, understeers within reason and the brakes work. The Honda gains in the tight sections and loses on the straights, where the experts say races are won and lost.

Plainly put, the Renault Encore GS wasn't happy on the track. Steering response is overly quick, as the front

wheels seem to tuck in while the back gets light and bouncy. Nor is there power to compensate, nor could the brakes be used hard enough in turns to make up for the engine's lack of suds. The harder the car was pushed, the less rewarding it became.

Off track, such as sports driving in the mountains or going about one's daily rounds in city or town, changes the focus.

Still working in lap-time order, the Mirage earned good grades on the road, less in town. Steering is heavier at lower speeds and the ride, so usefully firm on track, becomes jiggly on poor roads. There's torque steer in the lower gears and the engine responds at least as quickly as the driver needs, that is, careful with power in the corners or the tires squeal. Make that snitch. Display of speed is how the law sees it.

The heavy steering and some play in

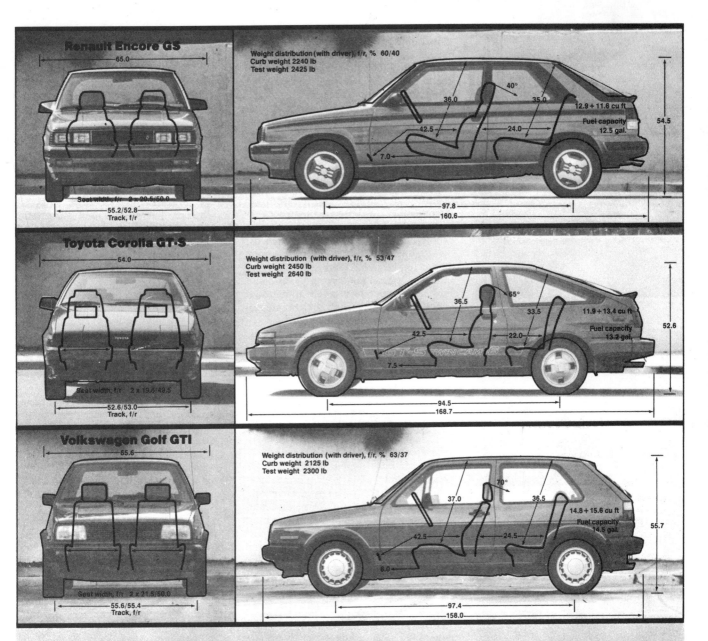

Renault Encore GS

65.0
Seat width, f/r 2 x 20.5/50.0
55.2/52.8
Track, f/r

Weight distribution (with driver), f/r, % 60/40
Curb weight 2240 lb
Test weight 2425 lb

40°
36.0
35.0
12.9 + 11.6 cu ft
Fuel capacity
12.5 gal.
54.5
42.5
24.0
7.0
97.8
160.6

Toyota Corolla GT·S

64.0
Seat width, f/r 2 x 19.6/49.5
52.6/53.0
Track, f/r

Weight distribution (with driver), f/r, % 53/47
Curb weight 2450 lb
Test weight 2640 lb

65°
36.5
33.5
11.9 + 13.4 cu ft
Fuel capacity
13.2 gal.
52.6
42.5
22.0
7.5
94.5
168.7

Volkswagen Golf GTI

55.6
Seat width, f/r 2 x 21.5/50.0
55.6/55.4
Track, f/r

Weight distribution (with driver), f/r, % 63/37
Curb weight 2125 lb
Test weight 2300 lb

70°
37.0
36.5
14.8 + 15.6 cu ft
Fuel capacity
14.5 gal.
55.7
42.5
24.5
8.0
97.4
158.0

the drivetrain make the Mirage a bit difficult to drive smoothly in normal use. Half the drivers objected to the driver's seat. Too much lumbar support, they said, an opinion contradicted by others. But nobody liked the lever by which one raises or lowers the entire seat. Even at its lowest, it was still too high for taller drivers. Further, the rear seat is cramped for adults, and all that glass—no wonder it's called a greenhouse—put the air conditioning on permanent overtime.

The GT-S also gains and loses when it moves from track to road. Most of the improvement comes from the highway's more relaxed pace; even going fast, one doesn't push to the limit. Thus there's more time to downshift and there's no need to be on the power all the time, so the wide ratios and peaky engine aren't as noticeable.

Rear drive helps here because no special technique is needed. The mild understeer works fine, plus it can be reduced, right to the point of hanging the tail out, by pushing the thin pedal.

However, engines that come on the cam at high revs are off the cam at lower revs. Pulling away from stops requires buzzing the GT-S engine and slipping the clutch.

On the open road the engine is revving high and demands 5th, even at 40 mph or so. Cruising at 65 or 70 spins the engine too fast for the driver's comfort. Not the engine's comfort: Toyota knows how to build longevity despite revs. But the driver keeps reaching for the taller gear that isn't there.

Inside, the front of the GT-S is great. Comfortable seats, light, usable controls in the right places, plenty of room. The rear seats are frankly occasional; i.e., crowded and spartan. And luggage space aft is no more than adequate.

The Omni GLH stays in character, as in souped-up sedan. It's a (relatively) big car and engine. The controls are heavy at road speeds and the gearshift is clumsy. The internal and final-drive gearing are suited to the engine and the car's intended use, and the engine is turning slowly at highway speeds. Except that this is a big, noisy engine and a lot of resonance comes through. The ride is solid but not harsh; this handling package wasn't overdone.

Our GLH was a 4-door, a true sedan. Overstuffed chairs, upholstery that will make your mother-in-law wonder if you haven't made the grade despite her predictions, plenty of leg, head and shoulder room. Chrysler has delivered the promised performance. They need to continue the development program, as in less boom and lighter controls. And surely it wouldn't take much to locate the turn signal stalk within reach of the human hand.

Dodge Omni GLH (above), Honda Civic S (below).

PHOTOS BY JIM BROKAW, II

Mitsubishi Mirage Turbo (above), Renault Encore GS (below).

Toyota Corolla GT-S (above), Volkswagen Golf GTI (below).

The GTI easily takes the prize for Most Improved. Because the Golf-based version arrived in the middle of all this, it and the Rabbit-descended GTI were driven in comparison with the others in group, and with each other.

The older car was fun, but demanding. The new plain Golf is nearly as quick as the Rabbit GTI, while the new Golf GTI is quicker yet. The extra power is added to the top and middle of the rev range, at the expense of some torque way down toward idle. The GTI demands just a bit more throttle from rest than you'd expect. Beyond that, no temperament at all. The gearing gives a choice of passing moves and a relaxed cruise on the open road. There's a computer reporting on average speed, miles traveled, elapsed time, even oil and outside air temperatures. The optional air conditioning also gives the most effective cooling system in the group.

The rear passenger area is now usable by adults, albeit drivers with children of car-seat age reported the rearrangement of the rear seatbacks and cargo bin lid, nice to have, of course, demanded more hands than the parent has free.

The GTI doesn't have the best ride in group. The sporting nature of the suspension makes the car rough on poor roads. We found some combinations, as in chopped slab, rain grooves and gentle curves, combined into a rhythmic pitch-yaw that fell somewhere beyond uncomfortable and disquieting. True, the fault was more with the road than the car, but we must drive on what we've got.

The Honda loses almost nothing transferring to daily use. It was nimble but not fast on the track, ditto for city or town. Steering is heavy at parking lot speeds but that goes away. The 1500 S is a willing engine with a light gearshift. The Honda is a light car and it feels light. Not cheap or flimsy, but the Civic gives the impression of having been built to a target weight. No surplus material anywhere. That could mean wear in the long run, although Honda's designers have been singing this song for so many years it's hard to imagine their not having it right by now.

The relative lack of speed is compensated by the willingness of the engine to give all it has got. Downshifts take care of passing or climbing hills. The engine's good cheer in the face of adversity makes light of how far the needle has gone to the right side of the dial. City work is less pleasing, as the Honda really doesn't go very fast and getting up to speed can be, sorry, boring.

In our context the Encore has two virtues: suspension and gearing. As befits a French car, there's lots of wheel travel. Heaves, bumps, potholes, etc almost disappear. The steering that was too responsive on the track goes just quick enough in ordinary driving. The Encore rewards a bit of effort with secure and easy response.

In 5th gear the Encore is loafing. Real downhill gearing, *route nationale* stuff. At 70, where the GT-S is revving and the GLH is booming, the Encore is quietly getting on with the job. It's got good manners in town and the controls work. The irritation caused by flicking the wipers on by accident in the dry is balanced by the ease with which they can be controlled on purpose in the rain. No one liked the driver's seat too much, as it was too short for all sizes, but the interior is cheerful, neither plush (GLH) nor MTV (Mirage). And adults can spend the day in back.

The Boxes' Ballots:

THIS GROUP test began with several assumptions; that a collection of upgraded family cars could be judged as bargain performance cars; that they could be evaluated against each other; and that they all could be used for unfair advantage, as in outrunning cars of higher price and reputation.

These assumptions were wrong. Instead, we found two of the entries, the Mirage and GT-S, to have been improved beyond upgrading. They are true sport coupes, and they look the part. Any snob of the open road who doesn't see the dams, spoilers, flares and badges proclaiming 16-Valve or Turbo isn't unwary, he's asleep.

The GTI and GLH match the group's intentions. Sure, they wear identification. But they are performance versions of family cars, both deceptively quick.

The Civic and Renault are lightweights, in several senses. They're upgraded family/economy cars, no question. But they aren't terribly fast. Still less are they *deceptively* fast.

Elsewhere on these pages are the facts. There are plain facts, as in sticker price, wheelbase, test weight, times to speed and miles per gallon.

Those are the baseline facts. Next are the subjective facts. The drivers who took these cars around the track, down the road and back and forth between home and office rated each car on a collection of subjective qualities, as in ease of handling, driveability, interior design and so forth. The ratings were on a scale of 1 through 10, terrible through tops. The charts show averaged scores.

But because the six cars divided themselves into three pairs rather than one group competing for the same buyer, it wasn't fair to declare one winner on the basis of numbers.

Instead, each participant rated the group on the basis of which he'd rather drive. Not buy, necessarily. Different families would fit/not fit in, say, the Mirage vs the GLH.

In the Rather Drive It test, a car got six points for best, five for second and so on down the list. Again, the scores were averaged and the winner was the car with the highest average.

Here's the finishing order, and why:

Toyota GT-S:

Rear drive and no turbocharger put the Toyota against the trend. Nobody cared. The GT-S is fast, controllable and fits nearly everybody. The coupe body limits space but it's still large enough to qualify as a family car. Nor can the prospective buyer ignore Toyota's reputation for durability and good resale value.

Debits? Yes. Gearing, which all drivers agree could be improved, and styling, which some thought a bit too flashy.

Volkswagen Golf GTI:

The rules were laid down before the votes were cast. Honest.

And a good thing it was, too. The deciding factor between the GT-S and the GTI turned out to be fun; that is, more of the drivers enjoyed the classic rear-drive configuration of the Toyota than paid attention to the superior family sedanship of the GTI.

Other than that, it was a toss-up. Excepting perhaps the occasionally harsh ride, the GTI has no flaws in class. (Sportsmanship requires noting here that the GTI option package lists for $2000, rather a lot for an added 15 bhp and a set of upgraded underpinnings; if the GT-S is less practical but faster than the GTI, so is the GTI a bit less practical and not all that much quicker than the standard Golf.)

Mitsubishi Mirage Turbo:

The very model of a modern sporting motorcar, what with turbocharger, fwd and all aerodynamic devices, the Mirage is small, quick and a bargain.

Held against it were matters of personal interpretation; the flash of the body's new panels, and several drivers don't trust turbochargers or don't like front drive in the performance context.

Honda Civic S:

The Civic delivers more than one can expect in a car of its size and displacement. In the right hands it covers ground at a good rate. What the engine lacks in power it almost makes up for in willingness. This is an entertaining family car,

and certainly a nimble one.

It falls short, though, not of itself but because it isn't fast enough to surprise a driver of equal skill in a car with a bigger engine.

Dodge Omni GLH:

The hot rod and the car for the family that plays together and gets there fast. The GLH delivers what the ads promise. It's roomy and it's powerful.

The controls need work, though, and the effort-to-fun ratio is the worst in the group. Dodge says the new model year will have answers for this.

Renault Encore GS:

One flaw in comparison testing is that there's always a car in last place, implying that because it's last, it isn't good.

Unfair, in this case at least. The Encore is a pleasant car, with room for all and their luggage. It has a good ride and cruises easily as fast as you're likely to get away with.

Drivers of relaxed disposition liked the Encore. Drivers who push harder, didn't. The Encore doesn't feel secure on the edge; in short, hard chargers would do better elsewhere.

CUMULATIVE RATINGS—SUBJECTIVE EVALUATIONS

	Dodge Omni GLH	Honda Civic S	Mitsubishi Mirage Turbo	Renault Encore GS	Toyota Corolla GT-S	Volkswagen Golf GTI	Remarks
Performance:							
Engine	6	6	8	4	8	8	A tie among 4 valves, fuel injection and a turbo.
Gearbox	3	7	6	6	8	7	GT-S's is best defined; GLH's is the wobbliest.
Steering	5	6	7	3	8	9	The GTI's steering talks and listens to you.
Brakes	5	7	7	5	8	8	Balance and pedal feel score for GTI and GT-S.
Ride	6	7	6	7	6	6	Controlled ride is the key: a soft GS; a firm S.
Handling	6	6	8	3	8	9	A predictably taut GTI; a dodgy E-ticket Encore.
Body structure	5	6	7	5	7	8	No real drummers here, but the GTI is tightest.
Average	5.1	6.4	7.0	4.7	7.6	7.8	
Comfort/Controls:							
Driving position	5	8	7	6	7	7	Civic requires the least compromises of the lot.
Controls	4	8	7	5	7	6	Ditto for controls; the S has no annoyances.
Instrumentation	6	6	7	4	8	6	GT-S gauges give a lot of info at a glance.
Outward vision	7	8	8	7	6	7	Lots of glass and narrow pillars score here.
Quietness	5	6	6	5	6	6	Engine buzz, road noise; none is overly quiet.
Heat/vent/air cond	6	6	7	5	6	7	GLH's controls are driver-only.
Ingress/egress	7	5	5	6	5	5	Door size, seat/wheel orientation score here.
Seats	5	6	6	6	6	7	Lateral support up front, adequate room behind.
Luggage & loading	6	3	4	7	4	6	Usable volume, easily folding seats rewarded.
Average	5.7	6.2	6.3	5.7	6.1	6.3	
Design/Styling:							
Exterior styling	6	6	5	5	6	6	All boxes are not created equal, but nearly so.
Exterior finish	4	6	6	4	6	5	The Japanese continue to show a slight lead.
Interior styling	5	7	5	6	6	5	Form follows function nicely within the Civic.
Interior finish	5	7	7	4	6	4	Some interiors are simply more plastic than others.
Average	5.0	6.5	5.8	4.8	6.0	5.0	
Overall average	5.4	6.4	6.5	5.2	6.6	6.6	
Editors' "Rather Drive" Preferences[1]	8	13	15	4	23	21	

[1]First choice = 6 points, 2nd = 5, to 6th = 1.

What it has is what it is… A SUPER

With power increased by 47 per cent and torque up by 37 per cent this Golf GTi tops 130 mph — but don't ask about the fuel consumption!

David Windsor reports

THE STANDARD VW steering wheel writhes informatively in my hands as the narrow pale grey strip of ageing tarmac flashes under the Pirelli P6 tyres. The thin ribbon of road stretches ahead, winding across the bleak mid-winter Northamptonshire countryside, seeming to cut a swathe through the light mist, to hold it back and create a clear zone of excitement for this specially tuned Golf. This is ideal Golf GTi territory. Almost deserted lanes with long, undulating, poorly surfaced straights, a rich variety of corners, some with awkward cambers and chassis-testing patches of localised repair, many with clear lines of visibility through the leafless trees … present an irresistible challenge.

Driving a standard, but "born again" Golf GTi over the roads

A **blowin'** revival

Could superchargers be making a comeback?
Daniel Ward **looks at the various types of superchargers, and concludes that for the moment at least the turbo is firmly in the driving seat**

SINCE the early 1920s when the British Racing Green "blower" Bentleys won Le Mans, their bulky, aluminium-cased superchargers have been synonymous with prodigious performance. The sight of the row of butterflies on the top of a dragster's supercharger cracking open to unleash 1000 bhp has only reinforced the image.

Yet look at today's new cars and you will be hard pressed to find a positively-driven supercharger. In recent years only Lancia with its Volumex version of the Fiat twin-cam 2-litre engine has dabbled with supercharging.

The reason is that the traditional centrifugal or alternative Roots-type units are not the only superchargers, and it is exhaust gas-driven turbochargers which are currently proving immensely popular, with the pressure-wave Comprex supercharger showing some promise. All the devices are capable of raising an engine's power and torque by about 25 per cent, but it is the character of the improved performance and the relative cost of achieving it that explains their respective popularity. The boost in performance comes from the improvement in volumetric efficiency.

Without the forced induction of supercharging, a four-stroke engine will suck in no more than 80 per cent of its swept volume, even when the throttle is fully open. As a norm, supercharging will raise the induction pressure by at least 0.5 bar above atmospheric pressure, with the extra volume of air/fuel mixture producing a boost in output, though there is some loss of thermal efficiency.

Of the positively-driven superchargers, the Roots-type used on the "blower" Bentleys and Volumex Lancias is the most popular design. It consists of two dog-bone shaped rotors geared together so that they can rotate with small clearances without ever touching. The rotors are belt-driven at 1.32 times the engine speed on the Lancias.

Two other types of supercharger have never been used on more than a few models. They are the centrifugal supercharger, with a modest boost in power achieved over a small rev range; and the vane type, where the out-of-balance

CHARGER

around Silverstone this morning would be a real pleasure — piloting Richard Lloyd's latest creation was much more than that. It was both fascinating and immensely satisfying, despite the car being a development workhorse and not a carefully prepared and pampered demonstrator. All-red, it looked neatly purposeful in its recently fitted Hella body styling kit. A little understated perhaps and in need of some visual sparkle. But conspicuous performance has its pitfalls in this speed-limit land, and while this newcomer from GTi Engineering certainly has Performance, it is delivered in an understated and highly impressive fashion.

Supercharging is what this Golf has and what it does! It represents a new departure for Lloyd and his resident tuning wizard Brian Ricketts, who have previously marketed ultra-reliable conversions based on enlarging the standard Golf's engine capacity as a means of creating torquey, relaxed horsepower. Those conversions are still available, offered in various stages to suit different budgets, and continuing development now sees the company offering a four-valve-per-cylinder tuning package for customers' cars, with 170 bhp, 146 lb ft of torque and a rebuilt gearbox, for a drive-away price of around £4200.

However, with VW working on its own 16-valver and most car makers offering the charismatic and/or real benefits of turbocharging on at least one model in their ranges, tuning firms must experiment more adventurously in order to better the constantly improving base vehicles. So Brian took the Oettinger 16-valve, 2000 cc engine out of GTi Engineering's 10,000-mile Golf II that doubles as the road-going test bed, returned it to the company's engine dynamometer, and slotted in his most demon tweak...

First impressions when lifting the Golf's bonnet are of the mass of wiring criss-crossing the engine bay and of how small the standard 1781 cc engine appears. And why is the alternator dominating the centre stage? The VW fuel injection is retained, but relocated in the front offside of the nose, mounted atop the Magnacharger supercharger unit imported from the USA. Fabricated trunking leads from this unit in a giant U down under the driveshaft and up behind the engine to its intake manifold. Invisible changes include a ported and polished cylinder head, compression ratio lowered to 8.5:1, an oil cooler, a camshaft with slightly revised timing and a very large diameter exhaust system. Everything in the transmission and chassis outside the engine ▶

---

eccentric carrying the vanes limits operating speed.

Today's turbocharger uses a centrifugal compressor to raise the pressure of the intake mixture, but instead of being directly driven from the crankshaft it uses an exhaust gas turbine on the same shaft to power the compressor at speeds up to 150,000 rpm. The gas turbine works by converting the heat energy of the exhaust gases — up to 1000°C for a petrol engine — into kinetic energy, which turns the turbine wheel. The beauty of

the system is that you are making use of energy that would otherwise be wasted.

The Comprex (pressure-wave) supercharger received a lot of attention when Ferrari tested one in 1981 and it showed considerable promise. However it has been left to Opel to announce, at the recent Geneva motor show, the first production car with a Comprex unit. It is fitted to a 2.3-litre diesel, which now produces not only 90 bhp, but more important 90 per cent of ▶

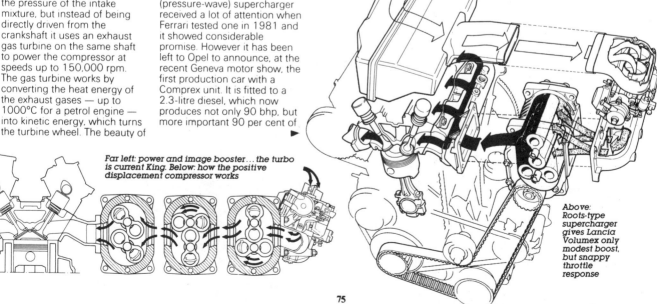

Far left: power and image booster... the turbo is current King. Below: how the positive displacement compressor works

Above: Roots-type supercharger gives Lancia Volumex only modest boost, but snappy throttle response

is standard Golf GTi.

The engine starts first time, but has a very lumpy idle and an incredibly deep, almost growling exhaust note that sounds like it means business without shattering any ear drums. In the engine test house this supercharged power unit has given 165 bhp and 150 lb ft of torque, but produces slightly more of both installed in the car with a different four-branch exhaust system. The standard Golf GTi does very nicely thank you on 112 bhp and 114 lb ft...

Blip the throttle and the engine rockets round the rev band, even more eagerly than the standard car. Move off and

immediately you become aware that this is both a very fast machine and an amazingly tractable one. Hold each gear to 6000 rpm where the charger gives its maximum boost of 7 psi, and the scenery becomes a blur. The gearchange is still delectable, the clutch still light and progressive, the massive torque surging the car forward in one continuous rush towards the horizon. Progress is deceptively rapid because it is genuinely effortless: the standard VW chassis can obviously handle it and retain its poised handling finesse. The steering is direct and precise and no more prone to torque steer than the standard car.

The engine's curious noise stays surprisingly level as the revs climb, disguising the car's true powers of acceleratation, so that you can easily find yourself travelling at 100 when you thought you were doing 60 mph...It's a wonderful machine to drive quickly but, like all really great sports cars, you don't have to work to maintain a brisk pace and can potter along if that's the mood you're in or forced to adopt. Floor the throttle in fifth gear at 30 mph and this Golf pulls like a train all the way to 130 mph!

Before the Hella body bits took hold, Lloyd's men timed their supercharged creation at 135 mph, and they talk of

acceleration times like 5.4 seconds (50 to 70 mph in 4th) and 4.8 seconds (70 to 90 mph in 4th). Times that have to be experienced to be believed. But, with power up 47 per cent and torque increased by 37 per cent it doesn't take very much imagination! Comparable figures for the standard Golf GTi are 6.1 seconds (50 to 70 mph) and 8.0 (70 to 90 mph), both in fourth gear. The Supercharged device covers the standing ¼-mile in 15.5 seconds...a clear 1.0 second faster than the Golf in its straight-from-Wolfsburg form.

Body styling parts are entirely optional so this could be a real Q-car, packing a Porsche-style punch in a discreet exterior appearance. But this express-train transformation won't come cheap — if GTi Engineering decides to put it into limited production. At present the imported superchargers are rather expensive (a cool £1000 each...) and the fabrication work labour-intensive. Depending on public reaction and further test-bed running — a reversion to the standard camshaft seems likely — Brian hopes to offer his supercharged conversion for a £1500 drive-away price, using a British-made supercharger unit and castings in place of the fabricated components. On top of that £1500, of course, you provide the Golf GTi...

If you fancy being the owner of the ultimate Q-car give GTi Engineering a call or drop it a line...the more interest that's shown in the amazing Supercharger...the more likely it is actually to make you one. Contact GTi at Unit 9 Silverstone Circuit, Towcester, Northants, NN12 8TN or telephone 0327-857857.

its maximum torque at 1300 rpm. The unit itself is a wide paddle-wheel-like cylinder, which rotates and uncovers inlet and exhaust ports at opposite ends. Pressurised exhaust gases pass into one of the chambers and by virtue of travelling towards the inlet mixture at the other end at the speed of sound, compress the charge air which, as the cylinder rotates, escapes through the inlet port to the engine. A pressure wave then drives the exhaust gas out.

To evaluate the relative merits of the Roots-type, turbocharger and Comprex superchargers, VW applied them all individually to a 1.2-litre diesel, and compared the performance with a 1.6-litre naturally aspirated engine. On both power output and specific fuel consumption the turbo and Comprex with intercooler proved the best — and were closely matched. The Comprex has easily the best low-speed torque; the Roots has a flat

torque curve but the turbo suffers from poor torque at speeds below 2000 rpm. Response tests again emphasise the turbo's problem of having first to overcome the inertia of the turbine/compressor when the thermal energy available is low.

While work continues on overcoming the manufacturing difficulties associated with the Comprex for petrol engines, the turbo will remain the firm favourite on account of its good power and ease of installation. Engineers are learning how to improve the turbo's low speed response.

But for the ultimate in supercharging look no further than the Group B rallying Lancia 038. It has both a Roots blower and turbo; the supercharger provides the strong low-speed torque and snappy throttle response, but as the revs rise it is automatically disengaged and the turbo takes over to produce barn-storming power output of 400 bhp.

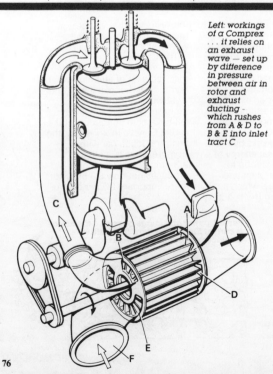

Left: workings of a Comprex ...it relies on an exhaust wave — set up by difference in pressure between air in rotor and exhaust ducting - which rushes from A & D to B & E into inlet tract C

Volkswagen GTI

A pocket pistol to win the West, and everywhere else.

• We don't know if Dan'l Boone ever gave a nickname to his best Pennsylvania Long Rifle, but we can be sure that whenever he ranged afield from his homestead in the Schuylkill valley near Reading, Pennsylvania, there was a graceful, accurate flintlock on his shoulder. Old Betsy, Roy Rogers's Trigger, Tonto at the side of his Kemo Sabe—the faithful traveling companion is an essential element of every great adventure.

Now, from out of the iron forges of the Monongahela watershed, just west of the Alleghenies, comes a new breed of personal weapon that a lot of us colonists are going to take down from the mantelpiece whenever we're really serious about a trek. This particular Pennsylvania German is not exactly a long rifle—it's more of a pocket snubbie—but it can bore a laser-straight hole through any obstacle on any journey, anywhere, any time. And be a faithful, amusing, uplifting partner every yard of the way.

It took Volkswagen only two years from the introduction of the original Golf/

Rabbit, in 1974, to create the GTI performance model for the Fatherland. It took the company's product planners another *six* years to admit that Americans might like it, too. The Rabbit GTI was such a smash hit, though, that Volkswagen is being nicer to us this time around: the new GTI follows the introduction of the new, U.S.-made Golf by mere months.

We covered the ways the Golf betters the Rabbit last December: basically, it's sleeker, smoother, and roomier. The GTI—which at bottom is a Golf, though it does not share the label—adds more power, more brakes, and more adhesion, as well as a variety of appealing details, such as a sporty interior and an informative dashboard computer. A little heavier than the old model but with the same torque rating, the new GTI is not quite as fast in a flat-out drag race, according to our timing gear, but it is superior in every other performance area—in top speed, in braking, in cornering, in subjective handling. It also offers a more refined driving environment in every way.

Cosmetically, connoisseurs of "wolf-in-sheep's-clothing" VW styling will be able to spot the new GTI by virtue of its larger, flush headlights, its fender-flare appliqués and bolder body-side moldings, its red accent trim and black bumpers, its hatch-top spoiler lip, and its 60-series tires mounted on larger alloy wheels. Inside, it has firmly bolstered bucket seats, a leather-topped

shifter, and the familiar Scirocco-style steering wheel.

Ahead of the fire wall, the 1.8-liter SOHC transverse four is basically the same as before, but several refinements enable it to pump out 100 horsepower now. That's ten more than the old GTI, at the same 5500 rpm, and fifteen more than the new civilian Golf (85 at 5250). Peak torque is the same 105 pounds-feet as before, but it peaks 250 rpm lower, at 3000. (The Golf has 98 at 3000.) The refinements include a Bosch KE-Jetronic fuel-injection system, hydraulic valve lifters, and larger intake valves. New pistons help develop mixture swirl and deliver a 10.0:1 compression ratio, significantly higher than the original GTI's 8.5. A digital ignition system senses knock and governs timing to suit different fuel grades and conditions.

The GTI package again includes a close-ratio five-speed. The changes from before are a taller final-drive, 3.67 versus 3.89, and a slightly taller top gear, 0.89 versus 0.91; all the other gears are the same. (The new vanilla version's final-drive ratio is also 3.67.) The tires are the same size as before, 185/60HR-14, but instead of Pirelli P6s they are Goodyear Eagle GTs.

There are disc brakes at all four corners,

vented in front (the older GTI had drums in back, as does the new Golf), and again the GTI is distinguished by anti-sway bars at both ends (the Golf has none).

Power rack-and-pinion steering is now available as an option. It quickens the overall ratio to 17.5:1 from 20.8 and cuts lock-to-lock steering-wheel turns to 3.2 from 3.8. Other options include air conditioning, cruise control, a sliding sunroof, and upgraded sound systems. The GTI shares the two-year mechanical, three-year rust-through, unlimited-mileage warranty of all 1985 Volkswagens.

The GTI also shares the new Golf's slightly greater bulk and weight. Compared with the Rabbit, the wheelbase is up to 97.3 inches, from 94.5; the overall length is 2.5 inches longer, at 158.0; and the width is 2.7 inches greater, at 66.1. The front and rear tracks are wider by 1.6 and 2.9 inches, respectively. Compared with our November 1982 test GTI, the new model's 2310-pound curb weight is 210 pounds heavier (though roughly 60 pounds of that difference is due to air conditioning and power steering that the older GTI lacked); VW spec sheets indicate that the GTI carries 50 pounds more equipment than the Golf.

On the plus side, the new body offers extra tape-measure room in virtually every dimension. The interior volume is up by twelve percent, the under-hatch space is 30 percent larger, and the gas tank holds 40 percent more fuel (14.5 gallons). Not to mention the wind-tunnel figure: 0.35 is the factory's Cd claim. That makes the GTI slightly less wind-cheating than the Golf, but still about fifteen percent cleaner than the old Rabbit.

Just as the new body style is slightly softer than the Giugiaro original, the GTI's on-road behavior is a bit more subdued. It's not a night-and-day difference—this is by

no means one of those enthusiasts' favorites that are ruined in their second incarnations—but it is enough of a difference to be noticeable. The earlier GTI wasn't exactly hard-edged, but the new one is slightly less so. While the suspension is tauter than that of average passenger cars, it seems a trifle more compliant than before, and the response to the various controls, while smooth and direct and immediate, subjectively is not quite as intense. The first thing owners of the old GTI comment on, however, is a welcome reduction in cabin noise. Our sound-level meter confirms this impression: the new car is quieter in every test we conducted. Idle noise is down by a whopping 8 dBA.

The 100-horse engine has very pleasant manners. A new mounting system improves the NVH readings; even at full bore, the engine remains almost unobtrusive. It's not a particularly wide-banded unit, though, nothing like the new sixteen-valve Toyota. It doesn't seem happy below about 1800 rpm, nor is it a top-end screamer. The rev limiter on our test unit cut in a bit earlier than the indicated 6750 redline, at about 6300, but even the lower figure is 800 rpm above the power peak, so this was no real handicap. In fact, this four is a distinctly torquey powerplant, and it does its best work in the 3000-to-4000 band, where it is so creamy-smooth and quiet that one can easily forget to change gears. It remains smooth at higher revs, but it seems to offer no real performance improvement there, even though it sounds as if it's working harder. Even when the driver's blood is up, flogging the engine much above 5500 seems pointless.

Given the GTI's increased weight and lower drag, we weren't surprised to find its acceleration down and its speed up. Compared with our 1982 tester, which did 0 to 60 mph in 9.7 seconds, the new model gave us only 10.1. But our quarter-miles were identical: 17.1 at 76. And our 114-mph top speed represents a rousing improvement of 9 mph.

Lateral adhesion was the real eye-opener. We found that the Goodyears gave our test GTI a skidpad grip of 0.83 g, which is a huge jump from the previous car's already good 0.78. In terms of pure grip, the GTI has just entered a rarefied stratum of performance machinery.

The beauty of all that g-force is that it's usable. All of it. So many cars, even some with pretty prestigious nameplates, start to feel squirmy when you take them to the edges. Think of the Porsche 911/930: its edges are well out there, but they're very ragged edges. It takes a great deal of care and attention—and talent, skill, and determination—to dance along them. But with the GTI . . .

Heck. All you do is steer. Once.

The steering precision is high, and the road feel and the effort level are very acceptable, even with the power assistance. The new Golf's rear suspension has had every trace of roll and ride steer engineered out, so you get exactly the amount of veer you ask for—exactly. The result is utterly viceless cornering behavior. It seems that no matter how fast you're going around a corner, if a rock or a pothole should appear on the line or if you perceive that your line itself is getting too wide, you merely tighten it. That's all. If you need to slow down, you merely lift your foot. If you decide, midcorner, that a little braking is in order, go ahead and brake. No problem, no wiggles, no sudden, vicious tail-happy breakaways. And, come to that, scarcely any noise from the superb Eagle GTs.

The feeling is one of total psychodynamic calm, total synergistic control, total confidence in self as in machine. The GTI is a car that practically drives itself. On a difficult road, it feels almost programmed. Mainly, it feels safe. At any speed.

This seamless excellence gives the car the personality of an ideal friend. No matter what mood you're in, the car seems to match it. Feel like an idle shopping expedition? A brisk canter cross-country? Flat-out mountain-pass storming? The GTI is happy to go right along with you.

Such handling perfection may not please

everyone. Drivers who like the 911/930 experience, who think it a heady challenge, will probably find the GTI about as thrilling as a well-designed kitchen appliance.

And no first issue of an all-new model is immune to determined nit-picking. The firmly Germanic seat is fine as far as it goes, but it should go farther in adjustability; the car deserves a really premium performance seat. (VW says that seat-bottom tilt mechanisms will soon be added.) For some physiques, too, the gearshift could fall more readily to hand. And there are cars with better pedal setups for heel-and-toe work, with more instantly legible gauges, with more capacious cubbyholes, with slimmer A-pillars (the new VW's is exactly fat enough to hide a small pickup at a junction; beware!), with more of an overall impression of ergonomic unity.

VW has muted the angry red glare of the prominently located hazard flasher switch, but it's a pity the company hasn't found some way to keep the heater from making the center console hot enough to burn the careless calf. The small computer display offers eleven items of interest, but only one at a time, and cycling among them can get *too* interesting. The Golf and the GTI also feature the world's nastiest-sounding key buzzer.

One of our samples exhibited freeway hop with a maddening rotational component on certain concrete surfaces. We suspect a duff shock absorber.

The list of minor annoyances is not long enough to spoil the enjoyment and the utility the GTI can give. This little derringer has enough strong points to overwhelm the few imperfections that come to mind. The bottom line is a very appealing little road weapon, a prime choice in traveling companions.

You'll want to give yours a nickname.

—*Pete Lyons*

COUNTERPOINT

• The Rabbit GTI is a hard act to follow. Its replacement is heavier and homelier, and it has no major engine breakthroughs or great leaps ahead in the chassis department to recommend it. How could the new GTI possibly be a better deal?

I can only recommend that you drive one and find out for yourself that, yes, it's a heck of a lot better. The new car is as great an improvement over last year's GTI as the previous model was over garden-variety Rabbits. The ride-and-handling combination is as good as any you'll find in a front-drive car. The flexible engine, the carefully spaced gearing, and the one hundred horsepower blend so nicely with the sure-footed chassis and the driver-oriented interior that this car will doubtless be held high as *the* new standard of affordable sports-sedan design.

Just to assure you that I haven't fallen off the deep end, I do have a short bitch list. I miss the old GTI's instrument-panel accent stripe. The pedals are a bit too widely spaced to give me sure heel-and-toe operation when I stab at them with my narrow feet. In our test car, the fourth-to-fifth gate was poorly served by a vague-feeling shift linkage. And, oddly enough, this car says "Oldsmobile!" when you hit the horn button. Something a bit more stirring—like *"Ausgezeichnet!"*—would sound better to me.

—*Don Sherman*

Any good chef knows that presentation is half the meal. The most perfectly cooked *médaillons de veau* with julienne vegetables wouldn't seem nearly so delicious if they were heaped artlessly on your plate.

That's the new GTI's problem exactly. This little whizzer is one of the world's tastiest small sedans, but you could fall asleep looking at it. Even in meltdown red, our test car had me reaching for the NoDoz. The breadbox shape that VW pioneered with the Rabbit—smoothed in the wind tunnel or not—now looks a generation old compared with the latest from around the globe. The new GTI even lacks the bulldog stance of the old Rabbit GTI.

Of course, when I plunk myself into the wonderful driver's seat and shut the door, my whole perspective changes. Suddenly, this is a car to be savored.

If only the GTI looked as good as it tastes. On the one hand, it's "My compliments to the chef." On the other, it's "Man does not live by performance alone."

—*Rich Ceppos*

Volkswagen's new American-built GTI is a better car in every way than the one it replaces—the one we loved so much. It is tighter, tauter, faster, and it now lopes along with a lot less stressful engine noise, thanks to a longer final-drive ratio. There's been a lot of intemperate whining from the motor noters that it didn't look "different enough" when it finally arrived. It is difficult to imagine why it should look "more different" than it does, or how looking "more different" might have made it a better car. Its lines are clean and handsome and entirely appropriate for a car that sets out to do what this one does. What doesn't show up, in either its exterior appearance or its specifications, is how much fun it is to drive. It represents as much pure balls-out fun and frolic as it's possible to have in a moving automobile. It cannot be called a Q-ship, because everybody in the civilized world now knows exactly what to expect from little sedans with fat tires and GTI badges, but it is the fox among the chickens when it goes after pricey competitors like the Fiero or Ford's turbo EXP.

—*David E. Davis, Jr.*

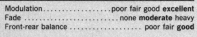

Vehicle type: front-engine, front-wheel-drive, 5-passenger, 3-door sedan

Price as tested: $10,410

Options on test car: base Volkswagen GTI, $8990; air conditioning, $695; AM/FM-stereo radio/cassette, $495; power steering, $230.

Sound system: AM/FM-stereo radio/cassette, 4 speakers

ENGINE
Type	4-in-line, iron block and aluminum head
Bore x stroke	3.19 x 3.40 in, 81.0 x 86.4mm
Displacement	109 cu in, 1781cc
Compression ratio	10.0:1
Fuel system	Bosch KE-Jetronic fuel injection
Emissions controls	3-way catalytic converter, feedback fuel-air-ratio control
Valve gear	belt-driven single overhead cam, hydraulic lifters
Power (SAE net)	100 bhp @ 5500 rpm
Torque (SAE net)	105 lb-ft @ 3000 rpm
Redline	6750 rpm

DRIVETRAIN
Transmission 5-speed
Final-drive ratio 3.67:1

Gear	Ratio	Mph/1000 rpm	Max. test speed
I	3.45	5.1	32 mph (6300 rpm)
II	2.12	8.4	53 mph (6300 rpm)
III	1.44	12.4	78 mph (6300 rpm)
IV	1.13	15.8	95 mph (6000 rpm)
V	0.89	20.0	114 mph (5700 rpm)

DIMENSIONS AND CAPACITIES
Wheelbase .... 97.3 in
Track, F/R .... 56.3/56.0 in
Length .... 158.0 in
Width .... 66.1 in
Height .... 55.7 in
Frontal area .... 20.7 sq ft
Curb weight .... 2310 lb
Weight distribution, F/R 62.3/37.7%
Fuel capacity .... 14.5 gal

CHASSIS/BODY
Type .... unit construction
Body material .... welded steel stampings

INTERIOR
SAE volume, front seat .... 46 cu ft
            rear seat .... 41 cu ft
            trunk space .... 18 cu ft
Front seats .... bucket
Recliner type .... infinitely adjustable
General comfort .... poor fair good **excellent**
Fore-and-aft support .... poor fair **good** excellent
Lateral support .... poor fair good **excellent**

SUSPENSION
F: ...... ind, MacPherson strut, coil springs, anti-sway bar
R: ..... ind, trailing arm integral with a transverse member, coil springs, anti-sway bar

STEERING
Type .... rack-and-pinion, power-assisted
Turns lock-to-lock 3.2
Turning circle curb-to-curb .... 34.4 ft

BRAKES
F: .... 9.4 x 0.8-in vented disc
R: .... 9.4 x 0.4-in disc
Power assist .... vacuum

WHEELS AND TIRES
Wheel size .... 6.0 x 14 in
Tire make and size .. Goodyear Eagle GT, P185/60HR-14

CAR AND DRIVER TEST RESULTS

ACCELERATION
	Seconds
Zero to 30 mph	2.7
40 mph	4.7
50 mph	6.9
60 mph	10.1
70 mph	13.7
80 mph	20.4
90 mph	33.2
Top-gear passing time, 30–50 mph	10.1
50–70 mph	11.9
Standing ¼-mile	17.1 sec @ 76 mph
Top speed	114 mph

HANDLING
Roadholding, 300-ft-dia skidpad .... 0.83 g
Understeer .... **minimal** moderate excessive

BRAKING
70–0 mph @ impending lockup .... 182 ft

Modulation .... poor fair good **excellent**
Fade .... none **moderate** heavy
Front-rear balance .... poor fair **good**

COAST-DOWN MEASUREMENTS
Road horsepower @ 50 mph .... 14.5 hp
Friction and tire losses @ 50 mph .... 6.0 hp
Aerodynamic drag @ 50 mph .... 8.5 hp

FUEL ECONOMY
EPA city driving .... **26 mpg**
EPA highway driving .... **32 mpg**
C/D observed fuel economy .... **23 mpg**

INTERIOR SOUND LEVEL
Idle .... 53 dBA
Full-throttle acceleration .... 82 dBA
70-mph cruising .... 74 dBA
70-mph coasting .... 74 dBA

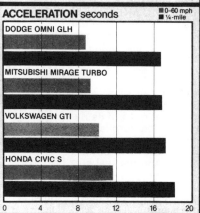

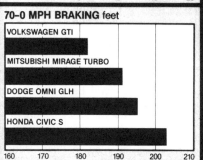

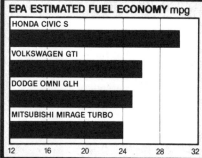

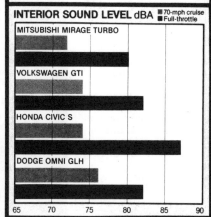

VW's number one iron

Despite all the competition the Golf GTi is still widely accepted as the bench mark for small sporting saloons … until recently, that is. Now the talk is of the GTi's grey hairs. It's been said that it is no longer king-pin and that the latest batch of rivals — Vauxhall Astra GTE, Peugeot 205GTi, MG Maestro EFI, to name but three, are out to get it. Do these upstart pocket-rockets have the bottle to beat the best, we asked ourselves…

On the road

The GTi may lack the seductive curving lines of most of its rivals but you'd be surprised at just how efficient its stolid-looking lines prove to be in a wind tunnel. And the real surprise — and delights — come when you turn the key and start to roll. But first the bad news. GTi engines aren't at their best when left to idle. 'A bit rough and a bit lumpy', was how one of our less urbane testers summed it up. And then there's the exhaust drone. It sets in at 4000rpm, never to go away thereafter. Still, all law-abiding GTi drivers in the UK will be some 500rpm short of the din when cruising on the motorway in fifth.

Learn to live with these and you won't find much else to complain about. Indeed, despite its shortcomings the GTi engine is probably the most civilised, yet exciting four-cylinder engine ever to be built on a mass-production scale. Its combination of breathtaking performance, enthusiasm for hard work and sheer versatility is remarkable. The Golf is capable of charging from a standing start to 100mph in under 25 seconds. Fourth gear will whisk you from 30-70mph in an equally impressive 12.6 seconds. If you don't study facts and figures, you can take our word for it that that's very quick. Yet it does it all with such zest and a complete lack of temperament that none of its rivals can begin to match. And, as if that weren't enough, the GTi is just as happy trundling the kids to school or pottering round to the shops. Indeed, it's so forgiving you could even use it for driving lessons.

Of course, the well-engineered controls must take some credit here. The sweet-acting gearchange, for exam-

ple, is one of the most helpful you could hope to meet, and other controls, such as the clutch and steering, are easy-going and flatteringly smooth.

The former notorious heart-in-mouth brakes are much improved on the latest cars. They are a little too sharp for our liking, but gone is the long and spongy pedal travel and response is now quick and the car stops all square.

Neither is there any stodgy ploughing on into a bend for this powerful front-wheel drive car. Handling is razor sharp, with a hint of a seductive tail wriggle that never develops

into oversteer no matter how hard it is provoked by clumsy footwork. We had the GTi hurtling round the test track steering pad on three wheels yet felt in complete control. The GTi must be the most exciting trike we've ever driven. The steering is light and always very informative.

Less impressive was the grip of the 60-Series Pirelli P6 tyres, which seem to be altogether too keen to slither and slide on a damp surface for our liking. It is in this area that the new GTi is supposed to have improved. We remain unconvinced.

The dampers are more on

top of the job nowadays, with less inclination to float. The suspension is set on the firm side as one might expect, although a lot of people will be surprised at just how well the GTi takes the sting out of poorly-surfaced roads.

They will get a pleasant surprise when it comes to fuel bills, too. The Golf GTi is, without a doubt, the most fuel-efficient performance hatch-back on the market. In fact, it uses no more fuel than many a more mundane family hatch. What's more, the new 12-gallon tank gives this latest model a very useful range between fill-ups.

Inside story

The GTi is one of those cars that feels right the moment you sit behind the wheel, and although you sit very high, you still have good headroom. There's plenty of space to stretch out, and the wrap-round, rally-style seat grips with reassuring comfort. The controls seem well related, too, and work with a precision and smoothness that only the Japanese can better. The minor switch gear is easier to use nowadays but silly little warning lamps still live on. Most annoying of all are the wipers that are no longer set up for righthand drive.

If the back seat is going to be

VW Golf GTi 3-door

Price £7699   On the road £7903

HOW GOOD

At-a-glance

DRIVE's testers' verdict on the VW Golf GTi 3-door, taking into consideration its main rivals, its price and what kind of car it's *meant* to be.

Out of ten

PERFORMANCE
●●●●●●●●●○

FUEL ECONOMY
●●●●●●●●●●

HANDLING/STEERING
●●●●●●●●●○

COMFORT/REFINEMENT
●●●●●●○○○○

INTERIOR/LUGGAGE SPACE
●●●●○○○○○○

PASSENGER AIDS
●●●○○○○○○○

DRIVER AIDS
●●●●●●●●○○

ACCIDENT/INJURY SAFEGUARDS
●●●●●●●○○○

RUST RESISTANCE
●●●●●●●●○○

EASE/COST OF REPAIR
●●●○○○○○○○

sed a lot we'd advise buyers to opt for the recently introduced four-door GTi — the two-door model makes life very difficult for rear seat passengers getting in and out. There is a lot more room in the back on Golf 2, kneeroom is particularly good.

Luggage still needs to be lifted over a sill, although that is at least lower on the latest cars. We didn't think much of the uneven floor and wondered why VW doesn't use a false floor arrangement, Fiesta-style.

The heater is quick to respond but smells when in use. There's rear footwell heating now — which is nice to have — but we wish the supply of cold, fresh-air ventilation was not warmed by the heater.

Living together

The Golf is very well assembled and finished, but some parts prices are beginning to look cheeky. Thank goodness items such as the exhaust and brake pads are now being made from long-life materials. Service and repair times will

come as a welcome relief after the shock of the parts prices.

DIY types are probably better off employing their skills on the house or garden; there's a lot of complicated technology under the GTi's bonnet.

The new alloy wheels should look better for longer than the previous type — they are certainly a darned sight easier to clean. The GTi is a messy beast in wet weather, however, with the door sills and tailgate getting especially filthy.

 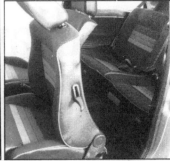

Padded wheel, hugging hot seat   *Reaching back seat is awkward*

GTi has clear dials and well-related controls   *Pity about the sill and the boot's uneven floor*

Verdict

Unlike most of its rivals the Golf GTi will do absolutely nothing for your ego when it's standing at the kerb or when the inquisitive peer inside. But once under way it proves to be the master of the understatement. It's versatile, civilised and well built, but most of all it's exciting, which is what a hot-hatch is all about. We aren't sure who put about the malicious rumour about the GTi's grey hairs but as far as we're concerned the VW Golf GTi rules ... OK.

We like
- superb power train
- razor-sharp handling
- build quality
- ability to excite

We don't like
- rear entry and exit
- uneven load floor
- screenwipers set up for lefthand drive
- parts prices

Costs 🔧
Parts/repairs (inc VAT)

clutch (exch) (fitting 0.7hr)	£84.91
exhaust (1.3hr)	£189.34
headlamp unit (0.4hr)	£26.51
front bumper (0.4hr) (cover only)	£26.73
laminated windscreen (0.7hr)	£59.80
alternator (0.5hr)	£91.16
set of rear dampers (1.0hr)	£78.08

Servicing per year/12,000 miles (2.0hr av)

Insurance Group 7
Warranty 1 year, unlimited mileage, plus 6 year anti rot-through corrosion and 3 years on paintwork

Running costs £ at Feb '85

Petrol 12,000 miles (£1.89 per gal)	£605
Insurance (av)	£334
Road tax, AA sub £90 + £36.50	£126.50
Servicing/replacements	£291
Total running costs (11.29p per mile)	£1357

Fuel 🅰 4-star/97 octane min

Consumption — normal range

hard driving, heavy traffic	26mpg
short journeys in the suburbs	30½mpg
motorway — 70mph cruising	37½mpg
brisk driving, mixed roads	37½mpg
gentle driving — rural roads	42mpg
Typical mpg overall	**37½mpg**
Realistic tank range	400 miles/10½gal

Performance ▶▶

Max speeds **116mph**/5th (5770rpm), **106mph**/4th (6700rpm), **83mph**/3rd, (6700rpm), **56mph**/2nd (6700rpm), **34mph**/1st (6700rpm)

Acceleration (time in seconds)
0-30mph 3.1; 0-60mph 8.9; standing ¼-mile 17.0

mph	through gears	in gears 5th/4th
30-40	1.5	4.6/3.2
30-50	3.2	9.0/6.2
30-60	5.8	13.3/9.3
30-70	8.6	18.1/12.6

Weights and measures

Outside:
kerbweight (full of fuel) 19¼cwt
overall length 13ft 1in
overall width 5ft 6in
overall height 4ft 7in

Inside:
front headroom 37½in
front legroom 32¾in-41in
rear headroom 36in
rear seat width
 (between armrests) 50½in
typical rear legroom 37½in
typical rear kneeroom 29¼in
load length 31in-51in
load width 36¾in-51¼in
load height
 with/without canopy 16½in-31in
load sill height
 (inside/outside) 8½in-30½in

Specifications

ENGINE
Type front-mounted 4-in-transverse-line 81.0mm x 86.4mm = 1781cc. Iron block/ alloy head
Fuel Bosch fuel injection
Valves belt-driven overhead camshaft
Max power 112bhp at 5500rpm
Max torque 114 lb ft at 3100rpm

TRANSMISSION
Type 5-speed, front-wheel drive
Mph/1000rpm 20.08 in 5th: 15.80 in 4th

CHASSIS
Suspension front: independent struts and coil springs. Rear: torsion beam with trailing arms and coil springs. Dampers: telescopic all round
Steering rack and pinion with 3¾ turns between locks; 32¾ft turning circle (1 turn gives 60¼ft)
Wheels 6J alloy with Pirelli P6 185/ 60HR14 tyres
Brakes servo-assisted discs all round

Brakes ◯

Pedal load	Efficiency
lb	(%g)
20	30
30	70
40	100
60 (wheels skidding)	90

Fade test pedal load needed for 75% stop: **32 lb** at start; **32 lb** in constant use; **40 lb** in severe use

HOW IT COMPARES	TOTAL ON-ROAD PRICE	ENGINE CAP/POWER (CC/BHP)	FUEL OVERALL (MPG)	MAXIMUM SPEED (MPH)	30-70MPH THROUGH GEARS (SEC)	30-70MPH IN 5th/4th GEARS (SEC)	BRAKES BEST STOP (%G/LB)	OVERALL LENGTH (FT/IN)	MAXIMUM LEGROOM FRONT (IN)	TYPICAL LEG/ KNEEROOM REAR (IN)	STEERING TURNS/ CIRCLE (FT)
Volkswagen Golf GTi	£7903	1781/112	37½	116	8.6	18.1/12.6	100/40	13'1"	41	37½/29¼	3¾/32¾
MG Maestro 2.0EFi	£7492	1994/115	34	117	9.3	18.4/14.2	96/55	13'3½".	39¾	39/27	4¼/35¼
Ford Escort XR3i	£7497	1596/105	36	116	8.3	20.7/14.8	100+/90	13'3¾"	39¼	39¾/28½	3¾/33
Peugeot 205GTi	£6882	1580/105	35	118	8.7	17.1/12.7	98/50	12'1¾"	40½	37/29¼	3¾/33¼
Vauxhall Astra GTE	£7560	1796/115	33	123	8.9	21.8/15.4	N/A	13'1½"	42	38/26½	4/33½

Callaway VW GTI Turbo

Bullet of the byways.

• Our almost unbounded affection for the Volkswagen GTI has been tempered only by our concern for its ultimate lack of poke. We looked forward to the day when the man who has turbocharged a thousand Volkswagen four-cylinders would pump more ponies into the company's latest GTI. When Reeves Callaway applies the ringed tails to his whizzers, the rings are generally symmetrical and the tails are usually tight. Callaway focuses on cars built in or inspired by Germany. They dovetail with his idea of the finer things in life. His turbo conversions are not free of flaws (an impossibility), but among performance privateers, this Connecticut Yankee is known for putting some of today's most astute turbo packages into the hands of people who feel, as he does, that the pedal on the right is for pouncing. Callaway leaped at today's GTI the moment VW released a pre-production model into his care. The result is your basic bullet of the byways.

The red-coated bullet we've been reloading at the Mobil station and firing at will for the past week is clad in a BBS trim package. The smoothly finished air dam, fender flares, and side skirts propel the GTI from "barn" toward "bullet," and BBS claims that the pieces slick down the GTI's aero ballistics by ten percent in the wind tunnel, despite the increased frontal area and the fat 205/50VR-15 Goodyear Eagle VR50s (a.k.a. "gatorbacks"), which are mounted on BBS's famous alloy wheels. Our coast-down testing shows that the Callaway GTI is indeed slightly better than the stock machine in aerodynamic drag but slightly poorer in rolling resistance. At higher speeds, the Callaway car's advantage should increase somewhat.

Speaking of high speeds, the turbo pushes the GTI's terminal velocity from 114 mph to 122. At that point, VW's rev limiter is itching to put a lid on fifth gear, though our test car's tachometer still read

short of the indicated redline. Whatever the effect of the body pieces, stability is first-rate.

The Callaway's headlong ballistics begin with muzzle velocity through a Nissan 300ZX Turbo hood scoop. Fresh air feeds an air box sandwiched between the hood and an air-to-air intercooler. In the past, Callaway's intercooler was buried below the battery; now it perches above the "Callaway" cam cover, and the resulting short runs of plumbing do a better job of cooling and delivering the denser air to the cylinders. VW has increased the GTI's fuel-delivery capacity by switching from Bosch K- to KE-Jetronic fuel injection, so Callaway eliminates its own proprietary Microfueler, relying on a one-time manipulation of the new electronic control box to feed an increment of extra fuel. A copper cylinder-head spacer reduces compression from 10.0 to 7.8:1, taking away some low-speed response but allowing the 10-psi boost that pumps the delightful 1.8-liter four to an estimated 150 hp.

Estimated or not, the power produces a 7.2-second 0-to-60 sprint amid a quarter-mile burst of 15.5 seconds at 88 mph. And it's easy, whooping up in a hurry with no sign of detonation (on unleaded premium pump fuel) and with only a brief hiccup if the throttle is quickly lifted. Fuel economy under a light foot is reasonable, but we

managed only 18 mpg overall. Temptation is a spiteful thing.

Although no official emissions testing has yet been done, Callaway claims that the retention of the stock emissions system allows the engine to remain at least 49-state legal. However, our test car's reluctance to start caused extended cranking and necessitated pedal babying, which might foul a full, by-the-bag emissions test. Company rep Scot Keller places the blame on an uncommon glitch in the brain of this prototype GTI.

Unlike many cars fitted with wide wheels and tires, the BBS-and-Goodyear-equipped GTI tracks true. Only when cornered hard over seams that mimic your general direction of travel does the car dance nervously. Despite the availability of a BBS suspension package, Callaway feels that the stock components provide the best compromise between day-to-day driving and ultimate adhesion. The fat-tired, stock-suspended version we sampled matched the stock GTI's 0.83-g skidpad performance but did not better it. Even on its original-equipment 185/60HR-14 Goodyear Eagle GTs, the everyday GTI sends shock waves through the top ranks of high-limit handling and world-class tracking. Two points: first, VW has done a fine job on the stock suspension; second, if the sweet limits of the stock car make you happy, you *could* save a bundle by leaving off the big booties and the extra body pieces. (If you *really* want to save money, a base VW Golf with Callaway's less expensive Stage I turbo can roll out the door for under $10,000.)

For about $9000, base price, the everyday GTI provides splendiferously heady behavior, and, except for its powertrain, it is dressed to kill. It's got dandy sport seats, suitably boffo trim, and the right heads-up dapper attitude. For an additional $4000 (which includes a heavy-duty clutch), Reeves Callaway's Stage II whizzer shows nothing but its ringed tail to row upon row of otherwise potent preen-and-strutters. Many and varied are the pompous asses who will be booted aside by the Callaway Turbo GTI, shot in the butt by the bullet of the byways. —*Larry Griffin*

Vehicle type: front-engine, front-wheel-drive, 5-passenger, 3-door sedan

Price as tested: $17,557

Options on test car: base Volkswagen GTI, $8990; Callaway Stage II turbo kit, $4000; BBS body kit, $960; BBS wheels, $940; Goodyear Eagle VR50 tires, $782; air conditioning, $695; AM/FM-stereo radio/cassette, $495; leather-covered steering wheel, $125; installation, freight, and dealer prep, $570.

Standard accessories: rear defroster and wiper

Sound system: Volkswagen AM/FM-stereo radio/cassette, 4 speakers

ENGINE
Type .... turbocharged and intercooled 4-in-line, iron block and aluminum head
Bore x stroke .... 3.19 x 3.40 in, 81.0 x 86.4mm
Displacement .... 109 cu in, 1781cc
Compression ratio 7.8:1
Fuel system .... Bosch KE-Jetronic fuel injection
Emissions controls ..... 3-way catalytic converter, feedback fuel-air-ratio control
Turbocharger .... IHI RHB5
Waste gate .... integral
Maximum boost pressure .... 10.0 psi
Valve gear ..... belt-driven single overhead cam, hydraulic lifters
Power (*C/D* estimate) .... 150 bhp @ 5500 rpm
Torque (*C/D* estimate) .... 160 lb-ft @ 3500 rpm
Redline .... 6750 rpm

DRIVETRAIN
Transmission 5-speed
Final-drive ratio 3.67:1

Gear	Ratio	Mph/1000 rpm	Max. test speed
I	3.45	5.2	31 mph (6000 rpm)
II	2.12	8.5	51 mph (6000 rpm)
III	1.44	12.6	75 mph (6000 rpm)
IV	1.13	16.0	96 mph (6000 rpm)
V	0.89	20.3	122 mph (6000 rpm)

DIMENSIONS AND CAPACITIES
Wheelbase .... 97.3 in
Track, F/R .... 56.3/56.0 in
Length .... 158.0 in
Width .... 66.1 in
Height .... 54.2 in
Curb weight .... 2323 lb
Weight distribution, F/R 62.8/37.2%
Fuel capacity .... 14.5 gal

CHASSIS/BODY
Type .... unit construction
Body material .... welded steel stampings, urethane-plastic trim

INTERIOR
SAE volume, front seat .... 46 cu ft
      rear seat .... 41 cu ft
      trunk space .... 18 cu ft
Front seats .... bucket
Seat adjustments .... fore and aft, seatback angle

SUSPENSION
F: .... ind, strut located by a control arm, coil springs, anti-roll bar
R: ..... ind, trailing arm integral with a transverse member and an anti-roll bar, coil springs

STEERING
Type .... rack-and-pinion
Turns lock-to-lock 3.7
Turning circle curb-to-curb .... 34.4 ft

BRAKES
F: .... 9.4 x 0.8-in vented disc
R: .... 9.4 x 0.4-in disc

WHEELS AND TIRES
Wheel size .... 7.0 x 15 in
Wheel type .... cast aluminum
Tires .... Goodyear Eagle VR50, P205/50VR-15

CAR AND DRIVER TEST RESULTS

ACCELERATION
	Seconds
Zero to 30 mph	2.4
40 mph	3.7
50 mph	5.2
60 mph	7.2
70 mph	9.4
80 mph	12.6
90 mph	16.5
100 mph	24.4
Top-gear passing time, 30–50 mph	11.5
50–70 mph	7.7
Standing ¼-mile	15.5 sec @ 88 mph
Top speed	122 mph

BRAKING
70–0 mph @ impending lockup .... 193 ft
Modulation .... poor fair **good** excellent
Fade .... none **moderate** heavy

Front-rear balance .... poor **fair** good

HANDLING
Roadholding, 300-ft-dia skidpad .... 0.83 g
Understeer .... **minimal** moderate excessive

COAST-DOWN MEASUREMENTS
Road horsepower @ 30 mph .... 5.5 hp
      50 mph .... 14.5 hp
      70 mph .... 30.5 hp

FUEL ECONOMY
C/D observed .... **18 mpg**

INTERIOR SOUND LEVEL
Idle .... 60 dBA
Full-throttle acceleration .... 81 dBA
70-mph cruising .... 76 dBA
70-mph coasting .... 75 dBA

PAR 16 GOLF

At a stroke, Volkswagen have regained their position at the top of the hot-hatch-back tree with the eagerly awaited 16-valve Golf. **Laurie Caddell** flew to Bavaria to try it out

Outwardly the Golf is little changed from the eight-valve car, which many will no doubt find annoying considering its substantial price premium. The Scirocco is still as pretty as ever, but is less refined than its saloon sister. Right-hand-drive conversion problems mean that the Scirocco will only be imported here on special order in LHD form

Nine years ago, when the Golf GTi exploded on the scene, it was unrivalled, being the first of the hot hatchbacks. Not surprisingly, however, with the proliferation of similar machines launched since then, the gulf has inexorably narrowed and even with an upgrade, three years ago, to 1.8 litres, the GTi now has plenty of rivals snapping at its heels. All sorts of claims of superiority have been made over the years, but no contender has come up with a better combination of performance, handling and refinement even if some have been able to outsprint the GTi to 60mph by a few academic tenths of a second.

It was at the 1983 Frankfurt Show that Volkswagen paraded a 16-valve Golf/Scirocco engine in public for the first time, but trepidation among competitors turned to relief as each new Motor Show came and went without a production version appearing. The delays, according to official sources, were due to the problems of meeting ever-more-stringent emission controls; it has also been suggested unofficially that the first examples fitted into cars for road evaluation were just too noisy and unrefined.

Whatever the case, the engine is now sorted and in production and will be seen in the Golf 16V, due to go on sale in Germany in November and to reach our shores early next year. The Scirocco will be similarly equipped in Europe at the same time, but this will only be imported to the UK on special order, in left-hand-drive form, due to the problem of resiting the 16V's enlarged brake servo with RHD.

There is some clever engineering in the 16-valve engine because it quickly became obvious during development that the eight-valve motor's belt drive to its single overhead camshaft couldn't cope with the strain of wrapping around a 'sprocket' for a second cam without an increase in its width. The solution was to drive the second cam from the first at its opposite end, thus allowing the standard belt-drive to be retained. First attempts used gears for this secondary drive, but this arrangement was too costly and proved noisy at tickover, so a simple chain coupling was substituted — and appears in production engines. Because the run of this chain is so short, expensive and unreliable tensioners or guide rails are not needed.

To make sure that the engine can cope with the extra stress and heat of the more powerful motor, sodium-filled exhaust valves are fitted while there are now crankcase oil jets to squirt lubricant up under the piston skirts when the pressure rises above 2 bars.

The finished four-valve head features a small, 25-degree, valve angle, which has two advantages: the head can be kept quite narrow and the combustion chamber design which best suits this layout is particularly insensitive to knock. Bore and stroke remain the same as with the eight-valve cars, as does the 10:1 compression ratio, so the new engine still sports a capacity of 1781cc.

Mechanical fuel injection is fitted — either Bosch KA-Jetronic on European-spec cars or KE-Jetronic for those sold 'Stateside, complete with their 10bhp-absorbing catalysts. European cars will not suffer such strangulation, and will be hitting the streets with no less than 139bhp at 6100rpm and just a shade under 138lb ft of torque at 4100rpm.

If we ignore the more expensive Scirocco which will only be sold in dribs and drabs here, then the main changes to the Golf

other than engine are as follows. The suspension has been lowered by 10mm, while both springs and anti-roll bars have been uprated to decrease roll and therefore improve ultimate cornering grip from 0.82 to 0.85g, according to the makers. There are uprated brakes (very good news for owners of vintage GTis) with ventilated items at the front, and there is a new deeper spoiler at the front with vents and ducting to those efficient stoppers.

Apart from the obviously different badging, the only other external difference for UK cars is a small radio aerial mounted at the rear of the roof. Volkswagen say that it needs to be that far from the distributor for good radio reception, but we think it is because it looks so twee there. Expect them to be *de rigeur* soon on all hatchbacks.

The *Autobahnen* and winding roads of Bavaria were to be hunting grounds for the lead-footed journalistic hordes at the launch and it was only a matter of minutes into the drive that one of the Finns in our group failed to negotiate a tree coming the other way. The car stood up to the impact extremely well...

Initial reactions were a little disappointing for a car that is expected to be all of £10,000 when it appears in UK form; there is little to give the game away on the inside, which remains too clinically bland for most tastes. When moving off there seems to be little extra urge over the two-valve car, but when the motor is given its head then in smooth GTi tradition the power comes flooding in and carries on long after the lesser variant would have been rev-limited into submission. The 16-valve unit spins freely to 7200rpm before the electrics cry enough, and so smooth is it at those revs that a red-lined tachometer on its own would not be enough to prevent overexuberance.

Volkswagen claim a top speed of 129mph for the Golf and 0-62kph acceleration of 8.5secs, while UK importers VAG claim a much less pessimistic 0-60mph time of 7.5 secs, which seems far more likely. Certainly, pushed hard in the lower gears the 16V feels that quick. Regarding top speed, we timed a one-way figure, on the flat in still conditions, of 137mph — not bad for an 1800.

'Ours' was one of the few cars available to us not to be fitted with power steering (which generally wasn't liked and will only be an option here) and its handling remained as sharp as ever, with the flatter cornering promised by the spec sheet minimising the three-wheeling normally found in a Golf when pressed hard. Braking is much improved and on the whole the 16V is incredibly rapid, if a little characterless, across country.

We sampled a Scirocco briefly, but with its strangely poorer aerodynamics (Cd 0.38 compared with the Golf's 0.35) and a noisier cabin it seems very much a poor relation. That is certainly not something justified by its price, however.

We were quite surprised when we heard just how much more expensive the Golf 16 Valve would be than the base GTi, but then we were reassured that UK-spec cars would have such fitments as electric windows and central locking as standard; we would hope so.

There is no doubt that the 16V is a blistering and unbelievably refined performer which will reward most drivers with 30mpg+ fuel consumption. It really does need a little more in its specification and a dash more personality to justify its price, but characterless or not this new Golf GTi 16V is still one hell of a motor car. ∎

PRIZE FIGHT

The forthcoming 16-valve Golf GTi and the Escort RS Turbo ought to be the deadliest of rivals, competing for the title of Hottest Hatchback. Here, Roger Bell compares them for the first time

IN THE red corner, the trim, clean-skinned Golf GTi 16V, limbering up like a confident underdog with hidden talents. VW is unequivocal about the pace of its latest championship contender, the looks of which belie machismo muscle. It calls the 16-valve Golf "by far the fastest production hatchback in its class." Top speed, is claimed as 130 mph, the 0-60 mph time as 8.2 seconds (our extrapolation from VW's 0-100 kph claim). Who can beat that?

The reigning champ is ready for its deference. In the white-or-nothing corner Ford's RS Turbo claims to be ace of the hot-hatch division. *Motor* test figures — 0-60 mph in 7.8 seconds, a Millbrook lap at 126.2 mph — secure its crown.

The 16V does not make its official UK debut until next spring; this was the first confrontation between the 16V and the RS Turbo, on suitably neutral ground at Prescott Hill, that narrow ribbon of treacherous tarmac that snakes up a wooded escarpment near Cheltenham. Not *on* the hill, because on this day that was a Golf 16V monopoly, when invited press guests competed for the honour of fastest ascent (which went to *Motor*'s rep on a non-qualifying run) and the coveted GTi cup (which went elsewhere), in five left-hookers imported especially for the occasion by VW.

As a gate-crashing intruder, the Escort was excluded from the climbing entertainment which, if nothing else, established the Golf as a formidable sub-56 second rocket — and a remarkably forgiving one, to boot. It is just as well that at and beyond the limit of adhesion (generally well beyond in the hands of those rotters who took it all a

The Golf 16V is still remarkably 'understated', compared with the overtly aggressive, all white RS Turbo. Some of the Ford's plastic addenda are rather untidily applied, too

mite too seriously), the 16V is tamely forgiving. Its user-friendly understeer imparts safe stability, though it was sometimes deceptively masked from the hands by the power assistance fitted as an option.

Had we slipped in a fast one with the RS, it would probably have pipped the pace-maker of the Golf quintet, the only one shod with Continental tyres rather than Pirelli P6s. Coincidence? Unlikely. The Contis seemed to give better traction out of Prescott's two decisive hairpins. Still, they didn't stop the scrabbling wheelspin altogether — as the limited-slip viscous coupling between the front wheels of the RS Turbo should have done; the Ford probably has more appropriate gear ratios, too.

But let's stick to facts, not conjecture. On the road, the two cars are quite different in feel and character, even though their makers had the same high-performance goals in mind, if not, one feels, exactly the same buyers.

As befits its butch looks, the Ford is the more overtly sporting of the two. It has the sharper acceleration — at least, it feels the sharper, with terrific bite from 2000 rpm on and so little throttle lag that you're never caught

napping by low-boost lethargy. This blown 1600 is a cracking engine — arguably the best thing about the RS Turbo. It spins so sweetly to the red line that many drivers could easily hit the abrupt ignition cut-out during eager acceleration.

According to VW's own figures, the 139 bhp 16V can't match the 130 bhp RS's 0-60 time. But the ultra-cautious Germans are inclined towards pessimistic performance data,

Internally the Escort is comfortable and reasonably civilised; wraparound Recaro seats provide superb lateral support but can make it awkward to change gear in a hurry

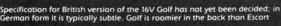

Specification for British version of the 16V Golf has not yet been decided; in German form it is typically subtle. Golf is roomier in the back than Escort

The RS Turbo needs careful handling and is easily unsettled; by contrast the Golf is relatively easy to drive and forgiving to the inexperienced

Driven with spirit, the Ford is dramatically fast on give-and-take roads. But it could frighten the life out of chicken-livered tearaways.

Put most of this agitated behaviour down to the transfer of strong turbo thrust to the front wheels through that FF limited-slip diff. Under normal driving conditions on a steady throttle, you are barely aware of its presence. The RS turns into bends crisply and holds a stable line.

which *Motor* usually betters in fifth-wheel tests. What-ever the makers say, expect sub-eight-second times for the 0-60 mph dash, comparable to those of the RS. That said, low and mid-range bite of the 16V doesn't feel so sharp as the Ford's turbo motor, which develops more torque at considerably lower revs. On the other hand, the VW's terrific top-end verve continues a full 1000 rpm above that of the RS.

All out, then, there cannot be much in it, though for normal brisk motoring, the RS seems to have the sharper, more responsive pick-up. On smoothness and refinement, again the two are pretty evenly matched, both engines spinning to their limits without frenzied hysterics or excessive noise. A brace of better fours than this would be difficult to muster in competition.

When it comes to changing gear, there are bonus points for the Golf, with its crisp, short-travel change and fluid clutch. The shift of the Ford is far from a

bad one, but the grippy lever's rubbery travel (not to mention its tricky reverse engagement) lacks the click-stop precision of the slippery Golf's. What's more, the superb wraparound Recaro seats badly hamper movements of your gearchange elbow.

The GTi's seats are of more conventional shape. They don't clamp you in place like a padded vice, as do the Ford's, but then nor are they lacking in adequate lateral location, not even for all-out attacks on the Prescott wiggle-woggle. You also sit taller in the Golf. The driving position in the Escort feels so low-slung that the fixed steering wheel — thick-rimmed and grippy, just like a racer's — could be an inch or so lower, even for tall drivers.

Competition breeding is more acutely evident in the nervous disposition of the RS Turbo. It's so highly strung in its handling that it can become edgily inconsistent, even unstable unless settled and soothed with deft, delicate flicks of the steering.

Open up mid-corner, though, and the viscous coupling transfers torque to the spin-prone inside wheel, causing to the car to tuck sharply on to a tighter line — exactly the opposite of the run-wide understeer behaviour expected of a front-drive car. It is not a fluid, progressive transgression but a sudden, darting one which often calls for sharp corrective action at the helm.

In the middle of a hard-charge overtaking manoeuvre, such throttle sensitivity is at best disquieting, at worst downright frightening. Yet for all that, perhaps as a consequence of it, the RS can be enormously rewarding to drive fast on twisty secondaries. It keeps you alert, at the peak of your form. It demands the best from the driver — and somehow inspires it.

There is no such teasing male-volence to the 16V's placid character. It is so well behaved, so predictably consistent that it feels quite tame to drive fast after the RS. That is not to condemn it

as the less appealing of the two. Far from it. Because it is so much easier to hustle without stressful concentration or sharp reflexes, eight out of ten drivers would probably have no hesitation in choosing it as everyday transport. The other two, perhaps revelling masochistically in the Ford's knife-edged nervousness, might well dismiss the 16V as too easy and forgiving (despite terrific roadholding) to stimulate the adrenalin glands, especially when equipped with uncommunicative power steering. What the superior feedback of an unassisted set-up would do for the 16V's role as macho driving machine remains to be seen.

The Golf has superb all-disc brakes, as good in their firm feel as they are in their stopping power. That disquieting sponginess which so flawed the old GTi's brakes has been well and truly exorcised. The Ford's disc/drum brakes are just as effective but marred on the car we drove by serious vibration when applied hard at speed. It was just one of several tremors, including that excited by the rather clonky suspension, that made the RS rougher round the edges (engine excluded) than the refined Golf, easily the sweeter of the two despite its indifferently firm ride.

The Ford is actually less flashy inside than the external plastic addenda (some of it rather tattily applied) would have you believe. In fact it's a comfortable and reasonably civilised car. In terms of decor and equipment, there is a touch more opulence here, some would say even more class than in the restrained, understated Golf. But that's a matter of personal taste. Reverting to objectivity, there's no doubt that the Golf is the roomier of the two in the back for long-limbed adults.

Ergonomically, both cars set high standards, with handy control layouts and clear instrumentation. Both have efficient heating and ventilation systems, too. The standard specification of right-handed 16Vs has yet to be settled but it will have to be lavish to outrank that of the Custompack RS Turbo, costing £10,070. Similarly equipped, expect a five-figure price tag for the top Golf.

So, where do we stand? That the two cars differ so markedly in their handling behaviour, if not in the way they perform, is just fine. It makes choosing between them comparatively easy. Even though Ford has doubled (to 10,000) the production target of the RS Turbo, its numbers will never be so great as to exceed its minority enthusiast appeal. With the 16-valve GTi, VW is casting its sales net well beyond the fringes of the hot-hatch division. It is the buyers of small Mercs and BMWs it is after. The RS Turbo is not that sort of animal. Perhaps, after all, the two cars are not the arch rivals they initially seem to be. In theory, they should meet head on; in practice they're surprisingly different.

Golf without handicap

Despite other makers' best efforts to catch up, the new Golf GTi is still the hot hatch to beat

VOLKSWAGEN'S Golf GTi — soon to go on sale in Australia in its latest Mark Two guise — was the European cult-car of the '70s. With the nimbleness and response of the Mini Cooper S, yet with performance levels better than most sports cars, the GTi invented a whole new car category — the so called hot hatchback — which has become the fastest growing class of car in Europe. The category has also replaced open-top two-seaters as the poor man's sports car. People who aspire to a Ferrari or Porsche will probably start their sports car owning days with a hot hatch, before moving on to the big league. The GTi is, if you like, the new MGB.

Despite an increasingly crowded market — with makers like Ford, Opel/Vauxhall, Citroen, Fiat, Peugeot, Renault, Austin Rover and established sports car manufacturers like Lancia and Alfa Romeo all trying to get a slice of the action — the Golf GTi in its larger and superior Mark Two form, still stands as the pre-eminent quick hatchback. The Japanese are also following the GTi's lead.

The heart of the GTi's excellence lies in its engine. Of 1.8 litres, and 78 kW in its lead fuelled form, it is an extraordinarily willing engine which reacts to the whip with a thoroughbred's alacrity, spins to just under 7000rpm, and has a wonderful band of strong torque. I haven't driven a better four-cylinder unit. Part of the Audi-designed four pot overhead cam family of engines as used in lesser Golfs, the unit is mounted transversely and sends its power to the front wheels via a five-speed gearbox. As its power figure suggests, this Golf engine also produces a hefty whack in the back. In European form, the GTi is capable of racing from rest to 100km/h in just under 8.5 sec and on to a top speed of some

190km/h. And while you're enjoying all this high speed fun, you can still expect to better 10.6 km/l. Not only will the car accelerate hard and have a high ultimate velocity; it also can cruise at high speed all day without fuss. As anyone who has visited Germany can testify, Golf GTis are likely to race by you on the autobahns, cruising comfortably at well over 160 km/h. They seem to have little trouble keeping up with most of the big Mercedes and BMWs, rocketing along like Jumbo Jets across the Atlantic.

Driving a GTi offers more good points than simply the engine response. The handling is manoeuvrable and, on its 185/60HR14 rubber — usually of Pirelli manufacture — the roadholding is excellent. Push the GTi very hard in a corner and it has the Mini-like habit of lifting its inside rear wheel, giving it a dog-at-its-favourite-tree type attitude. But, even with the inside wheel a good 30 cm off the deck, the car still grips the tarmac with determination. The steering — rack and pinion, with 3.5 turns lock to lock — is sharp, although rather heavy at low speed. It also suffers from that habit of all powerful front-drive cars: it has some torque steer. Although the torque steer is not bad, you are never in any doubt that the driveshafts are juxtaposed with the steering arms. Based as it is on a normal family hatchback, the GTi is forced to use front-drive.

This front-drive and prosaic lineage do have some benefits, however. They make the GTi a sports car with uncommonly decent levels of accommodation. The Mark Two version of the GTi — now getting on for two years old — is capacious in the rear, allowing a six-footer to sit upright and in the straight ahead position behind a similarly built driver. About the only rear-seat drawbacks are the rather awkward entry in the three-door model (the space between the front seat

squab and the B-pillar is not large enough) and the thick C-pillars, which give back seat passengers a claustrophobic 'hemmed-in' feeling. The boot is large, but partly spoilt by the high sill height. Like most hatchbacks, the GTi has a fold-forward rear seat — which is particularly easy to operate, even if its usefulness is compromised by the lack of split squabs.

Still inside, drivers won't get too much of a thrill

from the facia. The GTi has always suffered from a plasticky interior, insufficient instrumentation and a steering wheel which would look more at home in a family sedan than a sports machine. Unfortunately the Mark Two Golf offers no improvements. You get only the minimum instrumentation (no oil pressure gauge, or ammeter) and a plastic dashboard which is so insipid that you could just as easily be sitting behind the wheel of any old shopping-trolley Nissan or Toyota. As further evidence of the Golf's breeding, there is no left foot brace for your clutch leg. Granted the seats are Recaros, but they are a dime a dozen now. In sum, the inside of the GTi is unlikely to inspire confidence, even if it is uncommonly roomy.

Lots of people don't think too much of the outside of the GTi, either — particularly in its Mark Two Golf form. Its bodyshell is pure shopping trolley-Golf, with a few add-ons to give it a sporty flavour, and its alloy wheels are unsightly Pirelli designs — with their maker's trademark emblazoned around the rims. Quite why Volkswagen ever chose to advertise another company's wares on the wheels of its sporty flagship is one of motoring's great mysteries. Little wonder after-market BBS wheels are common on GTis.

These aesthetic black spots are soon forgotten though, as you pull in the horizon during your first miles of GTi motoring. The engine reacts instantly and briskly to any accelerator input, and will soon propel you through the back roads with uncommonly decent haste. It revs cleanly and sweetly, and sounds truly stimulating when the tachometer is bearing down on the red-line. Its throttle response and torque spread will remind you of the Alfa twin-cam unit, but it is a much sweeter engine at high revs than Alfa's gutsy four. It breathes through a Bosch fuel injection system, which ensures not only quick throttle response but also quick starting. Mind you, true to the GTi's rather lacklustre general presentation, the engine looks none-too-impressive when you open the Golf's snout for the first time. Hiding below a black tin cam cover, it could just as easily be one of Wolfsburg's more mundane fours.

The engine's briskness is helped greatly by a sharp, short throw gearchange and by intelligent gear ratios — unusual for a German car. Change through the five-speed box, and you're always likely to pick a spot in the engine's rev range where there is plenty of good, strong torque. The gear lever also falls nicely to hand. In every other way, the driving position is similarly good.

The steering, despite its obvious front-drive feel, is generally pleasing, becoming particularly responsive when the velocity gets higher. Going hard, the GTi is a very easy car to place accurately when cornering. It is always a paragon of nimbleness, and is the sort of car in which you purposefully seek sharp direction changes — even like driving quickly around flattened cigarette packets — further to reinforce its responsiveness. The brakes of the Mark One GTi were that car's great Achilles heel — with appalling pedal sponginess in right hand drive form — but in the Mark Two version the four wheel discs feel fine. They are also generally fade free. The car's old weakness is now one of its strengths.

The Golf GTi has been under strong attack in Europe recently, with various other makers trying to take its fast hatchback crown. The most serious challenges have come from:
● Ford, in the Escort XR3i, — a machine which is cheaper than the Golf and prettier, but lacks the performance
● the Fiat Strada Abarth, — which in typical Italian fashion has more brio than the Golf thanks to Fiat's powerful 2.0 litre twin-cam and rock-hard competition-type suspension, but lacks the day-to-day competence of the VW machine and isn't much faster anyhow
● the Lancia HF Turbo, — a Delta-based hatchback which, like the Strada, has tons of performance but also a terribly ugly interior and a rather all-or-nothing turbocharged engine
● and the Opel Kadett GSi (Vauxhall Astra GTE in Britain) — which looks futuristic and is aerodynamic but hasn't got much else going for it.

In sum, the Golf is still king. And in an attempt further to distance it from its rivals, Volkswagen in Europe has just released a 16-valve version of the GTi — which packs another 21 kW into the Golf shell. In Europe, the fast hatchback craze shows no signs of abating. The principle of offering sports car performance in a usable family type machine is still as clever now as it was when the original GTi first made its bow 10 years ago. And with the best example of the art about to make its debut in Australia, the Australian hot hatchback market is likely to jump in a similar way. □

RIGHT OF REPLY

A Golf GTi powered by a 16-valve engine is VW's hot hatch answer

VOLKSWAGEN GOLF GTi 16V

If the initials GTi conjure up visions of the spine-tingling performance usually associated with more exotic machinery, then VAG's latest little giant killer, the Golf GTi 16V, fills the bill perfectly. The seeds were sewn as long ago as 1978, when the original Mk I Golf GTi appeared and quickly established itself as something of a cult car. Other manufacturers were quick to follow, with the result that the high-performance hatchback sector is now heavily subscribed.

The new Golf GTi 16V does not break any new ground in its make up, but simply extends the appeal of the original car to help keep pace with the opposition. Toyota's efficient 16-valve, fuel injected Corolla GT has shown just what sophisticated head technology can produce in terms of power and economy, and more recent offerings like the Renault 5 GT Turbo and Ford Escort RS Turbo have elevated performance to an altogether higher plane.

The trouble with the existing eight-valve GTi unit is that, despite its extreme tractability, it runs out of steam very quickly if pushed beyond 5800rpm. If VAG could develop a more free-revving, better breathing combination then it would have a suitable weapon with which to fight back. This it has done with the new top model GTi, which uses the proven 1.8-litre short engine matched to an all-new light alloy 16-valve twin overhead camshaft cylinder head, the benefits of which have increased overall power output from 112bhp at 5500rpm to 139bhp at 6100rpm, coupled to a rise from 114lb ft torque at 3100rpm to 124lb ft at 4600rpm.

Bosch fuel injection is retained and hydraulic tappets are incorporated to reduce maintenance. Power is transmitted via a single plate clutch to the close ratio five-speed gearbox currently found in all other GTis, but in this case fifth gear is now slightly lower at 0.91, instead of 0.89.

Suspension modifications are limited simply to beefing up the original settings with thicker anti-roll bars, plus revised spring and damper rates that have effectively lowered the car nearly ½ins. The four-wheel disc brakes of the less powerful car are retained, but with larger pistons. The UK specification will be high compared with current GTis and will include 6 × 14ins alloy wheels and low profile 60 series VR-rated tyres, electric windows, central locking, ▶

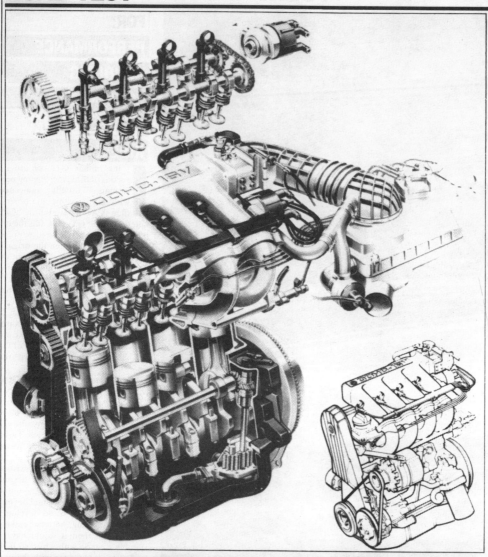

TECHNICAL FOCUS

The 16-valve engine is derived from the four-cylinder unit first used in the Audi 80, in 1972. In Golf GTi eight-valve form, the 1781cc power plant is fitted with fuel injection, and in GTi 16V configuration it benefits further from a new light alloy, four-valves-per-cylinder head with the valves operated by hydraulic tappets for reduced maintenance and the twin camshafts driven by a linked steel chain.

Originally a gear drive was incorporated for this function but to keep down engine noise levels a roller chain was adopted. Drive from the crankshaft pulley to the camshaft, on the other hand, is by the more normal expedient of a toothed rubber belt.

The head features an unusual valve layout for a twin overhead camshaft unit. The 33mm exhaust valves are vertical and the paired 40mm inlet valves are inclined at 25deg from the vertical enabling the cylinder head to be kept relatively narrow and allowing for an efficient mixture burn. The slightly convex tappet surfaces and a sloping cam contact face impart a rotary movement, thus avoiding premature tappet and valve seat wear and providing an optimum seal between the valve head and its seat.

The exhaust valves are sodium-filled for better heat dissipation — a design detail used in many current production turbo engines which has been borrowed from competition engine technology.

Engine compression is 10.0-to-1 and four-star fuel is needed.

◀ tinted glass, a radio/cassette player, steel sunroof, seat height adjustment for the driver and with further options of power steering, air conditioning and leather upholstery. In all other respects the specification is similar to current GTis.

A price for the Golf GTi 16V has yet to be finalised in the UK since the car will not be available in right-hand drive form until September at the earliest. However, we understand that it will cost no less than £10,000,

and as such will be pitched into the upper price bracket for performance hatchbacks.

Appointed VAG dealer, Colborne Garages, of Ripley, Surrey, gave *Autocar* a taste of things to come when it allowed us to test its personal import Golf GTi 16V.

PERFORMANCE

There's not much wrong with the performance of the current eight-valve Golf GTi but, as already

mentioned, if there is one area open to criticism, it is that a press-on driver might expect just a bit more power towards the top end of the rev range as engine power peaks at the relatively low figure of 5500rpm.

With the advantage in breathing afforded by the more efficient four-valve head, Volkswagen engineers have been able to raise both the overall power output as well as the peak, which now occurs at 6100rpm. And what a difference this has made

in the way the engine responds beyond 5500rpm; up to this figure there is not much difference, but now it is possible for a driver to hang on to the gears beyond 6000rpm and still feel an impressive surge of power. In fact, one can use this new-found 'revvability' and extra 'cammy' quality right up to 7000rpm before the cut-out comes into operation. This seems a little premature, since the red section of the rev counter, which starts at 6800rpm, does not become a solid red line until 7200rpm.

The change in engine character has had two effects on the vehicle's performance: firstly, sprinting ability is considerably better, and secondly, there is a slight loss in engine flexibility — this is not an immense amount, but the car is clearly slightly slower in the gears at low-to-medium revs compared with the eight-valve car.

Acceleration from 0-30mph is now below 3secs, and the GTi 16V reaches 60mph in 8secs dead. From a performance-measurement standpoint the fact that the rev limiter activated at 59.6mph in second gear meant we were prevented from achieving a mean of under 8secs. However, we did manage to record one 7.8secs pass to 60mph. The Golf's 'sprinting' ability is second only to the remarkable little Renault 5GT Turbo, which somehow manages near-supercar acceleration to 60mph (7.1secs) and goes on to a top speed of 125mph, a figure matched only by the Ford Escort RS Turbo. The GTi 16V is closer in this respect, managing a mean maximum speed of 123mph lower.

Despite this additional top-end performance, engine tractability and refinement remain very good; the car will pull from under 20mph without hesitation in fifth gear, and although it takes almost a second longer to cover each 20mph increment up to 80mph than the current GTi, from there upwards the more efficient cylinder head begins to pay dividends.

No less than 118lb ft of the maximum 124lb ft torque figure can be tapped between 2800 and 6100rpm, and this flat spread of power has cut the 90 to 110mph increment from 7.5secs, while the 70-90mph step in fourth gear has seen a staggering 10.5secs reduction to just 8.4secs.

The gearbox ratios are unchanged with the exception of fifth, which is now slightly lower. The result is that the GTi 16V's maximum speed of 123mph, developed at 6200rpm, is slightly over the 6100rpm power peak. The gearing change has presumably been made so fifth is more of a performance gear.

ECONOMY

Volkswagen claims an average fuel consumption figure for the GTi 16V of around 34mpg. We would describe this as slightly optimistic. Our overall figure of 25.3mpg, which included testing as well as driving on a variety

GTi 16V is distinguished by discreet badging and new alloy wheels

Seat height *adjustment is a feature of the 16-valve model*

Rear seat *legroom is adequate and seat belts are standard*

Unlike *many competitors, Golf's rear seat is a one-piece item*

of roads, reflects the sort of consumption an enthusiastic owner is likely to achieve, while our calculated average of 27.8mpg might reflect a less spirited driving style. The problem with this car is that there is always the temptation to use the additional power available.

If a driver succumbs to the temptation, then fuel consumption will suffer. However, the 16-valve head is undoubtedly efficient, and driven at a gentle pace may well reward the driver with better fuel economy than that of the eight-valve GTi.

In comparison with the Renault 5GT Turbo's 22.0mpg, the Ford Escort RS Turbo's 26.8mpg, and the Fiat Strada 130TC's 26.3mpg, the VW's figure is competitive enough, but compared with the 1.8-litre Astra GTE's 28.2mpg or the Peugeot 205GTi's even better 29.5mpg figure, the Golf begins to look a little thirsty. To be fair, our test car had only 1932 miles on the odometer when figured, and given increased mileage, VAG claims that both performance and economy are likely to improve.

The 12.1-gallon fuel tank of the current GTi is retained, producing a calculated range of just over 300 miles and a realistic mileage of perhaps around 250 miles, judging by the fuel gauge. A key-operated locking petrol cap is fitted behind the hinged flap, the tank accepting full flow from the pump nozzle without blowback and, due to the well-designed angle of the filler neck, trickle-brimming is an easy procedure.

REFINEMENT

Generally speaking, most of the 'hot hatches' currently available suffer in terms of refinement and therefore are quite tiring to drive quickly over long distances. The culprits are usually excessive exhaust or induction roar. The eight-valve GTi is one such example, and likewise the Toyota Corolla GT and Fiat Strada 130TC, with their sporting choice of ratios, means fifth gear motoring is often not a relaxed business.

Volkswagen has paid greater attention to this area in the GTi 16V; you can still hear the engine distinctly, especially between 3000 and 4000rpm, but the note is reasonably

muted and subsides at higher rpm. At higher speeds, window sealing remains excellent and road noise, too, is well controlled. Overall refinement levels are on a par with the Astra GTE, for instance, until one really begins to use the revs, and then that lovely healthy rasp takes over. Settle back on part throttle, and the note drifts into the background again.

Start-up from cold is instantaneous, although the engine hunts for the first 30secs or so before settling down to a smooth idle.

ROAD BEHAVIOUR

A criticism of the present GTi is the heavy steering at low speeds, which can make the car quite a handful when parking or attempting tight manoeuvres in town driving. The GTi 16V retains rack and pinion steering and there is now the option of power assistance — a welcome addition which was fitted to the test vehicle. We can only say that, having sampled this, we would recommend it.

Not only is low-speed manoeuvring vastly improved, but also the car's overall agility; however, this is at the expense of feel. Matching the light steering is a lighter clutch. It no longer requires a 40lb effort to depress the pedal. These two modifications have considerably altered the 'feel' of the GTi making it far easier to drive.

The suspension layout of MacPherson struts, coil springs and an anti-roll bar at the front and a semi-independent torsion beam at the rear with trailing arms, coil-over shock absorbers, and an anti-roll bar are common to current GTi models. In the case of the 16V, however, the car sits 0.4ins lower on uprated springs (from 120 to 130lb per inch front and 84 to 100lb per inch rear) and dampers, to the slight detriment of ride quality. There is now an obvious bias towards handling and grip.

On first acquaintance, the suspension imparts a feeling of suppleness over most surfaces, although there is clearly a 'nobbly' element in the ride, often the case when fitting low profile tyres, where the suspension does a less successful job of controlling frequent but small wheel movements ▶

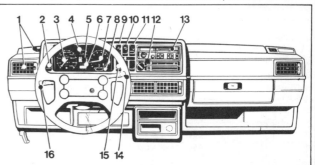

1 Ventilation outlet, **2** Lights switch, **3** Speedometer, **4** Temperature gauge, **5** Warning lights, **6** Trip computer, **7** Tachometer, **8** Fuel gauge, **9** Hazard warning switch, **10** Heated rear window switch, **11** Fog light switch, **12** Heating and ventilation controls, **13** Radio/cassette, **14** Wash/wipe, trip computer stalk, **15** Ancillary switches, **16** Indicators/main beam stalk

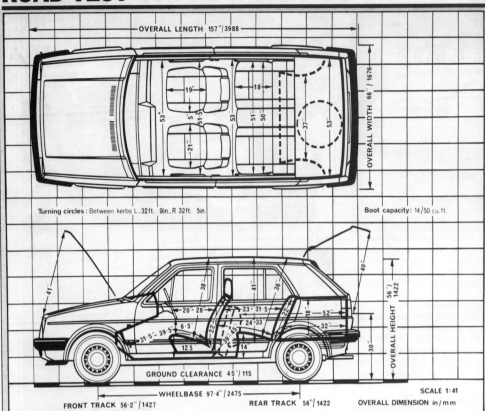

OVERALL LENGTH 157"/3988

OVERALL WIDTH 66"/1676

Turning circles : Between kerbs L. 32ft. 9in. R 32ft. 5in.

Boot capacity: 14/50 cu. ft.

OVERALL HEIGHT 56"/1422

GROUND CLEARANCE 4.5"/115

WHEELBASE 97.4"/2475

FRONT TRACK 56.2"/1427

REAR TRACK 56"/1422

SCALE 1:41

OVERALL DIMENSION in/mm

MODEL

VOLKSWAGEN GOLF GTi 16-VALVE

PRODUCED BY:
Volkswagenwerke AG, 3180
Wolfsburg, West Germany

SOLD IN THE UK BY:
Volkswagen Audi Group (UK) Limited,
Yeomans Drive, Blakelands, Milton
Keynes, Buckinghamshire MK14 5AN

SPECIFICATION

ENGINE
Transverse front, front-wheel drive.
Head/block al. alloy/cast iron.
4 cylinders in line, bored block, 5 main
bearings. Water cooled, electric fan.
Bore 81mm (3.19in), **stroke** 86.4mm
(3.40in), **capacity** 1781cc (108.7 cu in).
Valve gear 2ohc, 4 valves per
cylinder, toothed belt camshaft drive.
Compression ratio 10 to 1. Electronic
ignition, Bosch KA-Jetronic fuel
injection.
Max power 139bhp (PS-DIN)
(102kW ISO) at 6100rpm. **Max torque**
124lb ft at 4600rpm.

TRANSMISSION
5-speed manual. Single dry plate
clutch, 8.3in dia.

Gear	Ratio	mph/1000rpm
Top	0.91	19.80
4th	1.13	15.95
3rd	1.44	12.51
2nd	2.12	8.50
1st	3.45	5.22

Final drive: Helical spur, ratio 3.67.

SUSPENSION
Front, independent, struts, lower
wishbones, coil springs, telescopic
dampers, anti-roll bar.

Rear, semi-independent, trailing
arms and torsion beam, coil springs,
telescopic dampers, anti-roll bar.

STEERING
Rack and pinion, hydraulic power
assistance (optional). Steering wheel
diameter 15in, 3.2 turns lock to lock.

BRAKES
Dual circuits, split diagonally. **Front**
9.4in (239mm) dia ventilated discs.
Rear 8.9in (226mm) dia discs. Vacuum
servo. Handbrake, centre lever acting
on rear discs.

WHEELS
Pressed steel, 6in rims. Radial ply
tyres (Continental on test car), size
185/60VR14, pressures F29 R26 psi
(normal driving).

EQUIPMENT
Battery 12V, 45Ah. Alternator 55A.
Headlamps 120/110W. Reversing lamp
standard. 21 electric fuses. 2-speed,
plus intermittent screen wipers.
Electric screen washer. Air blending
interior heater; air conditioning extra.
Cloth seats, cloth headlining. Carpet
with heel mat floor covering. Screw
jack; 2 jacking points each side.
Laminated windscreen.

PERFORMANCE

MAXIMUM SPEEDS

Gear		mph	km/h	rpm
OD Top	(Mean)	123	198	6200
	(Best)	125	201	6300
4th	(Mean)	111	179	7000
3rd		87	140	7000
2nd		60	96	7000
1st		37	60	7000

ACCELERATION FROM REST

True mph	Time (sec)	Speedo mph
30	2.7	36
40	4.2	46
50	5.9	56
60	8.0	67
70	10.9	78
80	13.5	87
90	18.1	99
100	23.3	108
110	35.3	118
120	—	127

Standing ¼-mile: 16.2sec, 85mph
Standing km: 29.8sec, 107mph

IN EACH GEAR

mph	Top	4th	3rd	2nd
10-30	—	7.6	5.6	3.5
20-40	9.4	7.2	5.0	3.2
30-50	9.1	6.7	4.9	3.1
40-60	9.2	6.6	4.8	—
50-70	9.5	7.0	4.9	—
60-80	10.4	7.5	5.5	—
70-90	11.7	8.4	—	—
80-100	13.9	10.1	—	—
90-110	18.9	14.6	—	—

CONSUMPTION

FUEL
Overall mpg: 25.3 (11.1 litres/100km)
5.5mpl
Autocar constant speed fuel
consumption measuring equipment
incompatible with fuel injection
Autocar formula: Hard 22.7mpg
Driving   Average 27.8mpg
and conditions   Gentle 32.8mpg
Grade of fuel: Premium, 4-star (97 RM)
Fuel tank: 12.1 Imp galls (55 litres)
Mileage recorder: 2.2 per cent long
Oil: (SAE 10W/30) negligible

BRAKING
Fade (from 85mph in neutral)
Pedal load for 0.5g stops in lb

start/end		start/end	
1 21-21	6 31-35
2 22-21	7 35-37
3 24-27	8 36-39
4 25-30	9 36-39
5 30-34	10 40-43

Response (from 30mph in neutral)

Load	g	Distance
10lb	0.31	97ft
20lb	0.54	55ft
30lb	0.76	39ft
40lb	0.97	31ft
45lb	1.1	27.3ft
Handbrake	0.32	94ft

Max gradient: 1 in 3
CLUTCH Pedal 25lb; Travel 5.5in

COSTS

No information currently available

SERVICE AND PARTS
No information currently available

WARRANTY

12 months/unlimited mileage, 6-year
anti-corrosion

EQUIPMENT

Automatic	N/A
Cruise control	N/A
Electronic ignition	●
Limited slip differential	N/A
Rev counter	●
Power steering	○
Trip computer	●
Steering wheel rake adjustment	N/A
Steering wheel reach adjustment	N/A
Self-levelling suspension	N/A
Headrests front	●
Heated seat	N/A
Height adjustment	●
Lumbar adjustment	N/A
Rear seat belts	●
Seat back recline	●
Seat cushion tilt	N/A
Seat tilt	N/A
Split rear seats	●
Door mirror remote control	●
Electric windows	●
Heated rear window	●
Interior adjustable headlamps	N/A
Sunroof	●
Leather seats	○
Air conditioning	○
Tinted glass	●
Tailgate wash/wipe	●
Central locking	●
Child proof locks	N/A
Cigar lighter	●
Clock	●
Fog lamps	N/A
Internal boot release	N/A
Locking fuel cap	●
Luggage cover	●
Metallic paint	●
Radio/cassette	●
Aerial	●
Speakers	●

● Standard   N/A Not applicable   DO
Dealer option   ○ Optional at extra cost

WEIGHT
Kerb 19.8cwt/2226lb/1009kg
(Distribution F/R, 64.3/35.7)
Test 21.9cwt/2456lb/1114kg
Max payload 1036lb/470kg

TEST CONDITIONS
Wind: 7-12mph
Temperature: 18deg C (64deg F)
Barometer: 29.9in Hg (1015mbar)
Humidity: 72per cent
Surface: dry asphalt and concrete
Test distance: 872miles
Figures taken at 1932 miles by our own
staff at the General Motors proving
ground at Millbrook.
All *Autocar* test results are subject to
world copyright and may not be repro-
duced in whole or part without the
Editor's written permission.

FIAT STRADA ABARTH 130 TC £8036

With the arrival of 2-litre twin cam power the Strada has finally got the sort of performance necessary to make it a hot hatch contender. With 130bhp driving through the front wheels, understeer is a big problem when pressing on. Engine and wind noise are high in this thinly-disguised racer, and the ride is less supple than most of its hot hatchback rivals

Tested	29 Sep 1984
ENGINE	1995cc
Max Power	130bhp at 5900rpm
Torque	130lb ft at 3600rpm
Gearing	19.8mph/1000rpm
WARRANTY	12/UL, 6 anti-rust
Insurance Group	6
Automatic	N/A
5-Speed	●
Radio	DO
Sunroof	N/A
WEIGHT	2168lb

TOP SPEED	118mph	MPG	26.3
0-60mph	8.2secs	Range	320 miles

LANCIA DELTA HF TURBO £8499

Really might be classified as a hot hatchback for the driver who also wants refinement and an extra two doors. The turbocharged version of Fiat-Lancia's 1.6-litre twin cam endows the previously rather mundane Delta with excellent performance to complement its already good ride and handling. Rather cramped interior and less headroom than most

Tested	14 Jul 1984
ENGINE	1585cc
Max Power	130bhp at 5600rpm
Torque	142lb ft at 3000rpm
Gearing	20.95mph/1000rpm
WARRANTY	36/UL, 6 anti-rust
Insurance Group	7
Automatic	N/A
5-Speed	●
Radio	DO
Sunroof	●
WEIGHT	2387lb

TOP SPEED	121mph	MPG	25.6
0-60mph	8.2secs	Range	250 miles

PEUGEOT 205 GTI £7490

This little car is a standard-setter in the hot-supermini class. It retains the good ride comfort of the standard 205 but adds excellent performance and good handling. Interior is cramped by comparison with the Astra, but it is a smaller car; it could, however, be argued that the lack of rear space is not as critical in a performance-oriented car as it is in others

Tested	23 Jun 1984
ENGINE	1580cc
Max Power	105bhp at 6250rpm
Torque	99lb ft at 4000rpm
Gearing	18.77mph/1000rpm
WARRANTY	12/UL, 6 anti-rust
Insurance Group	5
Automatic	N/A
5-Speed	●
Radio/cassette	●
Sunroof	£180
WEIGHT	2004lb

TOP SPEED	116mph	MPG	29.5
0-60mph	8.6secs	Range	325 miles

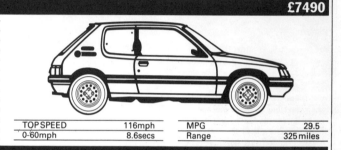

RENAULT 5GT TURBO £7360

This Renault undeniably sets new standards of performance for the whole, keenly squabbling hot hatchback brigade including the Golf GTi-Abarth 130 TC elite corps. Ride is stiffish, and it understeers a little with power, but straight line stability is excellent and cornering behaviour good. Visibility is not ideal, rear is very cramped. Engine incorporates latest technology

Tested	26 Mar 1986
ENGINE	1397cc
Max Power	115bhp at 5750rpm
Torque	121lb ft at 3000rpm
Gearing	21.75mph/1000rpm
WARRANTY	12/UL, 5 anti-rust
Insurance group	OA
Automatic	N/A
5-Speed	●
Radio/cassette	●
Sunroof	£140
WEIGHT	1749lb

TOP SPEED	125mph	MPG	22.0
0-60mph	7.1secs	Range	242 miles

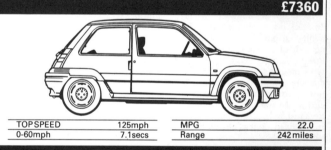

TOYOTA COROLLA GT 3-DOOR £8298

Now one of the quickest of all the performance hatchbacks. Toyota created this pocket rocket by fitting its 1587cc twin-cam, 16-valve engine to the competent, but rather mundane, Corolla hatchback. An impressive performer with 119bhp on tap. It possesses Japanese traits of good finish and generous equipment levels. Handling is easily up to the performance

Tested	10 Apr 1985
ENGINE	1587cc
Max Power	119bhp at 6600rpm
Torque	103lb ft at 5000rpm
Gearing	18.6mph/1000rpm
WARRANTY	12/UL, 6 anti-rust
Insurance Group	6
Automatic	N/A
5-Speed	●
Radio/cassette	●
Sunroof	●
WEIGHT	2091lb

TOP SPEED	120mph	MPG	28.9
0-60mph	8.5secs	Range	315 miles

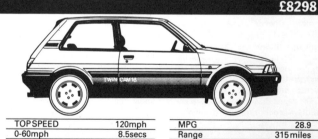

VAUXHALL ASTRA GTE 3-DOOR £8169

The on-paper specification looks formidable enough but performance is lacking in terms of acceleration. Top speed is another story however and the slippery Astra clearly sets new standards for a car of this power output. Rear visibility and headroom are both lacking. The digital dashboard layout is not to everyone's liking, but controls are well laid out

Tested	28 Nov 1984
ENGINE	1796cc
Max Power	115bhp at 5800rpm
Torque	111lb ft at 4800rpm
Gearing	19.76mph/1000rpm
WARRANTY	12/UL, 6 anti-rust
Insurance Group	6
Automatic	N/A
5-Speed	●
Radio/cassette	
Sunroof	£325.16
WEIGHT	2199lb

TOP SPEED	120mph	MPG	28.2
0-60mph	9.0secs	Range	255 miles

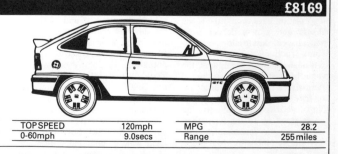

● Standard N/A Not applicable DO Dealer Option OA On application

Volkswagen has paid attention to refining the 16-valve unit

Uprated springs and dampers improve handling and grip levels

Neat facia is a little simple but ergonomically very efficient

◀when travelling at motorway speeds. This trait was noted in the original test of the Mk 2 Golf GTi, and in the 16-valve version this same aspect is further amplified.

In its favour, however, the GTi 16V clearly has a chassis to match the additional power output while the amount of grip available from the low-profile, 185-section Continental tyres mounted on 6ins-wide, 14ins diameter wheels is exceptional, not just in terms of cornering ability but also in the way the car accelerates from rest and can be brought quickly and safely to a halt when travelling at high speed.

Handling remains taut, with understeer prevailing at moderate cornering speeds, and changing to a near-neutral attitude close to the limit of adhesion which, as already mentioned, is very high. Two of the car's major attributes have always been performance and handling, and in the GTi 16V it is clear that Volkswagen has emphasised these points in order to enhance the driving pleasure aspect.

Four-wheel disc brakes, with the bonus of ventilated rotors at the front, are retained, but in this case larger pistons have been fitted to the calipers and a new deeper front spoiler has cut-outs to allow additional brake cooling.

In near-ideal test conditions, the car had little difficulty in recording an impressive 1.1g maximum deceleration figure for a slightly over-servoed 45lb of pedal effort. Similarly, the brakes stood up to the high-speed fade test with remarkable ease, recording variations in pedal pressure of only 22lb.

AT THE WHEEL

Ergonomically, the Golf design ranks among the best in its class, and with the useful addition of seat height adjustment for the driver via a control to the side of the base, occupants of all shapes and sizes are well catered for. As one has come to expect of VW products, the pedals are well arranged for easy heel and toe operation of the throttle and brake, and there is an excellent seat-steering wheel-pedals relationship. The gearchange is equally delightful, and although more friction-laden than mat of the Escort or Toyota, is nonetheless precise and easy to use.

The facia display is common to all GTis; it is a simple, neat, yet perhaps rather basic layout for this top specification Golf. One might have expected an oil pressure gauge at least, although the small on-board computer does reveal engine oil temperature. Two main insruments handle engine revs and speed, and these are separated by three stacked, rectangular displays containing water temperature, warning lights, and the trip computer display at the bottom.

The familiar four-spoke GTi steering wheel is retained, and apart from the different seating material — in this case, a smart hard-wearing striped cloth which is also used on the door trims—and a '16V' badge on the glovebox, there is little to distinguish this Golf GTi from its less powerful stablemate.

The ancillary switchgear is within easy reach of the driver and consists largely of push switches set into the facia, while column stalks either side of the steering column handle turn

indicators and headlamp main beam (left), windscreen wipers/washers and the trip computer (right).

Ventilation and heating is provided by an air blending system working in conjunction with slide controls for heat and direction and a three-speed booster fan. The output of hot air is plentiful, and in warm weather the fresh air flow through the vents can be augmented if the steel sliding sunroof is partially opened to improve the flow; otherwise, the cabin can become stuffy.

Forward visibility is good, but this is not the case when trying to leave angled T-junctions because of the thickish B-pillars and sizeable C-pillars which block out quite a large area of side and rearward vision. However, the situation is nowhere near as bad as for the Astra GTE with its highly aerodynamic, no-compromise shape.

CONVENIENCE

Rear passenger space is best described as adequate rather than generous, though it is no worse than the majority of the Golf's rivals. If the front seats are slid right back on their runners, rear passengers have to sit with splayed knees. Headroom, too, is limited and visibility severely hampered by the large front seat head restraits.

Oddment space is good, with deep door pockets, facia undertrays, a useful-sized lockable glove compartment, and cubbies in the centre console. The rear parcel shelf, which is divided into three sections, features a lipped outer edge, and can also be used to retain objects.

Unlike most of the Golf's rivals, the rear seats cannot be split to accommodate awkward loads as well as a third passenger; instead, the rear seat backrest folds forward in one piece. The load sill is at an unusual height, rather than being at bumper level; it falls somewhere around the car's waistline and loading is therefore tricky.

Predictably, the engine bay presents a rather complex picture, yet despite the addition of the more sophistcted, dimensionally larger cylinder head, the compartment is not too crowded. Looking at the clearance problems under the bonnet of a left-hand-drive example, however, it is no wonder that supplies of

right-hand-drive GTi 16Vs are taking longer than expected to arrive.

SAFETY

In the rear there are two reel-type belts, plus a third lap belt provided as standard. Remote-controlled, though manually operated, door mirrors are fitted, and these are set quite a long way back, behind the fixed quarterlights, to make smaller the usual blind spot where other cars can lurk unseen.

Front head restraints, a rear wash/wipe facility, a laminated windscreen, and tinted glass all round feature as part of the package. Electrically operated windows are convenient and time-saving features.

All VWs have a parking light facility, a single front and rear light illuminating when the indicator stalk is used without the ignition in operation. However, it is all too easy to leave this light on accidentally.

A rubbing strip which runs the length of the body is designed to save the paintwork from minor knocks and abrasions.

VERDICT

When you look at the VW's close rivals, most are priced at around the £8000-£8500 mark, with the two exceptions of the Renault 5GT Turbo (the least expensive) and the Ford Escort RS Turbo, (the most costly).

Oddly enough, these two outsiders are the class leaders in terms of performance, the former undoubtedly offering remarkable value for money if it is a 'point-and-squirt' machine that is required, and the latter offering more space in an equally exhilarating package.

VAG UK has yet to fix a price for the right-hand-drive GTi 16V, but it is likely to be more than £10,000, thereby just entering BMW 320i territory, a point worth considering if refinement is a prerequisite.

In the VW's favour is the responsive, lusty, and now high-revving engine, which has lost none of its edge in this high performance application. Set against this is the exhaust boom between 3000 and 4000rpm, a slight lack of steering feel with the power-assisted example we tested, and, perhaps, price. This is certainly the deciding factor, but even at more than £10,000, this latest Golf GTi will take some beating.∎